Urban Life and Urban Landscape Series

VISIONS OF EDEN

Environmentalism, Urban
Planning, and City Building in
St. Petersburg, Florida, 1900–1995

R. BRUCE STEPHENSON

Ohio State University Press
Columbus

Library of Congress Cataloging-in-Publication Data

Stephenson, R. Bruce (Robert Bruce), 1955–
    Visions of Eden : environmentalism, urban planning, and city
building in St. Petersburg, Florida, 1900–1995 / R. Bruce
Stephenson.
        p.   cm. — (Urban life and urban landscape series)
    Includes bibliographical references and index.
    ISBN 0–8142–0725–1 (alk. paper). — ISBN 0–8142–0726–X (pbk. :
alk. paper)
    1. City planning—Florida—Saint Petersburg—History. 2. City
planning—Environmental aspects—Florida—Saint Petersburg—History.
I. Title. II. Series.
HT168.S174S74   1997
307.1'216'0975963—dc21   96–39627
                                                                    CIP

Cover design by *Nighthawk Design*.
Cover photo: St Petersburg's public waterfront in 1927.
Courtesy of the St. Petersburg Historical Museum.
Type set in Goudy Old Style by Graphic Composition, Athens, Georgia.
Printed by Cushing-Malloy, Inc., Ann Arbor, Michigan.

9   8   7   6   5   4   3   2   1

Contents

Preface

To a large extent our environmental problems are caused by the expansion of our cities. Yet, "as the world becomes more urban," Rutherford Platt writes in *The Ecological City* (1994), "public and scholarly interest in the quality of the human habitat has become increasingly nonurban in focus."[1] Although scholars have generally ignored the functions of natural systems in metropolitan regions, America has a rich heritage of trying to reconcile urbanization and environmental protection. Early in this century, pioneer planners tried to mold the forces of urbanization around the constructs of nature.[2] Only recently, however, have practitioners looked to these planners for inspiration and guidance. This book explores the long-standing relationship between urban planning and environmental protection in St. Petersburg, Florida.

In February 1971, a billowing cloud of black smoke introduced me to the distinctive characteristics of Florida's natural environment. The state was in the middle of its worst drought in forty years, and the conflagration I saw that morning (and every morning for the next two months) was muck burning four to five feet below the ground. The earth was literally on fire! As I watched the St. John's basin burn, the Everglades were also ablaze, and saltwater was intruding into the water supplies of Miami, Tampa, and St. Petersburg. These events were attributed to natural causes, but I soon learned that they were exacerbated by the failure to include nature in plans for urban development. Between 1945 and 1970, thousands of acres of wetlands had been indiscriminately drained to provide living space for the state's rapidly expanding population. The drought revealed the fragility of the relationship between humans and nature in Florida. Yet there was no lack of planning; the problem came from not implementing the plans.

John Nolen, a founding father of the planning profession, drew up Florida's first comprehensive city plan for St. Petersburg in 1923, and the roots of this plan go back to the early 1900s. But St. Petersburg, like many American cities, preferred boosting a seductive image to the commitment of planning, and Nolen's plan was not adopted. The ecologically based conceptual plan that the city finally adopted in 1974, however, differed amazingly little from Nolen's. Nolen's groundbreaking effort in St. Petersburg provides an important link between past and present. If Florida's cities and counties are to implement their state-mandated growth-management plans effectively, it is important to understand why Nolen's vision of planning was taboo for half a century. Although planning controversies have become much more sophisticated since the 1920s, they still resemble the battle that ensued when Nolen's plan to structure St. Petersburg's expansion was attacked by realtors and subdividers demanding the freedom to build a city that met their needs.

In a state that is growing at a greater rate than China or India, the ideal of "sustainable development" remains problematic. Nevertheless, the environmental catastrophes that plagued Florida in the early 1970s forced municipalities to incorporate urban planning into the process of city building. Clashes between land speculators, regulators, and environmentalists continue; the degraded waters and lands within and surrounding our urban centers are a constant reminder of the need for environmental protection. But we have now reached a point where a pattern of development friendly to both nature and humans may yet emerge.

I also wrote this book so that my daughter might understand why she may never enjoy the same sense of place that I had, growing up on the shore of the Indian River Lagoon. On her second birthday we visited a park, purchased with funds from a natural lands referendum, near my boyhood home on Merritt Island. The visit recalled fond memories of days spent exploring the estuary's many wonders. I also remembered a few very special nights, when I lay in bed listening to porpoises breathing offshore, within fifty feet of my bedroom. The next dawn the water boiled as these sleek mammals worked their way through a school of bonita. Most mornings, however, were more peaceful. As I ate breakfast, I would watch "Oskhosh," the name my father had given our resident great blue heron, slowly work his way along the shore. My reveries had to give way to reality, however, when my barefooted daughter sprinted down the sandy beach and headed into the green, algae-infested water. Fortunately, I grabbed her before she made much headway. What we encountered was shocking. Our nature outing seemed more like a trek through an abandoned lot in the Bronx as we carefully worked our way around broken glass, concrete blocks, large bolts and nails, boards, and a dozen tires. While my daughter's exuberance was contagious, I could not shake the sensation that something had died. It was not only the demise of the lagoon that troubled me, but the fact that my daughter would never have the experiences that I so relished as a child. As our pile of debris accumulated, "Clean up, Da-da," I wondered if she would ever remember a place by giving names to the wildlife.

Acknowledgments

I am indebted to Emory University for funding my research at Cornell, to Rollins College for awarding me a Critchfield grant, and to the J. Gordon Barnett Foundation for funding several trips to St. Petersburg. I would like to thank my former associates at the Pinellas County Planning Department for sharing their knowledge and experience. Kathleen Jacklin and her staff at Cornell University's John M. Olin Library were especially helpful in my study of the Nolen Papers. I am grateful for the resources made available by Jay Dobrin, the former head of Special Collections at the University of South Florida, and the staff at the St. Petersburg Museum. Bill Olbrich, head of Government Publications at Washington University, St. Louis, was most trusting to send the weighty Bartholomew Plans to Rollins. Ken Woodburn and John Harvey were kind enough to share their personal papers and experiences with me. Andres Duany and Elizabeth Plater-Zyberk hosted a symposium on John Nolen that allowed me to appreciate the relevance of Nolen's work more fully. This forum also gave me the chance to glean some of John Hancock's immense knowledge of John Nolen. Finally, I am grateful for having had the opportunity to experience the candor and integrity of the late LeRoy Collins.

Harvey Young, Blaine Brownell, Gary Mormino, Dan Carter, Chris Silver, and Dana White provided important guidance during the early stages. Richard Miller, Barry Allen, and Wendy Brandon, colleagues at Rollins College, freely gave their time to critique this work. I also benefited from Reid Ewing's thoughtful and practical comments. Rick Musset, former planning director of St. Petersburg, and Brian Smith, Pinellas County's Planning Director, have been most helpful. Ray Arsenault's knowledge of St. Petersburg and Tim Clemmons's insights on Bay Plaza were also appreciated.

Zane Miller and Henry Shapiro were model editors. Their comments helped turn a cumbersome dissertation into a book that I hope meets their high standards. I am also grateful to Nancy Woodington for her precise editing.

Finally, I am indebted to Charles Holt and John Kleber for leading me on to the road of critical thought. It is to Charles and John that this book is dedicated.

Introduction

City Planning in Eden

His car full of family grows silent and dazed as he drives the miles, stopping now and then at the overhead lights that signal an intersecting road, a secondary road heading west to beaches and what mangrove swamps are left and east to the scruffy prairie being skinned in great square tracts for yet more development. Development! We are being developed to death.

John Updike, *Rabbit at Rest*

Florida epitomizes the potential of modern life. The forces of genius have transformed this once uninhabitable wilderness into an air-conditioned version of the American Dream. While modern engineering techniques have made Florida livable, the countless developments resting over drained swampland and filled bays are neither safe nor sustainable. Florida has become a preferred site for novels and movies that depict natural disasters destroying a fabricated Eden. Although "unscrupulous" developers are often blamed for Florida's poorly designed communities, the guilt is shared by all. Developers are wedded to the bottom line—and the bottom line is that people want to live in the Sunshine State. St. Petersburg, the principal city in Florida's most urbanized county, exemplifies how tenuous the relationship is between humans and the environment in a place shaped and reshaped by natural disasters.

This book examines the efforts of planners and their advocates to harmonize city building and environmental protection. Despite its geriatric image, St. Petersburg is a young city, the product of America's amazing twentieth-century prosperity. The city has grown in concert with efforts to impose a rational order on society.[1] Since the 1890s planners have combined utopian visions with regulatory techniques to channel development into desired urban forms.[2] Their plans, however, have often generated more conflict than consensus.

Planning for Survival?

American city planning is a paradoxical enterprise. How can planners impose controls that protect the public in a capitalist society based on expansion, property rights, and free enterprise?[3] And if planners are charged with protecting the public health, safety, and welfare, just what controls are necessary?

The noted urbanist Lewis Mumford confronted this issue in a speech at the 1927 National Planning Conference. There he urged planners to utilize an organic or ecological approach in their profession. The growing problems of urban America, Mumford felt, escalated when planners viewed cities as machines designed for production rather than biological organisms capable of reproduction. Unless cities were designed in accordance with natural constraints, Mumford warned, America's expanding urban centers would pass "the limits of functional size and use." In the past, when urban civilizations had exceeded natural limits, they collapsed. Initial periods of excessive growth were followed by ecological deterioration, catastrophe, and the demise of civilization. The "necropolis," or dead city, was the ultimate fate of any society that promoted unlimited growth. But fortunately, "at least one city planner," he declared, "realizes where the path of intelligent and humane achievement will lead during the next generation."[4]

Mumford was referring to John Nolen (1869–1931), one of the heirs of Frederick Law Olmsted's romantic environmentalism.[5] Like Olmsted, Nolen believed natural settings offered relief from the problems of urban life, but he had moved beyond Olmsted's belief that cities were inherently evil and that they formed "unnatural men." Between 1903 and 1919, Nolen wrote a series of pioneering works on urban planning that introduced the concept of a flexible, "organic city," where human life could evolve to new heights. The design of the organic city demanded that the human habitat be integrated within the surrounding landscape by following nature's guidelines.[6]

In 1919, after two decades of trying to reshape the American city, Nolen had despaired of the planning profession's ability either to erase the urban landscape's "cruel monotony" or to "check rank individualism," which dominated the city-building process.[7] But he still believed that the construction of a series of comprehensively planned "new towns" and "regional cities" would reveal the benefits of city planning to a wide audience. With a new urban model, development could proceed in a more efficient form.[8] In 1921, Nolen discovered a place to test his theories: Florida, America's fastest growing state.

In 1921, St. Petersburg experienced the first effects of the "Great Florida Land Boom."[9] The rush of building and land speculation intensified in that year, and William L. Straub, editor of the *St. Petersburg Times*, convinced the city commission to establish an advisory city planning board. In early 1922, the board hired John Nolen to prepare Florida's first comprehensive plan. After touring St. Petersburg and the Pinellas Peninsula, Nolen realized that he had found the ideal site for his prototype community.

St. Petersburg was a special place. Located in a site unsuitable for trade or industry, it was a city geared to consumption rather than production. The "Sunshine City's" subtropical environs offered the perfect conditions for leisure, the phenomenon feeding America's robust new consumer economy. The 1920s had ushered in a new reign of prosperity that allowed middle-class Americans to vacation in Florida's exotic locales for the first time.[10] If St. Petersburg hoped to maintain its lucrative tourist trade, the city's planning advocates believed, it needed a distinctive natural setting. In contrast to industrial cities like Chicago and Detroit, where the land was reshaped to promote industry and production, St. Petersburg would offer a new model, that of a resort city where humans lived in harmony with nature.[11] St. Petersburg was a site "blessed by a benevolent Nature," Nolen wrote, "and the enhancement of the beauty that already exists is a work that should be kept continually active, insuring for future generations the glories of today." Besides preserving the region's natural beauty, the plan he designed would "make St. Petersburg's suburban developments not only among the most interesting, but also the most unique and attractive in the country."[12]

The Nolen Plan was more than a design that was pleasing aesthetically; it also provided a strong economic rationale for restricting growth to certain areas. If followed, the plan would assure the vitality of the city's dominant industry—tourism. As America became more urbanized and prosperous the demand to visit enticing natural areas, Nolen contended, could only increase. Investing in tourism promised an immense return.

While the mayor, Straub, and the director of public works supported urban planning, the city's throng of real estate salesmen campaigned against it. Their desire to make quick profits outweighed any lofty notion of building a model city. The Nolen Plan's land-use controls and bureaucratic directives seemed ludicrous to the investors and salesmen reaping huge rewards from speculative land ventures. These men's hope for continued prosperity required a city with unlimited prospects for growth. In their minds, "property rights and personal rights," as President Coolidge fondly stated, were "the same thing."[13]

Florida's first experiment in planning went down to a crushing defeat in a referendum, but this setback did not mark the end of city planning in St. Petersburg. Instead it represented the beginning of a movement to bring order to a chaotic real estate market and to protect natural resources. Planners in St. Petersburg, however, did not approach Nolen's vision until a series of environmental catastrophes forced the state legislature to reconfigure the rights of property.

Paradise in Peril

Over the last century, Florida's subtropical environment has been central to an image that conjures up thoughts of Eden and visions of escape.[14] Its explosive growth and robust tourist economy attest to the Sunshine State's special allure. In 1920, not quite a million people lived in Florida. Over the next seventy years, the state's population increased by 1300 percent, to 12,937,926. This exponential growth rate is unmatched even elsewhere in the Sunbelt. Texas (16,987,000) and California (29,760,000) have larger populations, but their rate of increase over the same period (361 percent for Texas and 877 percent for California) pales in comparison to Florida's.[15]

To accommodate the crowds that flocked south, a tangled suburban maze replaced the state's expanses of mangroves, cypress swamps, freshwater prairies, and tidal marshes. Two hundred years ago, wetlands covered 54 percent of Florida; by 1990 that area had shrunk to 29 percent. Draining 9.7 million acres of wetlands allowed entrepreneurs to refashion the landscape into a jumbled mixture of tourist attractions, billboards, strip centers, crowded beachfront condominiums, and strings of characterless subdivisions.[16] While Florida has a few stellar developments, over the last half century speculation, misrepresentation, poor planning, and a general lack of collective responsibility have been the principal characteristics of city building in Florida.[17] Maybe John Nolen said it best in 1926, after he reviewed the state's cities: "Almost everything that is good and everything that is bad is to be seen there in the flesh."[18]

Florida's rapid urbanization has fostered an ecological crisis. The Everglades and the coral reefs are dying; mercury contamination has reached the most isolated waters in southern Florida; in Sarasota Bay shellfish have the highest concentration of lead in the United States; and even Disney World has been cited for illegal dumping of toxic wastes. There are perhaps a score of Florida panthers left. The bird population has dropped by 90 percent in the Everglades over the last two decades. And there are far more manatees on license plates than there are swimming peacefully in Florida's waters. The vast urban complex on both coasts continues moving inland to replenish diminishing water supplies. As inland water tables have dropped, sinkholes and saltwater intrusion have become more prevalent. "What we are seeing," John Ogden, director of the Institute of Oceanography in St. Petersburg, states, "are problems of an unprecedented complexity."[19]

In the last two decades, Florida has instituted a battery of progressive growth-management measures to mitigate the most abusive building practices. In response to the state's ecological crisis in the early 1970s, Governor Rubin Askew pushed through a package of reforms that moved Florida from a state devoted to boosterism into the national leader in environmental protection and urban planning. This movement culminated in 1985, when the legislature enacted the nation's most stringent growth-management bill.[20]

Florida is now a good laboratory for the business of city building and the art of designing cities. Besides its landmark legislation, it hosts some of the United States' most interesting communities. Innovative new towns like Seaside and Miami Lakes, and established communities like Winter Park and Coral Gables, show the state's charm and potential. While the prognosis for Florida's remaining natural habitat remains guarded, there is reason to believe that a balanced urban landscape may yet appear.

St. Petersburg: Florida's Bellwether

St. Petersburg embodies Florida's fortunes. Once a sleepy retirement community ringed by orange groves, it is now a packed conglomeration of subdivisions and strip shopping centers in Florida's most densely populated county. As people continue to funnel into the South and the West, this Sunbelt city offers the nation a glimpse of the future. With its large elderly contingent, rapid growth since World War II, service economy, high-tech industries, and fragile environment, St. Petersburg is dealing with the problems and prospects that will soon face the rest of the state and the nation. According to John Naisbitt, author of the bestseller *Megatrends*, Pinellas County is the nation's "bellwether county," an indicator of the future. "Those responsible for the state's growth management policy in Tallahassee," Naisbitt reported in 1985, "will learn important lessons presently facing the residents and leadership of the county."[21]

In 1990, Florida's chief planning agency, the Department of Community Affairs (DCA), presented awards for achievements in growth management. St. Petersburg's plan was recognized as the best among Florida's major cities. Not only did it meet the demanding criteria established by the 1985 Florida Growth Management Act; it also surpassed state standards in its efforts to preserve and enhance the natural environment. Since more than half of Florida's municipalities had failed the DCA's review, St. Petersburg's urban vision was exceptional.[22]

Located between the Gulf of Mexico and Tampa Bay, St. Petersburg occupies the lower third of the Pinellas Peninsula. A microcosm of the state, Pinellas's balmy temperatures, moderating breezes, white-sand beaches, and waterfront living serve as a year-round lure to tourists and a haven for retirees. Between 1940 and 1990, St. Petersburg's population has shown a nearly fourfold increase, from 60,812 to 239,000. Pinellas County's population has increased more than 900 percent, from 91,852 to 860,900. With only 280 square miles, Pinellas County's population density (3,075 people per square mile) is more than three times that of Broward County, Florida's second most densely populated county. It is also the most populous county in the St. Petersburg–Tampa metropolitan area, which, with 2,100,000 residents, is the nation's nineteenth largest metropolitan area. This figure represents an increase of over 1,000 percent since 1940. The national growth rate for the same period is only 90 percent. Among major Sunbelt cities, as defined by Bradley Rice and Richard Bernard, only San Diego and Phoenix are comparable. In addition, 2,900,000 tourists, the equivalent of 103,500 year-round residents, descend on Pinellas each year. While this translates into economic growth, it also places an added burden on the infrastructure and the environment. There is no indication of a slowdown, and during the 1990s Tampa Bay should remain one of the ten fastest-growing urban areas in the United States.[23]

A host of problems has attended Pinellas's rapid growth. Its roads are the most congested in Florida. During the winter, when multitudes of tourists descend from the North, they are virtually impassable. There is no rapid transit system, and plans for one are sketchy at best. To add to the problem, local governments, in particular the Pinellas County Commission, have been notoriously lax in regulating roadside developments. Miles of commercial developments lining the region's major thoroughfares, congestion, neon advertisements, and a mass of billboards all combine to mar the landscape.[24]

The more than seventeen million vehicles that travel the St. Petersburg–Tampa roads annually are the principal culprits behind the region's growing air pollution problem. Two pollutants—sulfur dioxide and ozone—plague the region, and in the early 1980s the EPA designated the Pinellas Peninsula a nonattainment area because the region failed to meet federal standards for these toxic automobile byproducts. While conditions have improved over the last ten years, the brown cloud hovering over the Pinellas Peninsula is a constant reminder of the threat to the regional ecosystem.[25]

The waters surrounding the peninsula have been especially endangered by urbanization. While St. Petersburg has operated a tertiary sewage treatment system (which recycles the effluent) for almost twenty years, a decade lapsed before other Tampa Bay cities also stopped pumping partially treated sewage into polluted waters that had been largely pristine in the 1940s. Dredge-and-fill operations have also laid waste to what was once one of Florida's most productive ecosystems. Despite strident protests, almost 25 percent of Boca Ciega Bay, which separates St. Petersburg from its outlying barrier islands, was filled in or dredged between 1940 and 1965.[26]

Boca Ciega Bay is now one of the most degraded bodies of water in the nation. Originally this shallow bay had crystal waters two to four feet deep, a sandy bottom, and large expanses of seagrass meadows supporting an abundance of marine life. Waters in these fill areas are now over ten feet deep and turbid, while the bottom of the bay is covered with layers of odorous anaerobic muck. The vast seagrass meadows are gone, shell fishing is prohibited, and the commercial fishing industry is nearly extinct.[27]

Even though the region receives more than fifty inches of rainfall a year, St. Petersburg and the rest of Pinellas must import over half of its water. As early as the 1920s, the low pumping capacity of the aquifer on the southern portion of the peninsula forced St. Petersburg officials to secure wellfields further inland. During the 1950s and 1960s, the region's rapid growth aggravated the problem, and by the 1970s all Pinellas communities depended heavily on inland counties for their water. Since a drought in the mid-1980s, year-round water restrictions have been in effect.[28]

Despite these problems, life could be much worse for St. Petersburg and its neighbors. In the early 1970s, environmental problems forced municipal officials to restructure St. Petersburg's planning system. In 1976, fifty years after the citizens of St. Petersburg first voted against planning, the city council received a strong directive from the electorate to adopt an ecologically based plan that bore a striking resemblance to Nolen's earlier work.

Nolen's work has lived on in another vein. He is one of the patron saints for the budding traditional town planning movement. Leon Krier, a classical urbanist and leading theorist of the movement, castigates our auto-oriented, sprawling urban form as "anti-ecological."[29] Andres Duany and Elizabeth Plater-Zyberk, two of the leading proponents of traditional town planning, designed Seaside, one of the most acclaimed new towns in the United States. Seaside's renown reflects the interest in a tradition that Duany and Plater-Zyberk are seeking to reinvigorate.[30] "If you want to understand what we are doing," Duany told a Philadelphia audience in 1990, "study John Nolen's plans."[31]

John Nolen's plan for St. Petersburg stands at the heart of this book. As a pioneer of the planning profession, Nolen helped formulate land planning principles still followed today. But before we can expect Nolen's work to inspire a revival of traditional town planning, we must discern why the people

Figure 1 John Nolen at work. Courtesy of the Division of Rare and Manuscript Collections, Cornell University Library.

of St. Petersburg rejected it, and why, fifty years later, the city adopted a comparable plan. To understand this turn of events, I examine the projects, visions, and plans that formed St. Petersburg and the impact of city building on the peninsula's environment. Finally, because St. Petersburg is almost entirely "built out," the city's efforts to revitalize the downtown, restore the natural environment, and recycle resources offer other Florida cities a model for solving the problems endemic to city building.

Planning is crucial, because our most pressing environmental problems no longer pertain to technological issues, but to questions of design.[32] The town planning principles that Nolen set forth still offer the best means to preserve the ecology of a region while allowing development to proceed on the most suitable lands.[33] Designing metropolitan areas for "reasoned growth," as Greg Easterbrook calls it, "holds out the hope of permitting an expanding economy and protecting natural habitats at the same time." Despite this promise, Easterbrook found that the "land-use planning taboo" continues to thwart efforts that would ensure America's long-term economic and ecological health.[34] While I look at the cultural tempest that accompanied St. Petersburg's various plans, I also thought it was imperative to provide some indication of the disaster that awaits us if those pushing the property-rights movement succeed in destroying growth management.[35] For anyone contemplating an alternative to reasoned growth, St. Petersburg's history offers an exemplary lesson explaining why, despite the most fervent protests, it became inevitable to accept planning.

In trying to unravel the complex relationships that constitute the phenomenon of urbanization, clear definitions are crucial. In this book, "urban (or city) planning" describes the effort to have the government systematically order development around a desired urban form or natural system to promote some concept of the public welfare. Most urban development in America, however, is not the product of planning but the result of countless uncoordinated efforts by individuals and corporate and governmental bodies ("city building").[36] I also wanted to give some indication of how city building[37] drove St. Petersburg's expansion and altered the environment. City building, in this book, describes not only the general urbanization process, but also the methods employed by businesses hoping to profit from intensified land use. Finally, I use the term *environmentalism* to refer to the endeavor to change the way public and private interests affect the environment.[38] To understand this collective effort to transform society, I include discussions of ecology, conservation, and the relationship between humans and those chaotic aspects of nature that they can neither fully control nor fully understand.

I

William Straub's Crusade for Beauty

It was in the wilds and virgin land where the encroachment of civilization has had no chance to mar the natural scenery, that the architect lin-
gered the longest. He made extensive notes all in the interest of
preparing the plans that if accepted and worked out will make this
county a veritable Garden of Eden.

St. Petersburg Times, 1914

In the 1890s, William Lincoln Straub's fiery editorials for the *Grand Forks Daily
Herald* established the young newspaperman as one of the Northern Plains'
leading journalists. Poor health, however, cut his promising career short. In
1899, after doctors told him he would die without major surgery, Straub moved
to St. Petersburg in the hope that he could regain his health in the mild Florida
climate. The town's "cleanliness, clear waters, and bright beaches" captivated
Straub, and after a regimen of sunning and outdoor activity his chronic
bronchial condition gradually disappeared. In 1901 he returned to work as editor of the *St. Petersburg Times.*[1]

Over the next thirty-eight years, Straub crafted a lasting, although con-
frontational, relationship with his adopted home. He was six feet tall, "with
a rugged, friendly face and gray eyes that peered through wire-rim glasses."
Straub's flamboyant prose and unbounded energy made him one of St. Petersburg's biggest boosters. While he joined in the chorus promoting the city's
beautiful locale, he constantly worked to alter the status quo in his desire to
shape the community's future.[2]

A determined civic activist, with, he claimed, "a hide impervious to anything said about" him, Straub, once he had taken up a cause, wrote editorials
and published cartoons that spared no one. According to Walter Fuller, a contemporary, "Straub was the greatest influence for the development of the
community ever to appear on the scene." In 1905 he played a key role in
the formation of St. Petersburg's board of trade, the forerunner to the Chamber of Commerce. Two years later he penned the "Pinellas Declaration of

Independence," a document that ignited a movement culminating in the peninsula's secession from Hillsborough County (greater Tampa) in 1913.[3] Straub also led campaigns to adopt a city-manager style of government, create a parks board, and build a library.[4] The longtime editor's most enduring commitment, though, was to city planning.

Like other planning enthusiasts, Straub's interest in city and regional planning grew from an initial involvement in park planning.[5] Over the years, his campaign to regulate the real estate market and protect the environment antagonized a large bloc of the town's conservative citizenry. In the face of continual criticism—and sometimes outright ridicule—of his stance, Straub remained determined to safeguard the place where he had found sanctuary.

Straub believed that Pinellas deserved reverent care and treatment. "We have no moral right," a *St. Petersburg Times* editorial stated in 1913, "to destroy any part of this great capital, instead it should be passed on with interest. To the extent that we wisely or unwisely use the heritage of millions now in their infancy or yet to be born, will this generation be blessed or cursed by its heirs." Straub constantly argued that this "struggle for preservation" would only succeed if the community "guarded and protected" the region's natural wonders.[6]

Pinellas: The Meeting of Land and Sea

Straub glorified Pinellas in his description of it: "Here stands the work of godly hands, the flowering peninsula of Pinellas, with her cluster of green islands and keys. Like gorgeous strings of emerald and jade, sweeping over the master plan of divine dreams."[7] The beauty that characterized the Pinellas landscape during Straub's lifetime was the result of a relatively recent geologic transformation. The Pinellas subpeninsula has emerged over the last 200,000 years as the shallow seas that once covered the Florida peninsula gradually disappeared. But these seas did not recede in either a uniform or a consistent manner. Sometimes they inundated the Pinellas Peninsula, leaving only a few small islands above sea level; at others they retreated to reveal large expanses of land. The interplay of waves and currents on the emergent land created marine terraces, generally level landforms with gentle seaward slopes. Three marine terraces (see figure 2) made up the general topography of the Pinellas Peninsula. The edges of the Wilcomico and Penholoway Terraces show where former shorelines were, while the Palmico Terrace abuts the waters surrounding Pinellas. Most of the Palmico Terrace is less than twenty-five feet above sea level, and its land is generally poorly drained. The Wilcomico and Penholoway Terraces' elevations range between thirty and sixty feet and from seventy and ninety-

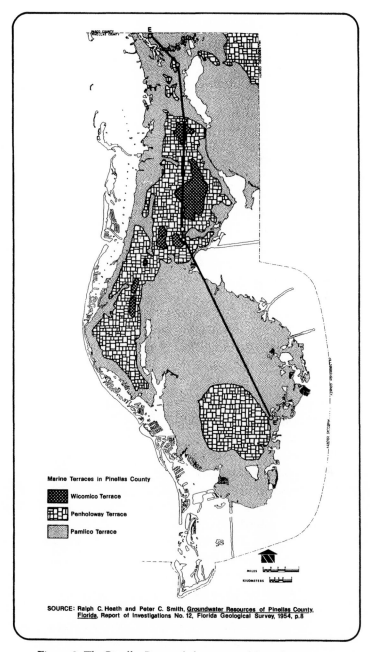

Figure 2 The Pinellas Peninsula has emerged from the sea over
the last 200,000 years. The land comprises a series of low-lying
marine terraces with gentle seaward slopes and low elevations.
Courtesy of the Pinellas County Department of Planning.

seven feet, respectively. Their nutrient-poor soils consist primarily of sand and shells. Below the ground lie beds of limestone a thousand feet thick.[8]

The peninsula's other landforms are the barrier islands running along the coast from north to south. They are separated from the mainland by a series of shallow lagoons. Once sandbars, the barrier islands formed gradually over three or four thousand years from sediment deposited by the waves. Sand accumulated around any obstacle, usually vegetation, to form dunes. The gulf's winds and waves fostered the sand dunes' continued growth and, once the dunes had reached a height somewhere between three and six feet, they acted as a stable foundation for the fragile barrier islands.[9]

Besides anchoring the beaches, the vegetation-covered sand dunes sheltered the islands' landward side, where colonies of bushes, shrubs, palms, and pines flourished. The barrier islands' seaward coasts featured white sand beaches, while the shores facing the bay held a mixture of mangroves and marine grasses.[10] Red mangroves played an especially important role in the estuarine ecosystem. Their prop roots trapped loose materials and leaf litter, creating habitats for marine life and buffering the island from storm tides. The mangrove was also a vital link in the food chain. When mangroves dropped their nutrient-rich leaves, the leaves nourished detritus consumers like shrimp, which were a primary food source for larger fish. The trees' prop roots also hosted scores of marine creatures—tunicates, sponges, barnacles, oysters, mussels, and other mollusks—that played an important role in the marine ecosystem that lay between the mainland and the beaches.[11]

A series of bays separated the barrier islands from the mainland. The largest coastal lagoon (today called Boca Ciega Bay) lay off south Pinellas. It is sixteen miles long, has an average width of two miles, and a depth of two to four feet. A dense mangrove swamp fringed the bay's ninety-mile shoreline. The mangroves' extensive root system restricted the seaward movement of upland sediments, helping to keep the brackish bay water clean and clear. The bay's vast underwater meadows of turtle grass prevented erosion of the sea floor while serving as both a nursery and a feeding ground for the abundant marine life.[12]

The barrier islands cushioned the coastal lagoons from the tropical storms and hurricanes that swept through the region. The dunes and the mangroves acted like shock absorbers and bore the brunt of the storms. Yet despite a dune system's amazing resilience, a barrier island could wash away in minutes when hurricane floodwaters or a storm surge made its eventual seaward return. Such a backwash occurs when hurricane winds change direction and combine with gravitational forces to force the storm surge over—and sometimes through—any obstacle in its way.[13]

In 1848, the worst hurricane ever to hit the west coast of Florida literally blew the water out of Tampa Bay, exposing large sand flats, during the back-wash stage.[14] The entire barrier island chain from Pinellas south to Captiva and Sanibel flooded when the Gulf of Mexico's waters rose 14.3 feet above normal. The hurricane's storm surge reshaped Pinellas's barrier island chain. It carved out two new inlets, washed away some keys, and built up others with sands dredged from both land and sea. Although the mainland escaped such punishment, two-thirds of the Pinellas Peninsula experienced heavy flooding. Fortunately, in 1848 Pinellas's barrier islands were uninhabited, and only a few hardy settlers lived on the mainland's higher elevations.[15]

Three centuries earlier, the first white men came to the Pinellas Peninsula on an ill-fated Spanish expedition headed by Pánfilo de Narváez. Although only Cabeza de Vaca and three others returned from this voyage, Narváez had four hundred men when he reached Tampa Bay on April 4, 1528. Three days later the explorers landed on one of Pinellas's southernmost barrier islands, near present-day Pass-à-Grillé. They splashed ashore across a wide expanse of open beach with unspoiled dune systems and thick clusters of mangroves. As they made their way to the mainland, the Spaniards encountered a primeval pine forest. They called their new discovery *punta pinal*, or pine point. It came to be known as Pinellas.[16]

The expedition trailed north and encountered a lush hardwood forest in the central portion of the peninsula, but the trek ended when the visitors encountered the mosquitoes that swarmed around Pinellas's freshwater swamps, creeks, and uplands. A host of wildlife lived in this varied environment, including bears, Florida panthers, deer, turkeys, and bald eagles. In immense offshore rookeries, such large wading birds as snowy egrets and roseate spoonbills flourished. The waters in and around the peninsula teemed with tarpon, bass, pompano, trout, mullet, redfish, and grouper. Shellfish—stone crabs, clams, oysters, scallops, and shrimp—also flourished in the local waters.[17]

After failing to discover any gold in their trek across the lower Pinellas Peninsula, Narváez and his disgruntled soldiers left the region to search for gold elsewhere. In 1567 Pedro Menendez de Avilés led another expedition through Tampa Bay, and these conquistadores fared no better in their search for mineral riches than their predecessors had. Menendez, the founder of St. Augustine, felt the area held some strategic importance and left behind a small garrison settlement. Two years later missionaries visited the site, but they were unable to find any signs of their countrymen. Although the Spanish constructed no permanent settlements, they left a dire legacy. The diseases they brought with them decimated the local Native American population; when other Europeans came to the area in the 1840s, they found only traces of human occupancy.[18]

In 1870, fewer than fifty families occupied the peninsula.[19] These early settlers, together with itinerant lumberjacks and hunters, harvested many of the region's resources. Large stands of pines, cypress, and hardwood trees were either cut for lumber or cleared for pasture and cultivation. Organized hunting parties systematically eliminated the peninsula's two largest predators, the black bear and the Florida panther, because they threatened the region's growing herds of cattle. Plume hunters, seeking to profit from America's millinery fashions, killed thousands of wading birds and pushed these species toward extinction.[20]

In 1880 only twenty-five of Pinellas's three hundred inhabitants lived on the southern portion of the peninsula.[21] Roads were practically nonexistent, and trips to Tampa were made almost exclusively by boat. There was only one commercial establishment, a small general store with less than $200 worth of merchandise. Despite these crude conditions, the settlers had laid the foundation for a prospering citrus industry. In addition, large herds of cattle grazed in the central and southern portions of the peninsula, and a few small commercial fishing operations mined the bountiful coastal waters.[22] While these pursuits provided a livelihood for the peninsula's early pioneers, the first indication that Pinellas could attract wealth came in 1885 at the American Medical Association's annual meeting. In a paper delivered to the full convention, W. C. Van Bibber declared that south Pinellas offered the ideal location for a "Health City."[23]

Ten years earlier, a group of English doctors had broached the idea of constructing such a city, and in the early 1880s they hired Van Bibber to find a site. After a year of research, he recommended that his clients purchase land on the southern portion of Pinellas, which he called Point Pinellas, where broad beaches stretched for miles. The region possessed a "peculiar, healthy climate" as attested to by its "natural products, the ruddy appearance of its few inhabitants" and its average winter temperature of 72 degrees. With "little upon its soil but primal forests," Van Bibber wrote, "there is a large subpeninsula, Point Pinellas, waiting for the hand of improvement." Although funding for the project collapsed, Van Bibber's findings set the tone for future generations of planners and city builders.[24]

Florida's First City Planning Experiment

City building on the Pinellas Peninsula began with the completion of the Orange Belt Railway in 1888. This narrow-gauge railroad ran the length of the peninsula, passing through Tarpon Springs, Dunedin, Clearwater, and Largo until it ended in St. Petersburg. On June 8, 1888, the first train ambled into St. Petersburg bringing only one passenger, a shoe salesman eager to snare clients in a boomtown. His hopes were quickly dashed when he saw a desolate village with a few ramshackle dwellings and fewer than thirty inhabitants.[25]

The Orange Belt's Russian builder, Peter A. Demens, had founded the small village only the year before. Its high ground and waterfront location made St. Petersburg, as Demens named the site, the logical point for the railway's terminus. Despite its inauspicious beginnings, a steady increase in rail traffic, its pleasant location on Tampa Bay, and the growing citrus market made St. Petersburg the peninsula's leading destination. In 1890, the population was 273, and by the turn of the century St. Petersburg had 1,575 inhabitants.[26]

Between 1900 and 1901 the town went through a construction boom, as a hundred buildings, worth $130,000, were built. In addition, the tourist industry enjoyed its best season. William Straub, in an early editorial for the *St. Petersburg Times*, envisioned an even greater season "as long as people who like a balmy climate in the winter continue to inhabit the northland."[27]

Straub argued that tourism represented the city's lifeblood because, aside from the surrounding waters, the region had few natural resources. A scenic setting and a pleasing climate attracted people from all parts of the country, and Straub believed that these features constituted the city's chief treasures.[28] The residents held a common pride in the town's natural amenities and its incomparable location on high, well drained ground that sloped gently to the water's edge. But although the townspeople boasted of St. Petersburg's waterfront location and how it attracted tourists, they had done little to protect or enhance this asset. "The sorry fact is," Straub reported in 1902, "our municipality has accomplished practically nothing for its improvement."[29]

Straub claimed that the community's negligence had allowed the waterfront to become an eyesore. An electric plant, a lumberyard, a warehouse, and unsightly debris cluttered this potentially scenic locale (figure 3). In addition, marine life in various stages of decomposition and other waste materials produced such noxious odors that shoreline residents feared for their health. The many rotting docks and boats added to this general appearance of decay and neglect.[30] Straub also voiced concern over the town's inability to provide tourists with a place either to stroll along the water's edge or to sit and enjoy the beautiful view across Tampa Bay.[31]

The sordid state of the waterfront provided ample proof, according to Straub, that the logic behind the building of a commercial or industrial city would not work for a city that wanted to cultivate the tourist trade. The waterfront represented St. Petersburg's primary asset, and enhancing the shorelines, Straub wrote, "can only come through municipal ownership."[32] He

Figure 3 An electric plant, woodyard, warehouse, and unsightly debris disfigured the St. Petersburg waterfront around 1900. Decaying seaweed, marine life in various stages of decomposition, and other waste materials produced such a stench that residents of the shore feared for their health. Courtesy of the St. Petersburg Historical Museum.

realized that he would "be called crazy for his plans" because "publicly owned waterfronts were almost unknown and unthought of in American cities." Nevertheless, in 1902 he started regularly running editorials that urged municipal officials to break from tradition and purchase the waterfront.[33] Straub also wanted the city's water commerce and industrial uses confined to Bayboro Harbor, located south of the city, so that the city could set aside the rest of the waterfront as a park where people could contemplate the surrounding subtropical beauty.[34]

Between 1902 and 1905, Straub's crusade for public ownership of the waterfront floundered. The owners of the frontage property, who were, as one reporter wrote, "without exception, aggressively interested in free enterprise and private profits," put little credence in the value of scenic vistas or public recreation. The city council also ignored Straub's editorials claiming that commercial exploitation of the waterfront would destroy the city's greatest assets. The townspeople seemed to be deaf. While the residents of St. Petersburg managed to take care of their own needs, Straub complained, "in affairs of great importance to all" the town held "as sleepy and lethargic a bunch as you can find in a month's journey."[35]

Straub continued his acerbic editorials, or "waterfront agitation," as some called it, decrying the shoreline's deplorable condition and the community's lack of civic enterprise. The city council eventually acceded to his constant badgering, and two committees were appointed to study the waterfront. Neither group resolved the issue and they both disbanded after one committee fell victim to apathy and the other to infighting. [36]

In late 1905 Straub gained a measure of success when he played a key role in founding the board of trade, the forerunner to the Chamber of Commerce. At the board's inaugural meeting in December, Straub urged members to join him in securing a municipal waterfront to aid the tourism industry. The gathering approved the measure and installed Straub as chairman of the Waterfront Committee. The committee members immediately endorsed a slate of city council candidates who supported the waterfront agenda. Over the next four months, Straub spearheaded an impassioned campaign for the "waterfront candidates," and in April they swept into office.[37]

On April 24, 1906, the new city council passed a resolution to acquire the waterfront. Since it did not provide for funding, however, the resolution merely represented the council's good intentions. Straub cleared the funding hurdle by persuading three members of the Waterfront Committee, developer Perry Snell, postmaster Roy Hanna, and A. F. Bartlett, the board of trade's president, to act as trustees and lend the city $3,120 to buy land. This money was enough to purchase one-third of the city's mile-long waterfront, and it also set a precedent for future council action. Shortly thereafter, an investor proposed to build cottages and an adjoining pier on the municipal waterfront. The city council responded by passing an ordinance that limited construction on the publicly owned lands to boathouses and bathing pavilions. This ordinance, according to Walter Fuller, represented Florida's first venture in city planning.[38]

After this success, Straub envisioned the creation of a "City Beautiful" that would radiate out from "the waterfront . . . the crowning glory of the city." During the summer of 1906, Straub pushed residents to support a $63,000 bond issue that would lay the foundation for the future. In addition to beautifying the waterfront, these funds could help city officials pave the streets, install water mains, build a sewage system, acquire land for parks, and even create a system for laying out new residential additions. He challenged citizens "to keep right at it" and to build a city that would conform "to the highest ideals of a beautiful city."[39]

The concept of raising taxes to enhance public life proved too extravagant for this backwater town of 5,000. Straub labeled his victorious opponents "a small town reactionary force" and chastised voters for not risking their capital to make necessary improvements. If businessmen in St. Petersburg readily used credit to enhance their enterprises, he argued, "Why should an entire community hesitate at a step that each individual would consider safe and wise?" Tax increases were inevitable in a growing city that lacked basic services, and rather than trying to escape responsibility, citizens needed to "work together for the City Beautiful," Straub wrote. "It will pay us, as nothing else will."[40]

After voters turned down the bond issue, the city council refused to consider raising revenues for acquiring the waterfront. The board of trade also failed to secure any monies and, in 1908, the city had still not reached consensus on the waterfront question. Residents had tired of the constant political haranguing, and they wanted the issue resolved. In the 1908 municipal election, a coalition vowing not to spend public funds on the waterfront dominated the returns. When the new city council convened, Hanna, Snell, and Bartlett received word that the money they had lent the city would not be repaid. They were incensed and immediately demanded restitution from either Straub or the city council.[41]

Straub was caught in a bind. His financial assets were limited, and the council adamantly opposed returning any funds. As a last resort, Straub organized a group of local entrepreneurs into the St. Petersburg Waterfront Company, which he represented in the *St. Petersburg Times* as interested in developing the waterfront. He believed that the threat of massive commercial development would stir public indignation and force the council to purchase the trustees' waterfront property. Straub's ploy worked to perfection. When the rumor went out that "Yankees" intended to build an industrial center on the waterfront, residents besieged the city council. The council and the electorate endorsed a bond referendum that not only paid off Hanna, Snell, and Bartlett, but also provided funds for the acquisition of additional land. On January 8, 1909, the city of St. Petersburg held title to one-third of the waterfront; by the end of the year it owned the rights to the entire waterfront except for two small parcels.[42]

Over the next fifteen years St. Petersburg backed bonds worth over $1,300,000 for developing and beautifying the waterfront. Between 1910 and 1918, the city dredged a channel for recreational craft, constructed a twenty-nine-acre yacht basin, a fifty-acre park, and a seawall. During this period the city gradually shifted all water commerce to Bayboro Harbor.[43] In 1918, St. Petersburg gained title to the two remaining waterfront holdings, and in the early 1920s, Perry Snell donated a mile of waterfront property to the north of the city. By 1923, citizens constantly boasted how their public waterfront had made St. Petersburg one of Florida's favorite vacation spots. The new park served multiple purposes, with its major-league (spring training) baseball sta-

Figure 4 Straub's crusade for a publicly owned waterfront in St. Petersburg lent legitimacy to the idea of government intervention for the community's welfare. Courtesy of the St. Petersburg Historical Museum.

dium, yacht club and basin, and tennis courts. Local citizens were adamant, however, that the waterfront's most attractive feature was the landscaped land hugging the coast (figure 4).[44]

Once the waterfront improvements were under way, Straub became even more unflagging in his promotion of the "City Beautiful."[45] "All other issues and improvements and industries and enterprises, public and private, combined into one," he wrote in 1913, "are not doing as much to make St. Petersburg great as the City Beautiful Movement." That same year, the *St. Petersburg Times* issued a "City Beautiful platform" that called for municipal ownership of all utilities, regulation of new building projects, the improvement and beautification of city parks and the waterfront, the acquisition of future parkland, and the building of a library. "The City Beautiful means," Straub told his readers, "the city *must* make these improvements itself, because private enterprises will *not* do it."[46]

As part of his new campaign, Straub wanted the city council to plan the city's expansion and to intercede when the community's general welfare was threatened. The City Beautiful philosophy, the *Miami Herald* reported, "was ingrained into the whole community" and "placed Miami and St. Petersburg at opposite poles."[47] After the waterfront park made St. Petersburg one of Florida's exceptional destinations, Straub decided to expand his vision of beauty to include the Pinellas Peninsula.

Pinellas: The County Beautiful

In March 1913, after leading the movement to form Pinellas County, Straub set out to establish the peninsula as a haven of "beauty and health." Six years earlier, Straub had penned the "Pinellas Declaration of Independence," a fiery call for the secession of the peninsular communities from Hillsborough County. The St. Petersburg Times's editor was "the man behind the gun who furnished the facts and figures which took a slice off this county to make Pinellas," a Hillsborough official noted, "and if we had not fought him hard and constantly, he would have stolen Tampa Bay, the Gulf of Mexico, and the flurry of clouds from out of our skies."[48]

Once Pinellas gained its independence, Straub wanted the peninsula's 15,000 inhabitants to band together to preserve the surrounding natural beauty. With more local control, the new county government could make certain that "our city and county landscapes be not left in the uncertain and selfish hands of real estate dealers." Straub proposed that the county commission appoint a board of disinterested citizens for the single purpose of "considering the City Beautiful and the public good, regardless of other interests." While property owners would make decisions "that shall seem good and sufficient to them," Straub asked, "shall the rest of the natural beauty be lost to the city?— The county?—The public?" On March 13, 1913, Straub announced, "Pinellas should have a county planning board."[49]

The impetus for Straub's proposal came from the counsel of the Boston architect Henry Long. Ten days before, Long had arrived in St. Petersburg to prepare plans for improving Bayboro Harbor. At Straub's request, Long delivered a speech on park planning to the board of trade. He recommended that the board appoint a committee to devise a plan that would enhance and protect the area's natural lands and vistas. The plan could also influence the pattern of development on the southern portion of the peninsula by creating a system of parks, gardens of native and tropical flowers, and scenic vistas for builders to incorporate into their projects. The board needed to convince city officials, Long told his listeners, to connect these public investments to the waterfront by a series of public driveways and boulevards. "Are you going to get hold of this peninsula," Long asked the gathering, "get control of the waterways and lakes around your city, lay out as many parks and boulevards as your artist may select?" If the board could manage such a feat, Long predicted, real estate sales would not only escalate, "St. Petersburg could be made one of the most beautiful cities in the world."[50]

The Bostonian's appeal heartened Straub. For a decade he had wanted an expert's confirmation of his aesthetic vision, which the townspeople tended to dismiss as a quixotic crusade.[51] After listening to Long, the city's businessmen realized that public investment in a park system could be profitable. At its April meeting, the board of trade passed a resolution to lobby the city council for the creation of a parks board that would oversee the implementation of a park plan.[52]

Long's counsel convinced Straub that an outside consultant could play an important role in promoting his City Beautiful agenda. After Long's eloquent testimony to the economic value of natural beauty, Straub made a point of bringing in an expert whenever it came time to design a public improvement plan. Before leaving, Long suggested that Straub contact the Olmsted Brothers firm, the nation's most prestigious name in landscape architecture, for guidance in park planning.

In May 1913, the St. Petersburg City Council voted in favor of creating an advisory parks board.[53] The parks board held its first meeting in June and elected Roy Hanna, the city's leading conservationist, to chair the group. After witnessing the wholesale slaughter of thousands of wading birds in the 1890s, Hanna had decided to establish a bird sanctuary and had purchased a small island, Indian Key, from the state. In 1902, Hanna contacted President Theodore Roosevelt when he heard that the federal government was interested in making Indian Key a bird reservation. After receiving a letter from Roosevelt, Hanna relinquished title to the government and, at his request, the Department of the Interior renamed the island Bird Key. After this triumph, Hanna founded a local chapter of the Audubon Society, and he continued working with the federal government to establish three additional small islands as part of the Bird Key preserve.[54]

At the parks board's second meeting, the group agreed that the city commission should contact the Olmsted Brothers to discuss the feasibility of creating a park plan. The commission gave its approval and sent Hanna to the Olmsted Brothers headquarters near Boston. When Hanna arrived at the Olmsted offices, he met with the landscape architect James Frederick Dawson. After reviewing some of the firm's projects, Hanna and Dawson toured the "Emerald Necklace" parkway, a famous Frederick Law Olmsted, Sr., project, which connected Boston Common and Franklin Park. After his New England sojourn, Hanna convinced the parks board to approach the county commission with the idea of creating a system of parks throughout the peninsula.[55]

Straub quickly lent his support to Hanna's proposal. The editor had cultivated connections throughout the peninsula when he led the independence movement, but now he faced a more difficult task. When he drafted the "Pinellas Declaration of Independence," Straub had spoken for a group of civic leaders united in their desire to see less interference in their private affairs. Now he needed their support to create a parks board with far-reaching powers. Fortunately for Straub, Pinellas lacked an entrenched elite with the power to crush his plans for the peninsula's development.

Straub employed a familiar strategy to build a broad-based consensus for park planning. In fall 1913 he spent two months convincing Pinellas's leaders that the new county needed a board of trade to promote issues vital to the "upbuilding of the county." In his newspaper he ran a series of editorials explaining the important role St. Petersburg's board of trade played in civic affairs and the tourism trade. On November 23, 1913, Straub's persistence paid off when the Pinellas County Board of Trade, at their first meeting, elected him president.[56]

The county board of trade's first resolution was a "declaration for the County Beautiful." They would make, the St. Petersburg Times reported, "Peerless Pinellas the most beautiful and popular playground in America." The gathering agreed that the quickening pace of development could mar the region's attractive setting. To prevent this and promote the tourism industry, the board declared, "It is in our opinion essential for the county to have definite plans for its development, as it is for advanced cities."[57]

Straub briefed the new organization's fifty-three members on the progress of the waterfront plan in St. Petersburg. Tourism had increased, profits were up, and the community shared a common bond in its efforts to build a more beautiful city. With Pinellas's newly won independence, Straub felt the board of trade could duplicate these accomplishments across the peninsula. Roy Hanna displayed examples of the Olmsteds' work and explained how a series of interconnected urban parks and natural areas would improve recreational opportunities and enhance property values. After concluding his presentation, the excited gathering elected Hanna to petition the county commission to hire the Olmsted Brothers. On January 5, 1914, using the same presentation, Hanna convinced the Pinellas County Commission to hire the Olmsted firm to design a park plan for the peninsula.[58]

By the next county board of trade meeting, enthusiasm for the County Beautiful had snowballed. The membership adopted a new resolution to set

Pinellas County off as "one beautiful garden." Stirred by this vision of Eden, members voted to help defray the costs of bringing a representative from the Olmsted Brothers to Pinellas.[59]

On February 16, 1914, James Dawson arrived in St. Petersburg. Initially, the landscape of the small city disappointed him. While duly impressed by the waterfront, he expected much more from a city in the "land of flowers." St. Petersburg offered only a small, overtaxed downtown park and, outside of a thin string of pines, there was surprisingly little foliage for such a temperate place. A few days later, Dawson's interest picked up when he explored Pinellas's hinterlands with Hanna. They encountered primeval stretches of swamp and forest, Hanna noted, "where the feet of white men seldom tread." The *St. Petersburg Times* reported that the landscape architect made his "most extensive notes . . . in the wilds and virgin land where the encroachment of civilization has had no chance to mar the natural scenery."[60]

In Pinellas's interior wetlands, Dawson found the essence of subtropical Florida. Giant live oaks encased in resurrection ferns and draped with Spanish moss marked the boundary where land and water met. As the elevation dipped the humid microclimate of the cypress dome produced a green, surreal world of knobby cypress knees emerging from a carpet of ferns. The nutrient-rich waters supported a host of such colorful plants as pickerel weed and duck potato, while countless pineapple air-plants decorated the ever present cypress. Above, the towering canopy of the bald cypress was punctuated by an occasional tupelo gum, a deciduous tree, with a bulging, bell-shaped trunk.[61] In this watery habitat, the two explorers encountered a wealth of species that equaled that of the tropical rainforest.[62]

The Dawson Plan

After a week of research and inspection, Dawson returned to Massachusetts. It took him six months to complete the project, which followed the traditional Olmsted format. The plan contained seventy-odd pages, without illustrations or maps, and described the virtues of a park system, the particulars of various sites, and the potential directions for real estate development. The final product also reflected the desires of Straub and his supporters to make the peninsula an Edenic reserve. A system of parkways connected urban "pleasure grounds," neighborhood parks, and natural preserves. The swaths of green that crossed the peninsula followed a formula that the Olmsteds had used in cities from Boston to Seattle.[63]

In Pinellas, Dawson wanted parkways to link the existing parks in St. Petersburg and Clearwater with the pristine bodies of water in the hinterland and along the coast. Scenic preserves were set aside in areas where creeks and lakes merged with marshland. These places had both abundant wildlife and the peninsula's last stands of old-growth hardwoods. If the plan was implemented properly, people would be able to relax in a landscaped park or explore the natural features that made the Pinellas subpeninsula unique in the Tampa Bay ecosystem.[64]

Dawson also encouraged the county to set aside an interconnected system of marshes and swampy areas for their usefulness as well as their sublime beauty. Since low-lying lands were subject to flooding and unsuitable for building, making such areas into parks was an efficient way of controlling floodwaters. In addition, parkways encompassing drainage canals and creeks were more cost effective for storing floodwaters than was the construction of underground conduits.[65]

The concluding section of the plan proposed a series of funding alternatives to implement the proposed park system. The Olmsted firm always recommended that local governments purchase parklands before property costs became so high that the public could not afford them. Municipal officials had a number of options: loans, bonds, special assessments, or tax increases. Usually local governments chose to raise money for land purchases by floating long-term bonds. By the time the bonds came due, the Olmsted firm predicted that the dollar value of the parks and the surrounding lands would far exceed the total paid on the loan. Although the expenditure of public monies would inevitably cause an outcry, the consultant thought that the returns would be especially lucrative in a county dependent on tourism.

Besides abetting the tourism industry, the Olmsted firm believed that a comprehensive park system would enhance the tax base because property values consistently escalated along parkways and parks. At the same time, the city might entice property owners holding lands designated for parks to sell portions at market rates to the city, provided they could reinvest their monies in comparable adjoining lands. Dawson urged those questioning this advice to visit Olmsted park systems in other cities and study the increased valuations in lands surrounding public green spaces.[66]

After reviewing Dawson's plan, Straub thought he had seen the blueprint for Eden. If the county commission adopted this work, the business of city building would take on an entirely different meaning. The Pinellas board of trade would work with the county commissioners to ensure, Straub wrote, that "natural and scenic beauties are conserved and not marred by helter-skelter real estate developments."[67]

Straub's optimism seemed well founded. St. Petersburg's municipal waterfront had brought the city national exposure. Among southern cities, it was a shining representative of what public planning could accomplish. In July 1913, the *Manufacturers' Record* reported why the people of St. Petersburg were "jealous of their waterfront." This prominent southern journal reported, "It is a thing of wondrous beauty and to the city a thing of wondrous value." With this public improvement, St. Petersburg appeared "to be rapidly reaching the dreams of its makers." Readers were urged to visit the city so they could "catch the inspiration of the place" and visualize how to improve their own cities.[68] In early 1915, the *Christian Science Monitor* commented that if other cities in the state followed St. Petersburg's lead, rather than Florida's being "commonly spoken of as the Italy of America, Italy might some day feel complimented on being called the Florida of Europe."[69]

Straub used this praise to promote the new park plan, especially when questions were raised over the expenditure of public funds. The benefits St. Petersburg had reaped from the waterfront had also attracted attention in Clearwater, the site of the new county courthouse. Civic leaders lauded the park plan and its backers as the "biggest thing Pinellas County had yet done," the *Clearwater News* reported. "When people from all parts of the county get together in one big, central organization and take up the work of developing the county along sane and sensible lines, the results will be far-reaching." By fall 1914, the board of trade had met four times, and with each meeting the membership grew and the rhetoric became more exuberant. "The Pinellas County Beautiful, the biggest and best movement for the upbuilding of the county, ever undertaken in Florida or the South," the *St. Petersburg Times* announced in October 1914, "will succeed."[70]

Florida municipalities and counties were not vested with the general powers of government (home rule). To gain these powers, local governments had to procure general enabling acts from the state legislature.[71] For Pinellas to establish a parks board that could disburse funds and acquire lands, the Pinellas delegation had to obtain enabling legislation from Tallahassee, and the county commission had to endorse the bill with a majority vote. The Olmsted Brothers drew up the necessary legislation, and the Pinellas delegation introduced the bill to the legislature for ratification in spring 1915.

The County Beautiful Bill, as it was named by its sponsors, called for a three-person county parks board with one member elected from each of the county's school districts. Members of the board would not be paid for their services, but they could employ an executive officer. The board would oversee the plan's production, but final adoption rested with the county commissioners. Once the plan was adopted, the parks board could implement it by acquiring land through purchase or condemnation. Financing the board would require a one-mill levy in the first year, a two-mill levy in the second year, and a maximum of a three-mill levy in its third year and every year thereafter. For any projects that exceeded budgetary constraints, the county commissioners could call a bond election, and the parks board would set the amount of the requisition.[72]

The Role of Natural Beauty in City Building

In May 1915, the Florida legislature passed the Pinellas County Beautiful Bill. The bill, however, received a far different reception in Pinellas. The euphoria over the prospect of turning the peninsula into a garden retreat quickly abated when boosters confronted the prospect of higher taxes. Straub wrote, "The idea was that it was nice but it would not pay—there was so much more that was practical and businesslike." While civic-minded residents could support volunteer efforts like the board of trade, many felt that subsidizing a bureaucratic initiative stretched the limits of democratic propriety.[73] The editor of the *Clearwater Sun* claimed not only that the creation of a park system was a waste of money, but that such an endeavor heightened the potential for political intrigue and the abuse of power. "[The bill] places more power in the hands of three men," the editor railed, "than is exercised by the president of the United States."[74]

The county commissioners also reversed their position once they realized that the executive manager of the proposed board could set up an independent domain that would influence the peninsula's development. While Straub blamed the demise of the County Beautiful Bill on "a 'don't care' Board of County Commissioners," the idea that beauty was valuable meant little in a region where it was common. Property owners and businessmen found it ludicrous that the government would raise taxes for parks when so many natural escapes were close at hand.[75] The peninsula's civic leaders had formed a new county to limit bureaucratic meddling, especially in the growing real estate market. In the rush to profit from the sale and development of land, those involved in city building could easily embrace a world with less natural beauty. Yet, whether they knew it or not, the failure to preserve a portion of the natural beauty that defined the region also had its costs.[76]

Straub learned some important lessons from the collapse of the County Beautiful movement. First, outside consultants provided valuable services, but their work still had to play on the stage of local politics. Next, idealistic visions might capture the fancy of local boosters, but pleasing notions counted for little when it came time to ante up. Straub, like other well-meaning reformers during this era, also discovered that expending public funds and instituting collective controls ran counter to the traditions of American democracy. He found that the sacred article of property rights and the pursuit of wealth could dissolve the bonds of the best plan, even one to create a new Eden.[77]

2

A Laboratory for Urban Planning?

In Florida we have the greatest opportunity of modern times to plan in
advance for the growth of our cities and towns, thereby eliminating forever the objectionable slums. . . . The state has every condition favorable for the soundest growth along lines exhibiting forethought in
planning.

George Gallup, 1926

In 1921 a tide of speculation and prosperity, now known as the "Great Florida
Land Boom," swept through St. Petersburg.[1] An increase in postwar domestic
spending, the Model T, modern advertising, the advent of leisure, and an unsurpassed spirit of financial optimism fueled an explosion in the real estate
market. St. Petersburg received national attention as tourists and speculators
swarmed into the city to buy land and bask in the subtropical surroundings.
Enthralled with both the city's natural and business climates, thousands returned after having vacationed there to take up permanent residence, and the
demand for public services quickly overwhelmed the Public Works Department.[2] Other Florida cities faced similar problems, but St. Petersburg's city
commission pursued a unique strategy to solve its predicament by hiring city
planner John Nolen. Nolen had watched the nation's fastest growing state
with, he wrote, "unusual interest. The settlement of other sections was
brought about by personal sacrifice and often danger, but Florida is being settled under modern methods, with almost unlimited resources of capital, experience and business enterprise." With just under a million residents in 1920,
this "last frontier," as Nolen called Florida, offered "a great laboratory of town
and city building."[3]

St. Petersburg Enters the New Urban Age

Among Florida's leading cities, only Miami (see tables 1 and 2) grew faster
than St. Petersburg during the 1920s. The accelerated growth of these two

Table 1
Population of Leading Florida Cities, 1900–1930

	1900	1910	1920	1930
Jacksonville	28,249	57,699	91,558	129,549
Pensacola	17,747	22,892	31,035	37,579
Tampa	15,830	37,782	51,608	101,161
Miami	1,681	5,471	29,571	110,637
St. Petersburg	1,575	4,127	14,237	40,425

Source: Bureau of the Census, *Fifteenth Census of the United States, 1930*

Table 2
Percentage of Population Increase in Leading Florida Cities, 1900–1930

	1900–1910	1910–1920	1920–1930
Jacksonville	103.0	58.7	41.5
Pensacola	29.5	35.0	1.8
Tampa	138.5	36.6	96.0
Miami	225.5	440.5	274.1
St. Petersburg	162.0	245.0	183.9

Source: Bureau of the Census, *Fifteenth Census of the United States, 1930*

Table 3
Florida's Population Growth, 1900–1930

	Population	% Increase from Previous Decade
1930	1,468,211	51.6
1920	968,470	28.7
1910	752,619	42.4
1900	528,542	35.0

Source: Bureau of the Census, *Fifteenth Census of the United States, 1930*

cities mirrored a phenomenon that occurred throughout the state. In 1900 Florida, with 528,542 residents, was the least populated state east of the Mississippi. By 1930 its population had almost tripled. While Florida's total population grew 51.6 percent during the 1920s, its urban population increased 114 percent (see tables 3 and 4). Over 80 percent of the state's 499,741 immigrants took up residence in cities and, by 1939, 51.7 percent of all Floridians lived in urban areas.

Table 4
Florida's Urban Population, 1900–1930

	Urban Population	% of Total Population	% Change from Previous Decade
1930	759,778	51.7	114.9
1920	353,515	36.7	61.4
1910	219,080	29.1	104.7
1900	107,031	20.3	38.4

Source: Bureau of the Census, *Fifteenth Census of the United States, 1930*

Table 5
Population Growth in Selected Southern States, 1900–1930

	1900	1910	1920	1930
Florida	528,542	752,619	968,470	1,468,211
Louisiana	1,381,625	1,655,388	1,798,509	2,101,593
Virginia	1,854,184	2,061,612	2,309,187	2,421,851
Texas	3,048,710	3,896,542	4,663,228	5,824,715
Georgia	2,216,331	2,609,121	2,895,832	2,908,506
Alabama	1,828,647	2,138,093	2,348,174	2,646,248

Source: Bureau of the Census, *Census of the United States, 1910, 1920, and 1930*

While a majority of Americans lived in cities for the first time in 1920, at the end of the decade Florida was the first state from the former Confederacy to have a majority of its population classified as urban (tables 5 and 6). (Another twenty years would go by before other southern states reached this point.)[4] Other southern cities acted as crucibles of change for the region, but in Florida the opportunities for city building proceeded from a different premise.[5] The booming Florida real estate market pushed St. Petersburg into a vibrant new world that held possibilities unforeseen not only by Southerners, but by an entire generation of Americans.

The 1920s, though often portrayed as a reactionary decade, were actually a time of unabashed optimism. "There was in the twenties," Clarence Stein, a member of the Regional Planning Association of America (RPAA), recalled, "a tremendous enthusiasm to build a new and better world."[6] The luxurious lifestyle accompanying the world's first economy of mass consumption fostered a new sense of hope in a nation anxious to repress the horrors of World War I. In the early 1920s, Americans enveloped themselves in a common aspiration to build a new civilization founded on industrial efficiency, scientific progress,

Table 6

Percentage of Urban Population in Selected Southern States, 1900–1930

	1900	*1910*	*1920*	*1930*
Florida	20.3	29.1	36.7	51.7
Louisiana	26.5	30.0	34.9	39.7
Virginia	18.3	23.1	29.2	32.4
Texas	17.1	24.1	32.4	41.0
Georgia	15.6	20.6	25.1	30.8
Alabama	11.9	17.3	21.7	28.1

Source: Bureau of the Census, *Census of the United States, 1910, 1920, and 1930*

and consumerism. Corporate America's technical wizardry and avowed mastery of the marketplace was changing the world, fueling the notion that a new people's capitalism would eliminate class divisions, and that a middle-class utopia would arise once Americans had acclimated themselves to abundance.[7]

Consumerism, modern technology, and the corporation were not only changing American life, but creating a world that yearned for change. The nation's rising standard of living produced a stream of innovations that grew from the search for profits and competitive advantages. Every individual or group competing for consumers contributed to this stream; the fluctuating market economy soon made any business not actively seeking change obsolete. In St. Petersburg, change meant vitality and progress. Almost every issue of the city's newspapers carried news of businesses that were reorganizing, shifting emphasis, and moving into new areas. "New blood is entering old firms," a business reporter noted, "men from older firms are branching into new enterprises, men are moving from one business to another."[8] If these changes were startling, they were also healthy. In an age of growth and prosperity, change equaled progress.

Prosperity had its price. If the people of St. Petersburg wanted to enjoy their new blessings, they needed to adjust to a place where disruption and modern-world vitality constantly intermingled as technical advances and shifts in the market offered new opportunities for growth and development.[9] They needed desperately to form, William Straub believed, new and imaginative responses to the rapid transformation of the city's life and landscape. In their pursuit of easy riches, citizens had left many important issues unattended. If they continued to boost and gamble rather than plan, Straub wrote in 1921, "we may perish by our own ostrich-like ignorance."[10]

Many in St. Petersburg believed that they could escape change because they lived in a place that was supposed to elude the hectic pace of the new age.

Local boosters claimed that the city's good fortune came from the decades of hard work it had taken to create an environment suited to the needs of modern America. They believed that their subtropical sanctuary provided the perfect escape, as poet Sidney Lanier had written a half century earlier, "from that universal killing ague of modern times—the fever and the unrest of trade."[11] In St. Petersburg many thought that securing the future merely required leading others to the new Eden.

Florida: The "Eden of the South"

After the Civil War and Reconstruction, Florida reentered the Union intent on reshaping the state's image and attracting northern capital and business skills.[12] Like other former Confederate states, Florida adhered to the "New South Creed," a philosophy of progress and optimism that mixed the traditions of the Old South with the mores of Social Darwinism. The creation of a new South depended on building an industrial empire that would rival the North's and return a measure of self-esteem to a defeated people. To resurrect their dormant economy, new South promoters advocated cooperating with northern business interests to exploit the region's abundant resources. New South champions, such as Henry Grady of the *Atlanta Constitution* and Richard Edmonds of the *Manufacturers' Record*, predicted that when northern entrepreneurial skills combined with the South's traditional values, the region would emerge as a paragon of productivity and virtue.[13]

At the dawn of the twentieth century, Florida remained peculiarly southern. Like the rest of what had been the Confederacy, Florida had failed to make the necessary structural changes that would enable its economy to compete with the rest of America. The state's Democratic leaders extolled the virtues of a new South, but poverty, single-party politics, Jim Crow, and an agrarian conservatism held sway over the state's overwhelmingly rural population. Even with these obstructions, however, it was possible to get a glimpse of the new South's most elusive commodity—prosperity.[14]

In 1888, Standard Oil tycoon Henry Flagler built the Ponce de León Hotel in St. Augustine, the first in a series of luxury hotels that furnished exotic escapes for travelers on his Florida East Coast Railway. Flagler placed his modern Moorish palaces in garden settings and near pristine beaches to create images long associated with Oriental decadence. Like the Crusaders encountering Arabia, tourists were primed for a land of sweetmeats, lush gardens, servants, and trickling fountains.[15] By 1900, Flagler's architectural marvels had captivated a wealthy set who regularly ventured to the small islands of civilization he had created in Florida's primitive subtropical wilderness.[16]

Flagler's ventures improved Florida's economy and gave it a new direction. Publications released by the government, railroad lines, and land companies used the state's tropical landscape and the myth of the Fountain of Youth to entice newcomers into what Elliot Mackle has called the "Eden of the South."[17] Many believed that nature's rejuvenating powers existed in their purest form in Florida, where one could also find elegant hotels, such wealthy winter residents as Andrew Carnegie and John D. Rockefeller, and a profitable real estate market. Whether newcomers came to enjoy themselves or to make money, the state's natural environment enraptured them. Profits had become "Eden's" most enticing fruit.[18]

The state's changing fortunes and the completion of a comprehensive rail network spurred an 83 percent population increase, from 528,542 to 968,470, between 1900 and 1920. But despite the surge in population and economic activity, Florida remained a poor, underdeveloped state. The few elegant resorts had undoubtedly improved Florida's image and prospects, but these pleasure palaces remained out of reach for the middle class until the 1920s. In the early 1920s, the nation underwent a momentous shift to become the world's first mass consumer economy. Coolidge prosperity gave Americans more leisure and money, and they used these gifts to escape the routine of business and banality of life. In Florida, Americans found a vacationland that combined American sport with subtropical beauty (figure 5).[19]

After spending two generations cultivating an image geared to escapist fantasies, in the early 1920s Florida succeeded in capturing the nation's imagination. America's newest vacation spot was the "Headline of America," according to the *New York Times*. Henry Grady's prophecies were finally being fulfilled: "The South is a miracle," *Collier's Weekly* announced, "a pretty fairy tale which no one if he can be carried aboard the Florida train or on a litter can afford to miss."[20] "The future of Florida is roseate with potentialities and possibilities beyond the power of the mind to fully grasp," proclaimed Richard Edmonds.[21] The image of swaying palms, tropical waters, and the Fountain of Youth still defined Florida, but the state now offered new pleasures that reflected the transformation in American life.

In the 1920s Americans faced an unusual problem. The advent of prosperity had given them an abundance of free time. As a people, Americans were so accustomed to pouring their energy into getting ahead that even vacationers needed structure and something to do.[22] Resort cities accommodated tourists' needs by incorporating new activities into the Florida lifestyle. St. Petersburg's

PRESIDENT HARDING DISCOVERS THE "FOUNTAIN OF YOUTH"
IN FLORIDA'S SUNSHINE, FRESH AIR AND EXERCISE

Figure 5 During the boom years, St. Petersburg mixed the racist image of
the Old South with the Fountain of Youth myth to sell itself as the "Eden
of the South." Bushnell, 1923, St. *Petersburg Times.*

Chamber of Commerce reminded visitors to prepare for "the robust activities
that are a part of your life. Pack your summer clothes, golf sticks, fishing tackle,
bathing suits, camera, and tennis racquets for a land of perpetual sunshine."[23]

In the early 1920s, it seemed as though Ponce de León's dream had come to
fruition in St. Petersburg. "I staked my all on this land, my fortune, my friends,
and finally my life. Now I have come back that I might know it was not in
vain," the conquistador states, in Ruth Crawford's inventive account of Ponce
de León's visit to St. Petersburg. The surprised explorer found that a "land of
youth" actually existed where "there was no age" because the "spirit of youth"
and the "generosity of the land" erased generational differences. In St. Peters-

burg, families lived together, "played together and made work their play." "Men went to work not as drudges, but as those who took joy in their workmanship." After surveying this paradise surrounded by water, where "the sun invited the people to play on the beaches," Ponce de León realized that he had "dreamed true." When the time came for the famed explorer to depart, he speculated, "Perhaps if I hid myself in the park near the water, I could stay one more day. Surely when there are so many dreamers, one who had gone back to his dreams would not be missed."[24]

The image of the early explorer accompanied the thousands who journeyed to Florida in search of Eden. "Not since the Great West was opened up," Perriton Maxwell, an editor for *Suniland*, reported, "has history recorded such an amazing growth of civilization as in Florida."[25] Whether seeking a hiatus in the Garden or a bucolic, suburban residence, world-weary people yearning for the rewards of modern life found a seductive lure in St. Petersburg: "Homes contribute to the fascination of the suburbs. Yet they attain no small degree of their surpassing beauty from rare natural attractiveness of location. Picture bits of South Sea Islands, Palms on Golden Beaches, swaying to the trade winds, the sweeping shore of the French Riviera, Italian sunsets, glowing on a community of perfect homes and hovering overall is the atmosphere of ancient Spain. This is Beach Park on Old Tampa Bay."[26]

Realtors published thousands of advertisements like these as they mixed selling and seduction. This new twist in promotion swelled the pages and bolstered the sales of St. Petersburg's leading newspaper, the *St. Petersburg Times*. In 1925, at the height of the boom, the *Times*'s twenty-five million lines of advertising ranked second nationally only to the *Miami Herald*'s record forty-two million lines. On November 22, 1925, the Sunday *Times* allocated ninety of its 134 pages to real estate advertising, with fifty-five pages listing vacant lots for sale. Nationwide speculation in Florida real estate more than tripled the circulation of the *St. Petersburg Times* between 1920 and 1927.[27]

Both public and private initiatives contributed to the proliferation of advertising. In the 1920s, every city in Florida actively engaged in advertising or otherwise boosting the community.[28] The people of St. Petersburg made such activity a communal project. "It takes boosting to get ahead," the *St. Petersburg Times* declared, and because of this, the "Chamber of Commerce is the most important industry in the city."[29] The civic leadership's preoccupation with boosting reflected an acute discernment of the marketplace's new proprieties. The leaders understood that the city's vitality did not depend on producing goods, but on the promotion and creation of a fabricated environment where visitors could pursue their fantasies. C. B. Axford, a leading builder, wrote of the need to attract tourists: "We have no factories, no vast industries

. . . we are solely dependent to take wealth and tribute from all the world to make our city grow."[30] Boosting qualified as a civic duty.[31]

The journalist Frank Stockbridge found boosting so intense in St. Petersburg that he called it "the city that advertising built." He reported, "There is no community in all Florida [in which] the united efforts of the entire citizenship [have] been so acutely and intelligently concentrated upon advertising its advantages."[32] In the early 1920s, St. Petersburg imposed the state's first special tax to pay for advertising.[33] The Chamber of Commerce spent the funds raised, allocating a statewide high of $8,000 on advertising in 1921, $27,000 in 1923, $45,000 in 1924, $160,000 in 1925, and $270,000 in 1926.[34]

These expenditures seemed well-placed. In late 1921, the Automobile Association reported that it received more inquiries for routes to St. Petersburg than any other Florida point. Two years later, John M. Bowman, president of New York's Biltmore Hotel commented that, "the amazing growth of St. Petersburg is in direct proportion to the unusual and widespread advertising the city received."[35] In 1924, the city gained recognition as a vacation Mecca in the *Saturday Evening Post, Literary Digest, National Geographic, Travel, Vogue, Vanity Fair, Homes and Gardens,* and *Cosmopolitan.*[36]

Locals and visitors alike were mesmerized by St. Petersburg's growth. "It seems almost like looking at the dramatization of a fairy tale to view the wonderful development that has taken place in St. Petersburg," Senator Walter F. George of Georgia concluded after his twenty-five-year absence from the city. In 1923, L. F. Epplich, president of the National Realtors' Association, was "simply astounded" by what he saw. "The progressive spirit of the city is evident everywhere—in the wide streets, new churches, and buildings under construction."[37] If the city continued to grow at its present rate, one realtor predicted in 1923, its population would jump to almost 150,000 in a decade: "Thousands of families in the North are bound to settle in this 'Fountain of Youth' section with its wonderful climate." The secret of this rapid growth, the Chamber of Commerce revealed, "is found in the simple fact that in one community have been combined in a remarkable manner those advantages and attractions, natural and man-made, which civilized mankind dreams of and desires."[38]

Planning for Prosperity

Despite all that was written idealizing it, St. Petersburg suffered from many problems. Land speculators, or "subdividers," purchased vacant land, then divided it into small (forty-foot wide) lots because such lots' return per square foot was two to three times that of larger ones. Because no planning guidelines had been laid down, the city had turned into a confusing patchwork of disconnected subdivisions by late 1921. Lots ran in every direction, while streets and alleys were laid out haphazardly, often failing to meet at intersections—or just running into dead ends. When the Department of Public Works tried to extend urban services to a subdivision, the engineering obstacles were often insurmountable.[39]

On July 5, 1921, the city commission hired E. C. Garvin as the first director of public works. The commission hoped that Garvin, a licensed civil engineer with degrees from George Washington and Case Western Reserve Universities, could bring some order to the city's chaotic expansion. Garvin quickly realized the difficulty of his task after tract owners flooded his office with demands for public improvements: sewers, sidewalks, and especially streets. These investors were anxious to sell their lots at the market's inflated prices, and they believed that a better infrastructure would impress prospective buyers that the Florida Riviera, Paradise Park, Elysian Fields, or Seminole Estates stood at the vanguard of civilization. "In that day," Walter Fuller recalled, "a lot was something to sell the avid speculator and not something on which to build a home." All the subdivider wanted was a "contract or deed, a street and an imposing entrance."[40]

Without a plan to follow, the Department of Public Works faced an awesome task in trying to meet the increasing demand for public improvements. In some areas where Garvin's staff were called on to provide services, they had no idea how the land would be used in the future. He desperately needed a city plan to get a fix on the location of subdivisions, so that his office could implement an efficient design for streets, sewers, and other improvements.[41]

Once Garvin came on board, Straub began a drive for city planning. A few months earlier he had helped form a local chapter of the Rotary, and this group served as his springboard for reform. Straub was the group's president and, a week after Garvin's hiring, he petitioned the city commission, on behalf of the Rotary, to establish a city planning board. After twenty years, local politicians were well acquainted with Straub's crusades. Although city planning was a subject foreign to most of the commissioners, they acceded to Straub's request, although more to "shut him up," as one member recounted, "than anything else."[42] After a unanimous vote, on August 15, 1921, the mayor appointed Straub, Annie McRae, and a realtor, T. J. Heller, to sit on the new advisory board. A week later, Straub chaired the Planning Board's opening meeting, with Annie McRae as secretary.[43]

At the Planning Board's second meeting, its members sent the city commission a resolution asking for funds to hire a consultant. The commission consented and, in late November 1921, after reading one of his books, Annie McRae wrote John Nolen that the city needed his services. Nolen responded by congratulating the city for establishing Florida's first planning board and informing McRae: "The opportunity to plan seems to me most unusual and I would be more than happy to cooperate with you and the City Planning Board." Although St. Petersburg was not a new town, more than 90 percent of the city stood vacant, and it was, as Nolen wrote, "bound to grow."[44]

John Nolen: Pioneer Planner

John Nolen's vision of urban reform helped pioneer the planning profession. Although separated in age by a quarter of a century from Lewis Mumford and his colleagues in the RPAA, Nolen was a kindred spirit. "What we may have had in common," Stein stated, "was a tremendous enthusiasm to build a new and better world."[45] Nolen's utopian quest led him to city planning. Born in Philadelphia in 1869, Nolen was admitted to the University of Pennsylvania in 1890, where he majored in economics and public administration. Simon N. Patten, the Wharton School's professor of political economy, captivated Nolen with his theories of social engineering. Patten believed that America's economic transformation gave urban reformers the opportunity to enhance the quality of the public realm. He thought that the provision of municipal art, parks, lectures, and concerts would help the urban masses adjust to a new prosperity that would make leisure a given in life. Like other Patten students— Herbert Croly, Walter Weyl, and Rexford G. Tugwell—Nolen went into the world confident that, through the cooperative efforts of the public and private sectors, Americans were destined to enjoy a higher standard of living.[46]

After graduating from the University of Pennsylvania in 1893, Nolen spent ten years serving as the executive secretary of the Society for the Extension of University Teaching. Nolen honed his public-relations skills and spent an increasing amount of time studying municipal affairs. In 1901, Nolen left his job to pursue a new career in city planning. He spent two years in Europe studying innovations in land-use zoning and town design. Immediately after his return to the United States, Nolen enrolled in Harvard University's newly formed School of Landscape Architecture.[47]

At Harvard, Frederick Law Olmsted Jr. instructed Nolen in the art of landscape design. Olmsted and his star pupil also spent many hours discussing the potential of America's fledgling city planning movement. A decade earlier, a tour of Europe with his renowned father had introduced the younger Olmsted to English and German experiments in urban planning, and by the early 1900s, he was the leading spokesman for America's city planning profession. Besides teaching Nolen the intricacies of urban design, Olmsted introduced him to the idea that planners could unify the complex elements comprising the "organic city."[48]

Although Nolen's theory of planning evolved over the years, his design technique centered on the Olmsteds' ideal of harmonizing natural and urban landscapes.[49] After leaving Harvard, Nolen worked as a consultant on park plans and municipal improvement projects in the South, the East, and the Midwest. By 1907 he had joined Olmsted and a small cadre of like-minded reformers in promoting comprehensive city planning as a tool to ameliorate the nation's urban ills.[50]

Between 1907 and 1919, Nolen helped establish the theoretical constructs of comprehensive planning. Nolen, Olmsted Jr., and other pioneer city planners saw the world in ethical terms. For them, the landscape encompassed a communal good that the speculative real estate market failed to value properly. The American city's haphazard expansion, sordid living conditions, inadequate public services, and lack of amenities were telling indictments against the laissez-faire approach. The planning profession wanted to replace America's chaotic method of city building with a planned land-use system. In 1917 Olmsted defined city planning as "the attempt to exert a well-considered control on behalf of the people of a city, over the development of their physical environment as a whole."[51]

The new profession expanded the urban vision of earlier reformers by wedding beauty to utility. While they continued to emphasize civic responsibility, park planning, and formal design in their work, they also wanted to address a wider range of issues.[52] "There is a danger in making city planning look like merely a 'city beautiful' scheme," Nolen warned the eminent British planning theorist Patrick Geddes in 1915, "instead of the practical, hard-headed recommendations for the permanent betterment of city life."[53] But Nolen never sought to dismiss beauty from the city; instead he thought that comprehensive plans following natural lines would produce a more efficient urban system.[54]

The planning profession promoted comprehensive planning as a systematic procedure that could guide urban expansion and curtail the excesses of free enterprise. Plans usually included both text and a land-use map that depicted an idealized conception of the city's future. "In a word, we should frame a concept, an ideal of what we wish the city to be," Nolen advised, "and then we should make it one of the controlling purposes in the development of the city plan."[55] The plan coordinated transportation systems, park systems, and the use of land, while establishing the character of development, Olmsted explained, "in so far as it is practicable for the community to control or influence such developments."[56]

The planners also sold their new idea as a means to improve the efficiency of the free-market system. Since the land-use plan reflected the "highest and best use" of urban property, entrepreneurs seeking to maximize land values would benefit from following it. At the same time, the plan's transportation network and schedule of improvements would make the inevitable public outlays more economical. Planning also offered the means to improve the working classes' congested and insanitary living conditions by separating residences from factories and giving easy access to public parks and transit lines. For those questioning the legitimacy of public planning, reformers responded that the improved living conditions would foster a more productive work force and, in turn, higher profits.[57]

In designing and implementing plans, planners had to work closely with municipal officials and city planning commissions, the quasi-governmental agencies that focused exclusively on issues surrounding city building. In theory, their autonomy insulated members from the mundane affairs of municipal government and freed them to concentrate on the visionary aspects of city building. To maintain a measure of independence from elected officialdom and local political scheming, urban reformers wanted knowledgeable volunteers to sit on planning commissions. Often the planning commission hired a professional planner to prepare the plan, which was submitted to public review. Once an elected body adopted the plan, the planning commission reviewed new building projects and coordinated expansion of improvements in the infrastructure. Although only an advisory board, the planning commission helped the city commission enforce the city's zoning code.

While the comprehensive plan provided a conceptual design of the city's future mixture of land uses, zoning regulated the construction industry and the real estate market. The zoning code set the standards for the height and bulk of buildings and separated different land uses into a system of hierarchical urban cells, or zones. Height and bulk regulations gave municipalities a means to control population densities and protect property values. Citizens who wanted to change their property's zoning classification were required to seek a variance from the planning commission. The burden rested with the property owner to show that the proposed land use would not become a nuisance to the surrounding properties or impair the intent of the plan. If the planning commission rejected the petitioner's plea, property owners could bring their case before the city commission.[58]

The technical details of planning and zoning were by no means the planner's most difficult task. In a society where property rights are preeminent, implementing a plan required the consultant—and the planning commission—to strike a balance between civic needs and market demands. Otherwise, local governments could never enforce the land-use controls needed to implement the plan.[59]

The idea of city planning was in tune with the political reforms that swept through the United States between the turn of the century and World War I.[60] "The promise of American city planning is bright," John Nolen proclaimed numerous times between 1909 and 1917, "because of this new spirit of democracy . . . of which . . . city planning is only one meager expression."[61] The chaos of the land market, which lacked any controls, was ample justification for enlisting the planner's aid. Between 1910 and 1920, 42 percent of the nation's fifty largest urban centers, and 13 percent of all cities over 25,000, turned to comprehensive planning.[62]

While the planning profession managed to initiate the planning process and educate civic leaders, it generally failed to obtain backing for public housing, site planning, and residential design. In a speech at the 1919 National Planning Conference, Nolen stated that, aside from Chicago, no major city had seriously pursued planning. If the profession was to shape urban America, practitioners needed to lobby state legislatures and obtain legal standing for their plans.[63] Nolen also felt that the profession needed to improve its record on plan implementation. To improve the existing procedure, he advocated using the right of eminent domain (although selectively), charging assessments for planned improvements, and issuing bonds for purchasing parks. For city planning really to advance, he concluded, planners needed "better ways of forming intelligent public opinion and of giving it effective expression."[64]

John Nolen: Theorist and Practitioner

Nolen worked tirelessly to promote city planning. By 1919 he stood at the apex of his profession. He had edited two books, written two more, and published more than fifty articles and plans. He was the sole proprietor of the nation's largest planning firm. Nolen's success arose from a blend of idealism and business acumen, which allowed his work to be both innovative and pragmatic.[65]

Nolen's books—*New Ideals in the Planning of Cities, Towns, and Villages* (1919) and *New Towns for Old* (1927)—owed a great deal to the opinions of his friend and confidant, the English planner Raymond Unwin. Nolen and Unwin first met in 1911, and soon became fast friends. Close in age and interests, these two pioneer planners corresponded regularly for twenty-five years, exchanging social views and planning expertise as well as more personal information. Both men rose to the pinnacle of their profession, holding the presidency of their respective national planning associations. In 1931, Nolen replaced his close friend as president of the International Federation of Housing and Town Planning, a post Unwin had occupied since 1928. Nolen's last letter, written on his deathbed, went to Unwin.[66]

Unwin's English garden cities at Hampstead and Letchworth, and his writings on town design, greatly influenced Nolen. Unwin advocated building clusters of garden cities connected by rail as an alternative to the "huge aggregation of units ever spreading further and further from the original center." For Unwin, a disciple of Ebenezer Howard's garden city movement, planning allowed local governments to allocate land for the various components of a city in accordance with the land's characteristics.[67] Adherents of the garden city concept believed that planners could break down the complexities of urban life by designing communities around natural forms and at a human scale (defined as no more than twelve units per acre). In contrast to the rectangular monotony of the traditional checkerboard plan, Unwin's neighborhoods followed the contours of the land. He grouped residences, often garden apartments, on the land most suited for development. This allowed him to set aside the most fertile soils for agriculture and to preserve the more fragile lands for recreation or as common open space.[68]

Nolen's *New Ideals*

In *New Ideals in the Planning of Cities, Towns, and Villages*, Nolen blended Unwin's theories with his own experience to propose a new agenda for the American city. Besides analyzing planning procedures, Nolen made a strong plea for using urban planning as a tool to protect the natural environment. After a half century of urban development, Americans had finally started to realize, he wrote, "the necessity of respecting and conserving natural features, to which they owe not only their form, but often their very life."[69] Americans wanted safe, healthy communities, but Nolen felt that this goal would be unattainable as long as cities continued to expand in a haphazard manner. According to him, imposing a plan to check "haphazard drift" was only part of the planning process. It was also imperative to work with municipal officials to create a common culture by designing a future city that maintained local traditions and the health of the landscape.[70]

The first step in Nolen's idea of planning was to study the region's environment. This gave practitioners a base from which they could "unfold and perfect" a community's natural characteristics. Besides satisfying the "love of nature and the desire for outdoor life," a plan that more clearly echoed the landscape set the pattern for the city's future development.[71] Analysis of soil, topography, and natural features determined the best sites for intense development. By setting aside scenic areas unsuited for building—for example, floodplains and steep hillsides—a community could also protect important natural resources and make the urban fabric more aesthetically pleasing. Nolen recommended that a system of paths and parkways connect public lands so that urban dwellers could "enjoy the beauty and wonder of the nature [sic] world."[72]

After laying out the park system, Nolen designated lands suited for industrial, residential, business, and public uses, based on their function and subsequent use and maintenance. In a section of the city dedicated to industrial uses, for instance, it was important to incorporate efficient transport for goods and workers. "Foremost among the functions of practical city planning," Nolen wrote, "is to arrange a city so that its citizens can live and do business there with the maximum of comfort and the minimum of cost."[73] By planning the different components of an urban system around natural forms, he wrote, "It will invariably be found that utility and beauty go hand in hand and are virtually inseparable."[74]

Nolen also wanted American cities to follow the European practice of providing municipal improvements to benefit the entire public, not just private investors. The Old World presented an impressive array of public buildings, city squares and plazas, playgrounds, parks, parkways and boulevards, art museums, and theaters, all available to the citizenry. Besides giving urban dwellers an escape from "the grind and fatigue of the day's work," Nolen believed that a beautiful and functional public realm helped expand civic consciousness.[75]

Nolen's excursions to Europe convinced him that what he called "collectivization" was an indomitable historical force that had arisen in response to the urban and industrial revolutions. In modern urban society, collectivization conferred the planning powers local governments needed to enhance the public life and protect the common welfare. The striking contrast between cities on the two continents resulted from Europe's fifty years of collectivized action "to meet the requirements of modern life." Since the 1870s, the collaborative efforts of private and public enterprise had furnished a wide array of improvements that left citizens with "a more intimate knowledge of noble examples of human life and beautiful products of human work."[76]

Nolen believed that America stood at an important crossroads in the early 1920s. The nation's technological acuity had revolutionized city building, but the forces transforming the country's once graceful agrarian landscape followed no guide but profit. Technology had accelerated the urbanization process to the point that it was no longer safe, Nolen believed, to leave the intricate details surrounding city building "to chance or speculation or mere private aggrandizement." While delegating collective powers to municipalities and experts represented a dramatic change of focus in American democracy, it was an inevitable response to the profound changes sweeping the nation. Planning gave municipal officials the means to educate and motivate people who, Nolen wrote, "have stood listless, without the business sense, skill or courage to begin a work that must sooner or later be done."[77] If America's outdated system of urban governance—predicated on "selfish individualism"—were to continue, American life would hold little promise. Nolen's *New Ideals* concluded with a ringing denouncement of the country's urban ills, which to him clearly indicated the need for planning: "The faults of the street system, the ignorant and ugly conditions of waterfronts, the failure to link various agencies for transportation, the demoralizing influence of slums—these represent the neglect of any large planning authority to control and check rank individualism and to exercise collective power in the name of the entire community."[78]

A Test Case in the "Eden of the South"

By 1921 Nolen had concluded that it was a hopeless task to replan the American city or alter the patterns of development. The nation's cities were cursed, he wrote, "with nearly insolvable social and political problems."[79] He was also frustrated because most planners, instead of designing a new standard for urban living, spent their time drawing up zoning ordinances that ensured mediocrity. Nolen had started to explore, he wrote Patrick Geddes, "the beginning of a much more hopeful character in the way of planning new communities."[80] After Annie McRae sent Nolen a telegram to retain his services in late 1921, he thought that St. Petersburg might be the proper laboratory in which to test his theories.

In February 1922, Nolen signed a $6,500 contract to produce a comprehensive plan for St. Petersburg and its environs.[81] He immediately hired Frank B. Williams, author of *The Law of City Planning and Zoning* (1922), America's first treatise on planning law. Nolen could put Williams's legal expertise to good use. He could write both a general enabling act for planning for the state of Florida (which had none) and also legislation that would give St. Petersburg control over the platting and planning of the city and county lands slated for annexation. In March 1922, Nolen wrote Williams: "I am much pleased with this arrangement as an unusual opportunity for you to exercise a good influence on city planning legislation." "This seems," he confessed, "to be an opportunity to do rather more than we have ever been given the chance to do before."[82]

3

St. Petersburg Today, St. Petersburg Tomorrow: A Model Plan for the Modern City

> If we cannot create better urban conditions without changing our present methods and institutions and controls, we must be prepared to change them: To hold that the present means are sacred and untouchable is to succumb to a superstitious taboo.
>
> Lewis Mumford, 1923

In January 1923, John Nolen wrote Lewis Mumford: "I am enjoying and profiting by *The Story of Utopias*," which was Mumford's first book.[1] The book was especially helpful to Nolen's project in St. Petersburg because it justified the criteria he had employed in designing Florida's first comprehensive city plan. Nolen's vision of a resort city that followed the lines of a "benevolent Nature" represented more than just a blueprint for development. It also incorporated, as Mumford noted of all designs for a better life, "a new set of habits, a fresh scale of values, and different set of relationships and institutions."[2] For St. Petersburg to come close to the desirable future Nolen envisioned, the city-building process would have to change. "One of the problems of the St. Petersburg of tomorrow," Nolen wrote, "is the adequate control of private development.... The future character of this larger city and its environs ... is very much a question of what the present generation wishes it to become."[3]

St. Petersburg: A Laboratory for Planning

In the 1920s a tranquil alternation of land and water characterized St. Petersburg's subtropical landscape. Clear, temperate waters bounded the city to the east, while a mixture of live oaks, pines, palms, and citrus bordered the rest of the city. This sublime setting displayed, Nolen wrote, "much the same character as that of southern France."[4]

Figure 6 The traditional Cracker frontier home was designed to accommodate St. Petersburg's hot, humid climate. Courtesy of the St. Petersburg Historical Museum.

Although it was hardly Nice or Cannes, by 1922 St. Petersburg was becoming one of America's favored resorts. An established town of nearly 20,000, it radiated from a central urban core on Tampa Bay to cover eleven square miles. As a result of the land boom the city extended about a mile inland, in a progressively less linear and compact form. Thanks to the greater mobility made possible by the automobile, subdivisions were appearing next to new roads almost overnight. At the same time, the downtown was growing upward as two seven-story buildings, the Sumner Building and the Ponce de León Hotel, neared completion. These landmarks were the beginning of St. Petersburg's skyline.[5]

Interesting groupings of vernacular architecture covered the landscape surrounding downtown. The Cracker-style home (figure 6) traced its origins to Pinellas's earliest pioneers. This simple, two-story frame house was designed for maximum comfort in Florida's hot climate. It sat on concrete blocks for better air circulation and to minimize flood damage during the seasonal downpours. The wide front porch and many windows provided cross-ventilation, while the steep tin roof allowed hot air to be drawn upward. Although the Cracker home remained an option, in the 1920s St. Petersburg's prosperous middle-class citizens were more likely to build bungalows (figure 7). Larger and

Figure 7 The bungalow was part of the American Dream in pre–World War II St. Petersburg. Courtesy of the St. Petersburg Historical Museum.

more ornate than the Cracker home, the bungalow with its deep porch, wide eaves, and low, overhanging roof gave its residents both shade and ventilation. The many windows offered an entrance for winter sunlight, while its roof blocked the intense summer sun. Wood floors and stucco walls stood natural and unpainted, while the unplastered ceiling exposed structural beams for a decidedly different interior appearance.[6]

The Mediterranean Revival style (figure 8) was the most elegant (and also the most expensive) adaptation to the region's environment. Open court-yards, tiled roofs, stucco walls, high ceilings, and arched windows and door-ways were the principal components of an architecture that combined practi-cality and beauty. The grand homes and lavish hotels embellished with secluded gardens, iron gates and grills, open balconies, and hand-painted tiles marked the rise of an affluent class. The city's expanded housing stock hinted at St. Petersburg's potential, but, at the same time, new development was cre-ating problems that required immediate attention.[7]

When Nolen arrived in St. Petersburg in March 1922, he found a city in bloom. Hibiscus, azaleas, camellias, and dogwoods lent the town a special beauty, while vines grew, he wrote, "wherever opportunity is afforded and bril-liant mats of color are produced by such climbers as the purple bougainvillea, orange and red trumpet flower, yellow and white jasmine and the golden alla-manda."[8] At the same time, the groves surrounding St. Petersburg permeated

Figure 8 The magnificence of the Soreno Hotel's Mediterranean Revival style captured the spirit of the boom years. The hotel was razed as part of the ill-fated Bay Plaza project. Courtesy of the St. Petersburg Historical Museum.

the air with the scent of orange blossom. Besides citrus, Nolen encountered "on every hand the fruits of the tropics; mangoes, avocadoes, guavas, papayas, bananas and pineapple."

On March 3, 1922, a crowd of approximately two hundred attended Nolen's presentation on city planning at the high school auditorium. The slight, mustachioed speaker began by defining his profession as "the substitution of art, scientific skill, and foresight for chance and a haphazard and piecemeal procedure." Nolen explained that his plan for St. Petersburg would encompass the southern third of the peninsula, because this represented the city's "natural boundaries." His firm would analyze the region's topography and environment, inventory the existing land uses, and then gather information from St. Petersburg's citizens to determine the plan's "controlling purpose." While the final product would "properly regulate" the city's growth, it would also reflect, Nolen concluded, "the people of St. Petersburg's best impulses and highest conceptions."[9]

On March 4, 1922, Nolen flew over the Pinellas Peninsula to get a feel for the region. He emerged from the plane ecstatic: "What a site for a city!" With the peninsula's blend of land and water, there were "few if any situations like it in the world. . . . Waterfront, almost endless in extent and variety, lakes large and small, with unspoiled tracts of tropical jungle and miles and miles of good building land give one the thrill of the possibilities. . . . There is a good reason," he wryly concluded, "for so many realtors." Since his contract with the St. Petersburg Planning Board called only for planning "greater St. Petersburg," Nolen asked for a meeting with the Pinellas County Commission to draw out a general conceptual plan for the peninsula. This exercise, Nolen wrote, would be "relatively inexpensive," and "the advantages in the future development of the County and its property would be considerable." In Nolen's view, regional planning was the best investment the commission could make to ensure future prosperity.[10]

The quickening pace of urbanization was closing the gap that had once separated urban areas from their hinterlands. "Where the country was once simply an agricultural region, producing food for cities," he wrote, "it has now become, through the use of motor transportation, part of the city." The increasing commuter traffic between cities and suburbs corroborated his opinion that "the potential urban possibility is rapidly becoming a reality." Given these new circumstances, Nolen felt that regional planning offered the best means to design a city and its supporting lands as a single unit.[11]

Shortly before Nolen left St. Petersburg, the county commission rejected his offer. The consultant, however, could not turn away from the promise the peninsula held for future business. In his plan for St. Petersburg he decided to include a regional study of planning issues, for example, road connections and the acquisition of park sites, that faced both the county and the city.

Nolen returned to his Massachusetts office with a once-in-a-lifetime opportunity. In a profession that gave "too much attention to caring for the mere wreckage of society, and too little toward establishing a better social order," he could finally design a regionally scaled plan for a city with untold potential.[12] He brought back a cache of materials to work with: Chamber of Commerce pamphlets, Van Bibber's report from the *Journal of the American Medical Association*, the city's official directory, Sanborn maps, the county soil survey, and geological maps.[13]

During his stay, Nolen had met with key community leaders: Mayor Frank Pulver, Herman Dann, president of the Chamber of Commerce, Roy Hanna, developer C. M. Roser, and J. P. Lynch, president of the Board of Realtors. Only one influential figure, Lew Brown, editor of the *St. Petersburg Independent*, chose not to meet with Nolen.[14] Aside from Straub, Nolen learned the most about St. Petersburg from Perry Snell, a developer, Annie McRae, the planning board's secretary, and E. C. Garvin, the director of public works.

Annie McRae, a quick-witted stenographer and notary public, was St. Petersburg's resident expert on municipal affairs. In 1915, McRae gained a seat on the Advisory Committee for the National Municipal League. Her writing appeared in various magazines, including *The American City* and *The National Municipal Review*.[15] As the planning board's secretary, she corresponded with Nolen regularly and also drafted pro-planning editorials for the *St. Petersburg Times* when Straub was out of town.

While McRae lent her literary skills to the project, E. C. Garvin furnished Nolen with valuable technical advice and a list of the numerous problems that had accompanied the city's expansion to date. Garvin had found that private enterprise, when it had no plan to go by, created as many problems as profits. "There is an obvious need," Garvin wrote Nolen, for "the better control of property and subdivisions. The absence of control is apparent in many parts of St. Petersburg to the lasting detriment of the city."[16]

The *St. Petersburg Times* also looked unfavorably on the way the city was growing. While land speculators argued that they could use their property as they wanted, Straub countered that the good of the community equaled that of any individual. Given St. Petersburg's chaotic expansion, city planning could only be an improvement on "the private undertakings being organized and put over us constantly."[17] He urged citizens to assess the damage the community "had sustained and will sustain from the lack of a planning power so that the work of City Planner John Nolen will be approved and adopted."[18]

Like Straub, Perry Snell had an idealistic vision of the city. In 1913 he had visited the French Riviera to add to his growing art collection. While there he became enamored of the idea of modeling St. Petersburg after Nice, a pleasing city of pastels and parkways along the Côte d'Azur. Snell thought the vista from Nice's coastal promenade was similar to the view from St. Petersburg's waterfront. While St. Petersburg had set aside about the same amount of land for beautification as the French city's waterfront park occupied, the scale of improvements differed dramatically. St. Petersburg offered a pleasant stroll; in Nice walkways curved through a shoreline park artistically landscaped and bounded by a broad promenade that ran to Monte Carlo. Designing St. Petersburg along the same lines as Nice, Snell thought, would make it the centerpiece of an American Riviera.[19]

After his return from France, Snell tried to imbue St. Petersburg with a subtle Mediterranean beauty. His early work on the municipal waterfront and his groundbreaking use of the Mediterranean Revival style made St. Petersburg a more interesting and gracious place. Snell had donated a mile of shoreline to the city, and the elegance of his ongoing projects set a new standard for the Tampa Bay region. His plan for Snell Isle blended a Beaux Arts boulevard with winding residential streets to create a pleasing pattern for living (figure 9). Snell's site plan grouped neighborhoods around amenities, and his

Figure 9 During the 1920s, Perry Snell's designs for Snell Isle blended the classical Beaux Arts boulevard with curving natural lines. Courtesy of the St. Petersburg Historical Museum.

architectural controls and landscaping requirements infused his project with a special character. In the 1920s, the graceful contours, quality housing, and scenic vistas of Snell Isle testified to the benefits of urban design.[20]

Although Straub and Snell dreamed that their city would come to rival the great Mediterranean resorts, little had been done to preserve the natural beauty that was the foundation for St. Petersburg's future. If citizens failed to protect a portion of the region's beaches, lakes, and forests, Straub feared that prospective visitors would go elsewhere "to find any semblance of Florida scenery in its natural state." "It was for guidance and instruction in these lines of beauty and economy," Straub wrote, "that John Nolen was employed."[21]

Designing a Model City

In producing a plan, Nolen's office followed a well-thought-out process. Nolen devoted his time to coordinating the project, writing the text, consulting with clients, and promoting the finished product. Philip W. Foster, helped by Irving Root and Justin Hartzog, oversaw the design work. Once the members of the Nolen team completed their regional and general city plans, they collaborated on the more detailed site plans, which covered specific areas of interest. When local authorities requested it, Nolen also gave advice on utility placement, road grading and construction, architectural design, zoning, and planning law.[22]

The Nolen firm devoted special attention to their first Florida plan. While Nolen was writing the text and keeping up a steady stream of correspondence with the planning board, public officials, and civic leaders, Foster analyzed the peninsula's natural environment and mapped a broad conceptual plan for the entire county. The two collaborated on St. Petersburg's land-use map and on a park plan. Frank Williams drafted a platting ordinance, zoning code, and the enabling legislation which, if enacted, would grant St. Petersburg the authority to implement Nolen's plan.

In March 1923 the Nolen firm completed its ambitious project, which it called *St. Petersburg Today, St. Petersburg Tomorrow*. In addition to thirty pages of text, the document contained zoning and platting ordinances and maps of the regional study, the land-use plan, the park plan, and improvements for Central Avenue. Although St. Petersburg contained only eleven square miles, "the southern end of the Pinellas Peninsula is in reality one topographical unit," Nolen wrote, "and could best be developed in that spirit by the adoption of a comprehensive plan for the region."[23] Nolen's comprehensive plan covered a fifty-five square-mile area that corresponded with the city's plans for annexation.

The Nolen firm pictured the future St. Petersburg as a captivating place where urban and natural landscapes converged. The plan hinged on the "preservation of the natural advantages that belong to the St. Petersburg region," Nolen claimed, "and the enhancement of the beauty that already exists there." He thought St. Petersburg had the potential to "produce the sort of living that will make the St. Petersburg of Tomorrow one of the truly great resort cities of our country." The people of St. Petersburg, however, were not moving toward this goal.[24]

The haphazard outcropping of subdivisions spreading across the landscape demonstrated a "ruinous policy of drift with regard to the physical layout of St. Petersburg and the surrounding territory." Nolen urged the city to "grasp more securely its peculiar opportunity and to take such leadership among the Florida resorts as nature has accorded it." Otherwise, the town would become like other resort cities where unplanned growth had "despoiled the natural surroundings and turned what was once an attractive landscape into the most commonplace development."[25]

For Nolen, the landscape set the parameters for any plan. "The closer a town plan adheres to the natural conditions," he believed, "the more original and attractive it will be."[26] Given St. Petersburg's dependence on tourism, the city's need to develop along natural lines represented more than an aesthetic yearning; it was a necessity. "Man," Nolen warned, "is the only animal who desecrates the surroundings of his habitation."[27]

The Regional Study

Nolen devoted the first section of his plan to the regional study. This work provided "farsighted planning for a long time ahead," Nolen wrote, "representing improvements that will require, perhaps decades for full realization."[28] Foster used a county soils map to determine which sites were suitable for nature preserves and which for building (figure 10). Soil is a limiting factor for natural vegetation. From a soil's characteristics one can draw assumptions about an area's drainage capabilities and about the flora it can support. In a swampy, coastal area like Pinellas, tropical storms and occasional hurricanes have made land with poor drainage and high water tables unfit for intensive building.[29]

The regional study map listed seven soil classifications: coastal beach, Norfolk Sand, Loam Sand, Parkwood Sandy Loam, muck and swamp, Plummer Sand, and tidal marsh. The large concentrations of well-drained, sandy soils in the central upland area and near Tampa Bay provided the best lands for urban uses. The rest of greater St. Petersburg, about 60 percent of the lower third of the peninsula, consisted of swampy lands with poorly drained soils that were prone to flooding and erosion.

As for nature preserves, prices were still low enough, Nolen wrote, for the city to purchase properties "peculiarly suited for recreation and at the same time not of such a character as to be valuable for building property."[30] Most of the proposed reserves surrounded wetlands (identified on the regional study map as coastal beach, tidal marshes, and swamps) because they had the highest water tables and the greatest potential for severe flooding. If the proposed nature preserves were placed in the public domain, a greenbelt circling the lower third of Pinellas would furnish a natural boundary for Nolen's "St. Petersburg of Tomorrow."

The largely vacant barrier islands that bounded Boca Ciega Bay from

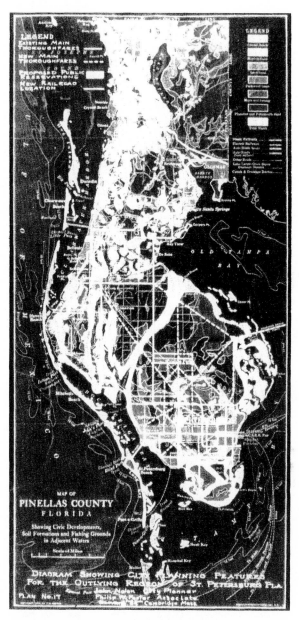

Figure 10 The Nolen firm's 1923 regional plan used a soil analysis to propose preserving flood-prone wetlands and creating a system of interconnected parks and nature preserves. Courtesy of the Division of Rare and Manuscript Collections, Cornell University Library.

Figure 11 Computer projections indicate that when a hurricane descends on the low-lying Pinellas Peninsula, damages will be greater than anywhere else in Florida. Courtesy of the St. Petersburg Historical Museum.

Indian Rocks Beach south to Pass-à-Grillé especially interested Nolen. While Boca Ciega Bay offered the city "wild natural unspoiled beauty," the appeal of the beaches was quite different. The offshore isles' great beauty was the result of a "long unbroken curve of white sand contrasting strongly with the deep color of the waters of the Gulf." In 1923, local builders considered the beaches unsafe for permanent residences because of the region's frequent storms. Only two years before, a hurricane had leveled beach homes and destroyed the existing bridge to the mainland (figure 11). Nolen wanted St. Petersburg and the other Pinellas municipalities to make the offshore isles public preserves. Once residents and tourists were drawn "to the unique and attractive character of these islands," Nolen believed, the peninsula would become the eastern United States' prime tourist destination.[31]

The Comprehensive City Plan

In Nolen's view the regional study framed the setting, while the more specific components (park plan, land-use map, and Central Avenue study) of the comprehensive plan established the future city's living patterns.[32] In the park plan

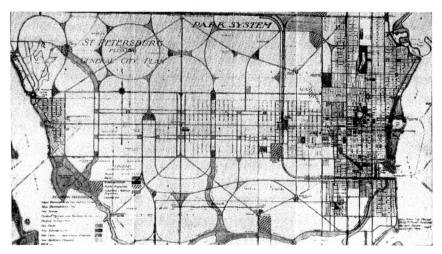

Figure 12 In Nolen's plan, a system of parks, parkways, and boulevards provided easy access to both recreational and natural areas. Courtesy of the Division of Rare and Manuscript Collections, Cornell University Library.

(figure 12), an interconnected series of parks and parkways joined the ring of nature preserves encircling the lower peninsula. The proposed park system formed a green rectangle of about thirty square miles that ran across the town for two miles north and south of Central Avenue. Nolen believed that this would encompass the range of development and public improvements.

The parkways included a series of pleasure drives that bordered the parks (which Nolen wanted landscaped with native trees and shrubs) and green corridors that followed meandering creeks and the Cross Bayou drainage canal. Nolen also recommended establishing a series of green squares, similar to Savannah's park blocks, that would stretch across the city. If the city implemented the proposed park system, all residents would live within half a mile of a natural escape.

Nolen used a mixture of street patterns. A series of axial boulevards led to the downtown, which was laid out on a grid. In outlying sections, curvilinear roads shaped new neighborhoods around natural contours. Nolen also recommended broadening the intersections of main thoroughfares with green areas to improve traffic safety and alleviate the dreariness of continual pavement. At major intersections, he envisioned a collection of traffic squares, plazas, and small greens. Besides enlivening the urban environment, Nolen thought these improvements would make right-angle crossings less dangerous.

Nolen and Foster made a special study of Central Avenue, the city's principal east-west connector, and the focal point of retail and commercial activity.

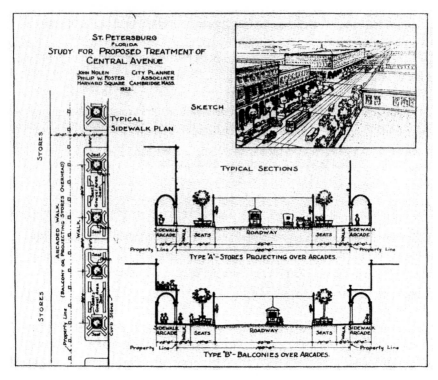

Figure 13 Nolen wanted to encourage social interaction and business by giving Central Avenue a strong pedestrian orientation. Courtesy of the Division of Rare and Manuscript Collections, Cornell University Library.

According to Nolen, Central Avenue set the "straight lines of communication" for the downtown's heavy pedestrian traffic. "The many seats along the street where thousands of people congregate and enjoy the activity of the crowd without actually being a moving part of it," Nolen wrote, "is unique and one of the distinctive features of the city."[33] He wanted to enhance this effect by making the avenue more appealing to pedestrians and retailers. Foster depicted an improved Central Avenue (figure 13) replete with arcades, plantings, sidewalk seats, balconies, and an excellent view.

To foster pedestrian traffic, Nolen recommended covering a twelve-foot walk with arcades. He also encouraged setting back some new buildings to provide balconies for outdoor cafés, businesses that he thought would immediately prosper. An eight-foot sidewalk, placed between the street and trees and the arcades, would give strollers a pleasant promenade for viewing the boulevard's sights.

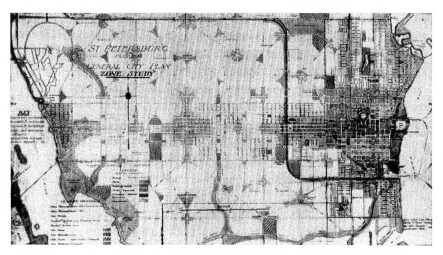

Figure 14 In Nolen's 1923 comprehensive plan, the existing urban areas followed a traditional grid, but the new suburbs were to follow natural contours. Courtesy of the Division of Rare and Manuscript Collections, Cornell University Library.

While Central Avenue received special treatment, the land-use map (figure 14) showed what Nolen had in mind for the remainder of the city. "Everything in the proposals for St. Petersburg," he wrote, "is in keeping with the character of the topography and environment of the city."[34] The proposed mixture of urban uses, natural areas, and parks sought to foster congenial relations, improve recreational opportunities, and minimize land-use conflicts. The land-use map depicted three different zoning categories: industrial, business, and residential. The accompanying zoning ordinance placed limitations on the height, bulk, and setback of buildings in each classification.

Nolen felt that the placement of businesses played a key role in designing any city. In St. Petersburg, it would be possible to concentrate the most intensive commercial activities in the downtown area, just off Tampa Bay, where buildings could reach eight stories. A second commercial category was located immediately to the west of the downtown retail section and in two other shopping districts. There buildings could reach a maximum of three stories. Support storage and warehouses would occupy most of the land zoned for industrial uses, and Nolen planned that these areas would lie along the railroad and near the terminal at Bayboro Harbor.

The placement of neighborhood commercial centers particularly concerned Nolen. "St. Petersburg has a wonderful opportunity," he wrote, "to make this side of civic development as it should be." If clustered at nonresidential-street intersections, within half a mile of all residences, "these local centers with their store groups, churches, clubs, and sometimes schools should be the real center of neighborhood activities and should be expressive of the life of the people in the surrounding sections."[35] On the other hand, if the city failed to structure neighborhood centers around focal points, commercial uses would sprawl out along the principal streets and create grave traffic and land-use problems.

Nolen placed a mixture of apartments and green spaces around the neighborhood centers, except near Boca Ciega Bay and Tampa Bay, where tourist apartments and hotels bounded the proposed shopping centers. Nolen believed St. Petersburg's future as a resort required a special zoning category to accommodate tourists and seasonal visitors. He also thought that concentrations of tourist housing would shield single-family homes from commercial properties.

The land set aside for single-family homes covered about half the city. The proposed design would ensure that new subdivisions would, Nolen wrote, "escape from the monotony and commonplace character of the gridiron plan." He derided the city's existing checkerboard layout as "having all the dreariness of the Midwest industrial town."[36] He found this especially troublesome because the city's flat landscape demanded that "variety and distinctiveness be injected to break the monotony."[37] In the undeveloped sections of St. Petersburg, Nolen broke up the grid plan with diagonal and broadly curving streets that followed the outline of natural features. He hoped this organic pattern would provide the "base from which to carry out the more elastic, freer method of subdivision" that could transform St. Petersburg into a model city.

The plan allowed for a variety of lot sizes ranging from quarter-acre to ten-acre holdings. Nolen placed one-acre estates behind the shoreline preserves to enhance property values and provide a verdant buffer. In the territory outside the thirty square miles slated for development, the plan allowed for ten-acre farms to cultivate "subtropical delicacies such as oranges, guavas, lemons, mangoes, and avocados."

Land-Use Controls

Nolen anticipated objections to his proposals from subdividers who would demand rectangular blocks because his design did "not produce as many lots to the acre and is more difficult to plan and lay out." But a city with St. Petersburg's potential "should be less interested in the number of lots it is producing" and more attuned to creating "attractive, convenient, well-planned places."

The sale of lots or homes in a planned community offered realtors ample opportunities; they just needed to change their pitch. Salesmen would have to "devote their energies more profitably to the selling of *location*, than merely to the selling of so many feet of property."[38]

For Nolen, the ultimate return of the planning process was to give a site "location." The value of a lot depended less on its size and more on its surroundings and its relationship to streets, parks, and scenic sites. The plan's combination of parks and natural preserves offered countless opportunities for developers to create subdivisions where property values would escalate over time. Nolen also designed neighborhoods convenient for pedestrians by positioning parks, playgrounds, schools, and shopping centers within walking distance of all residences.

A special section of the plan was devoted to the subdivision issue. Nolen realized that forcing subdividers to follow the plan's guidelines would generate controversy, but the public welfare required "some control of private enterprises." Many subdividers would undoubtedly try to circumvent the plan, laying out projects that altered "the lines of travel, the logical flow of traffic, and park locations for their own gain." Nolen predicted that subdividers would do their best to influence the city commission to pave streets in outlying districts, where they owned property, before paving proposed thoroughfares (figure 15). This would create "adverse conditions that the purchasers and residents of the section would have to contend with probably as long as the city exists."[39]

To prevent such abuses, the city planning board would have to monitor the city's expansion. While this group's powers would remain purely advisory, Nolen wanted the board to make a "rigid examination of (subdivision) plats before their acceptance." In addition, the board needed to review requests for public improvements or the expansion of utilities. If the board refused a property owner's request, individuals could seek remedy from the city commission.

Nolen also wanted to give E. C. Garvin, the director of public works, additional leverage in managing the city's expansion. The platting ordinance drawn up by Frank Williams installed the director of public works as the supervisor of plats and gave him a seat on the planning board. Although the city commission could override Garvin, he would review all proposed plats and public improvements. "This proposal," Nolen wrote, "cannot be too strongly emphasized."[40] The platting ordinance established minimum street widths, procedures for street and alley alignment, minimum lot sizes, and easement requirements. It also reinforced Nolen's proposals for preserving natural areas by recommending the dedication of properties (swamps, lakes, ponds, and creek bottoms) not suited for development.

The zoning ordinance provided the means to enforce the plan. The

Figure 15 Nolen warned that developers would try to alter "lines of travel, . . . logical flow of traffic, and park locations for their own gain." This street sign in an orange grove shows how accurate his prediction was. Courtesy of the St. Petersburg Historical Museum.

proposed ordinance came from the guidelines set forth in the Standard Zoning Enabling Act, which Frank Williams obtained from the U.S. Department of Commerce. Williams converted the Commerce Department's guidelines for state legislatures into a special enabling act for St. Petersburg. The New York attorney also suggested that a county commissioner sit on the planning board, because the plan incorporated county land set for annexation at a uniform distance of five miles from St. Petersburg's 1922 boundaries.[41]

The enabling legislation that Williams drafted for St. Petersburg became known as the Planning Law. Since St. Petersburg was not vested with home rule, the city commission needed a special act from the state legislature to establish a planning and zoning ordinance. If the legislature passed this act, a majority vote by the city commission would give the city the power to enforce a zoning ordinance.[42]

The passage of the Planning Law would also abet the city's policy of racial segregation. "Like all southern cities," the plan read, "St. Petersburg has its colored sections."[43] The planning board had received strong direction from the city commission to restrict black homes, 17.1 percent of the city's residents in 1920, to the southern portion of town. In January 1923, Straub wrote

Nolen: "We do not want to zone the colored people by law, we are hoping by persuasion and suitable arrangement for them to bring about such corrections in their locations as may be found possible."[44] A relieved Nolen replied: "I am quite in agreement with your statement about racial zoning." He had recently been embroiled in a debacle in Palm Beach, where the desire to establish racial zoning was the sole reason that a consultant was contacted. If possible, this was one controversy he wished to avoid.[45] Although the St. Petersburg plan contained no de facto racial zoning, the proposed industrial districts running along the railroad would effectively separate the black neighborhood from the rest of the community.

Selling the Plan

Nolen anticipated that the city's powerful lobby of realtors and subdividers would label the plan impractical and harmful to business. To preempt these attacks, he explained that the plan would enforce a "businesslike public policy" to replace the "haphazard and piecemeal fashion" in which the city furnished urban services. Once there was a plan, the Department of Public Works could schedule improvements in a way that would reduce costs and confusion.[46] By dividing the city into land-use districts, the plan would give realtors a better idea of a particular property's potential earnings. And the extreme highs and lows of the speculative cycle would even out as the land market stabilized and began to reflect "genuine real estate values."[47]

Nolen also assured the people of St. Petersburg that the adoption of a plan would not endanger the city's way of life. "The business of the city," Nolen wrote, "is first of all to supply the wants and needs of the thousands of visitors who come each winter."[48] The plan outlined a rational procedure for public investments in tourism well into the future. As the number of Americans searching for vacation destinations continued to increase, Nolen felt that a city with striking subtropical beauty and abundant recreational opportunities could only prosper.

Nolen was eloquent in support of his plan, but the onus of selling it rested with the planning board. For city planning to work in St. Petersburg, elected officials and civic organizations needed, Straub wrote Nolen, "to work in the most complete harmony and agreement possible."[49] Straub's most influential ally in this project was Frank Pulver, the city's eccentric unmarried mayor. The mayor's lifestyle raised a few eyebrows, but his business acumen was invaluable to the city. Pulver had made a small fortune in retail merchandising and, unlike most of the city commission, he had refused the favors tendered by land speculators. A strong mayor, Pulver did not hesitate to push Straub's agenda through the ranks of a reluctant group of commissioners.[50]

With Pulver firmly committed to planning, Straub spent most of his time lobbying the Chamber of Commerce and other civic clubs with roles in formulating municipal policy.[51] Herman Dann, the president of the Chamber of Commerce, owned the city's largest building supply store, and he had worked closely with the town's leading builders and Straub.[52] In November 1922, Dann acceded to the editor's persistent badgering and appointed him to head a Chamber of Commerce subcommittee to promote city planning. While the Chamber could raise thousands for advertising, it allocated no funds for this effort, and when Nolen completed his work the group had already disbanded.[53]

On March 7, 1923, Nolen informed the planning board that he had completed his plan for St. Petersburg. A week later, Straub wrote Nolen that he had arranged "a large public meeting" for March 29.[54] Straub could not have had a better person present Florida's first comprehensive plan. Nolen was "unsurpassed at promoting and producing plans," according to his fellow planner Earle Draper.[55] After many years in the public spotlight, Nolen had become adept at reading an audience. Depending on the circumstances, his message might be caustic or inspirational, simple or analytical. His goal, however, always remained the same: to inspire in his audience the civic spirit needed to implement any plan.[56]

"A very large and enthusiastic audience greeted John Nolen's lecture," the *St. Petersburg Times* reported, "on the planning to fulfill St. Petersburg's natural mission to be the greatest tourist city of all the South throughout all time."[57] Nolen's rhetorical dash, incisive appraisal, and visual aids played well, and energetic rounds of applause accompanied his presentation. St. Petersburg was unlike most cities, "where the door is closed to city planning." Instead, he told his listeners, south Pinellas's vast stretches of vacant land provided a clean slate for the construction of a model city.

The plan for the "St. Petersburg of Tomorrow" surpassed his audience's expectations. Nolen acknowledged that he had already received some complaints that his vision was too grandiose for St. Petersburg. "But the issues are large," Nolen stated, "the population is large and growing, and the wealth involved is large." He explained that the plan's broad regional conception sought to accommodate growth while still preserving vital natural resources. Maps and drawings depicted a future city where residents enjoyed outdoor activities and had convenient access to the services they needed. Although the nature preserves limited the amount of land open to development, they contributed to the beauty of the city's setting. To help the audience understand his vision better, Nolen showed slides of residential and recreational developments in the coastal resort cities of California, Italy, and the French Riviera. Because the Pinellas Peninsula's environs equaled—and in some ways surpassed—those of such cities, Nolen told the crowd, "Each of the views carry a suggestion of the beauty that could easily be achieved in St. Petersburg."

St. Petersburg had enormous potential, but aside from the waterfront, it had as yet few attractions—as soon became evident when Nolen asked the audience to list the city's features. The community's principal recreational area, Williams Park, was overtaxed by the growing populace. Nolen said that, by pointing out its shortcomings, he did not mean to "knock the city, but to find honestly where we stand. It is no use trying to deceive ourselves. We cannot deceive the tourists and visitors who come here."[58]

In presenting the regional study, Nolen took special care to emphasize the importance of restricting development and preserving lands on the outlying barrier islands. He felt that "the lack of control and planning was already detracting from the city's gulf beaches."[59] He also advised that the city purchase additional public lands in lieu of a proposal by Lew Brown, owner and editor of the *St. Petersburg Independent,* to build a giant pier.[60]

Nolen believed that the best investment for attracting tourists was to establish a system of public preserves, especially on the beaches. To prove his point, he included among his slides some of shoreline parks in Monte Carlo, Nice, and Santa Barbara. If St. Petersburg followed the example of these successful resort communities, Nolen assured his listeners, the community would not need a million-dollar pier to draw visitors. His proposal also made economic sense because the real estate boom had missed the beaches. In 1922 St. Petersburg Beach, a two-mile long barrier island, had been sold for $750,000.[61]

After explaining the mechanics of the adoption process and the details of the zoning ordinance, Nolen closed his presentation with a familiar charge: "The plan must be given the whole-hearted support even of those whom it may not immediately benefit. Everyone must cooperate to put it across." While it would take years of hard work to implement the plan, Nolen reminded listeners that its potential return was extraordinary. He concluded his presentation to thunderous applause.[62]

Straub was unprepared for the rousing reception that Nolen's presentation received. It was "much more than many have suspected." After two decades of continual prodding, he thought that the people of St. Petersburg had finally grasped the significance of city planning. Nolen's expertise "in this great modern specialty" could not have come at a more opportune time; in "no city in the world can such work be more useful." Straub made a special plea for the city's realtors to study the plan closely because they were in the position to reap the greatest rewards.[63]

Annie McRae could not match Straub's enthusiasm, as Nolen had admitted to her his disappointment with the plan's reception. Shortly after Nolen left, McRae wrote to him: "More perhaps than you are aware, I realized some of the difficulties which you have encountered, particularly in presenting the plan. I believe your work was thorough, honest, disinterested and sincere all through."[64]

The audience had not fully understood Nolen's message. When the *St. Petersburg Times* published the plan's text and asked for ideas and criticism, there was only one response, from C. M. Roser, an influential builder. Roser criticized the plan for failing to address adequately the "disposition of the colored population." He wanted a corporation of businessmen to secure a large tract of land and supervise the building of "a colored section with schools, churches, theaters, good roads, and easy transportation to the business section."[65]

Despite Nolen's foreboding, St. Petersburg's civic leaders seemed pleased with the vision of a city designed for comfort, leisure, and health. Of course, this was the same theme that was given constant play in local newspapers, Chamber of Commerce brochures, advertisements, and realtors' promotional material. Straub and his supporters still needed to persuade residents that planning offered the means to build the city everyone desired.

Nolen was well acquainted with advertising and public relations. Two weeks after his departure, he wrote to Straub asking him to exhibit St. Petersburg's plan at the National Planning Conference (which Baltimore was hosting to promote city planning in southern cities). Nolen felt that this plan represented an "especially interesting proposal" that "would give wide advertisement to St. Petersburg and its progressive policy for the future."[66] A month later, however, a disappointed Nolen wrote to McRae asking about St. Petersburg's failure to exhibit the plan in Baltimore and the city's inability to meet its schedule of payments. Even with the loss of revenue, Nolen could still "take satisfaction," he stated, "in the character of the work and in the belief that it will benefit St. Petersburg."[67]

While McRae understood the need to promote the plan, the planning board's energies were focused on getting the Planning Law over the necessary legislative hurdles. Despite much grumbling, in early May the city commission approved Mayor Pulver's request that Straub lobby the State Legislature for passage of the Planning Law. After a three-week absence, the editor returned from Tallahassee with Chapter 9915 of *The Laws of Florida*, the St. Petersburg Planning Law.[68]

For a local government to impose land-use controls, it had to obtain enabling legislation to delegate the legislative or policy-making power the Constitution grants each state to establish laws and ordinances that preserve public order and promote a community's general welfare.[69] Chapter 9915 granted these powers to the St. Petersburg City Commission for the expressed purpose of "promoting the health, safety, morals and general welfare of the community" through the institution of a zoning ordinance. The act also allowed the city commission to regulate development both in St. Petersburg and in the land bordering it at a uniform distance of five miles.[70]

In early June the city commission approved the bill, but the legislature added another hurdle. Tallahassee decided that Florida's first attempt at comprehensive planning required a referendum. The city commission set the Planning Law referendum for the middle of August.[71]

Shortly after the city commission's approval of the Planning Law, Nolen notified Frank Williams that St. Petersburg's payments were late and that the planning board had failed to publish the plan. But Williams, like Nolen, was more concerned with the printing of the plan than with badgering the planning board for payment. He generously forgave the debt and urged the planning board to use the monies owed him to publish the plan.[72]

The city commission never gave the planning board funds to print copies of the plan for public review, but on June 10 the Planning Law did appear in the *St. Petersburg Times*. An accompanying editorial urged all citizens to make a careful study of the measure as a piece of legislation drafted expressly for St. Petersburg. Although the plan would not be published, Straub offered the newspaper as an open forum for discussion.[73]

Ten days later, Straub resigned from the planning board because he did not want the new planning legislation to be perceived as another one of his quixotic quests. For the Planning Law to pass the referendum, Straub needed more support than he could gain through the *St. Petersburg Times*. In Frank Jonsberg, a gifted local architect, described as a "scholar and artist, and practical businessman," he found an able successor on the planning board. It also helped that Jonsberg was a personal friend of John Nolen's.[74]

The Planning Law referendum placed St. Petersburg at a crossroads. After three decades, a prospering city had emerged from the Florida wilds. Straub and his supporters wanted to temper the pioneering tradition that was building St. Petersburg. Although portions of the city showed significant improvement, a growing number of ill-conceived projects threatened the community's general welfare. Nolen's plan offered the means to deal with these problems and build a nonpareil resort city. His supporters, however, faced the unenviable task of trying to sell a system of land-use controls in a town where the allure of quick riches from land speculation ruled over all.

4

To Sell or to Plan Paradise?

The city planning election referendum was as abusive as any ever held
in St. Petersburg, and that is saying a great deal.

St. Petersburg Times, 1929

The power of the so-called Planning Board will be exercised over your
streets and parks and playgrounds; over all buildings; over all exten-
sions and services: lights, water, gas, sewers, street cars—everything
affecting your home life. . . . You had better get busy and protect your
home and your liberty.

St. Petersburg Independent, 1923

Despite the support of leading citizens, among them Frank Pulver, Perry Snell,
and Herman Dann, the Planning Law met stiff resistance from A. P. Avery, the
city's political power broker. Avery was the president of the American Trust
Bank and the majority shareholder in the city's largest paving company. He
feared that adoption of a comprehensive plan would threaten his lucrative
paving contracts, because the planning board would structure the city commission's outlays on capital improvements. With the aid of Lew Brown, editor
of the *St. Petersburg Independent,* Avery's campaign against the Planning Law
quickly gained the backing of St. Petersburg's powerful caste of realtors. Like
Nolen, these enterprising salesmen had a vision of the future, although it differed from his. In their vision of the ideal city, realtors did not sell lots, but provided admission through the gates of Eden.[1] Their paradise, in contrast to
Nolen's, was based on unbounded growth, not on control. They dreamed of an
ever-expanding city where profit always followed speculation.

Regulation and Conflict

Less than a month after the state legislature approved the Planning Law, St.
Petersburg faced a major crisis. In late June 1923, word leaked out that the city

commission intended to fire E. C. Garvin, the director of public works. Garvin had angered the commission by canceling a three-million-dollar paving project in an outlying section of the city. He believed it would jeopardize the city's finances. The commissioners disagreed and asserted that Garvin had gained "too much independence."[2]

Garvin retorted that the commissioners wanted him removed because he had refused to alter paving specifications for the powerful banker A. P. Avery. If he were fired, Garvin claimed in the *St. Petersburg Times,* the city's paving costs would double. The day after his assertion was published, the city commission terminated Garvin's contract.[3]

Straub immediately fired off an editorial proclaiming that Garvin's dismissal was not just a personal injustice, but a disastrous financial decision. Garvin's review of public projects was the taxpayers' only insurance against corruption, and his work, as even the city commission admitted, was proficient and punctual. But the commissioners did not present any justification for having fired Garvin, nor did they explain how a replacement could perform in a more professional manner.[4]

Frank Jonsberg, the new chairman of the planning board, moved to save Garvin's job. He realized that implementing the new plan would be nearly impossible without a sympathetic and competent director of public works. Jonsberg formed a group that petitioned the city commission to reinstate Garvin and secure St. Petersburg's fiscal health. "Any change in this important position," he contended, "would be to the utmost disadvantage of the community."[5]

Straub and Jonsberg's efforts proved futile. On July 6, 1923, the city commission fired both Garvin and C. C. Brown, the city's second most knowledgeable engineer. E. G. Cunningham, one of the commissioners and an influential realtor, took the lead in getting rid of these two men, but refused to comment on the proceedings. For Straub, the reason behind the firings was obvious: Garvin and Brown stood in the way of local businessmen's profiteering. "Nothing would or could have come of the Commission's objections," Straub contended, "if Garvin had not refused to put aside his own judgment to serve the wishes of special interests."[6]

The city commission had chosen their time well. Mayor Pulver, Garvin's chief supporter, was embroiled in a recall battle and was fighting for his political life. Those who wanted to recall him claimed that the mayor lacked the moral fortitude to enforce Prohibition. While this pretext went over well in the parlors of St. Petersburg, the real reason behind the recall was protecting A. P. Avery's interests. Pulver supported Garvin's efforts to regulate the city's expansion, and Avery saw any regulation as a threat to his lucrative paving business. In late 1922 Pulver had survived a first recall—as he did this one—but his political capital was exhausted, and he was unable to save Garvin.[7]

Avery was a formidable opponent. Cunning, resourceful, and ambitious, he was the consummate politician. He had first come to St. Petersburg in 1892 and found employment as a baker. With his regal bearing and commanding profile, he soon became a powerful figure in the fledgling community. Within a few years, Avery moved from baking to a more profitable career in real estate. In 1899 he was elected to the city council, and five years later he headed the board of trade. After he founded the American Trust Bank in 1910, his political star was in the ascendant. Although he served as a city commissioner from 1916 to 1919 and from 1928 to 1930, his real power rested on his position as broker for the local Democratic political machine.[8]

The *St. Petersburg Times* called Avery St. Petersburg's political boss—and more than once charged him with instigating "Tammany Hall rule."[9] His alleged takes from "honest graft" were legendary. During the boom years of the early 1920s, Avery worked in collusion with bond houses to pirate funds from the city's municipal bond program. He also controlled or influenced most of the paving contracts the city awarded. Between 1923 and 1927, Florida's average cost for paving a one-mile length of road ranged from $8,000 to $47,000. In Miami the cost was higher—$95,000— but in St. Petersburg the "Avery additive" raised the average cost per mile of pavement to $185,000.[10]

Lew Brown, the editor of the *St. Petersburg Independent,* was in Avery's corner. Brown had started his career in Louisville, and he came to St. Petersburg in 1908 as owner and editor of the *Independent.* Major Brown (the title he preferred after organizing a local militia unit during World War I) favored blue laws, red-blooded American values, and white Anglo-Saxons. In 1916, he earned the title "father of the white primary" after he championed the exclusion of black voters. "When Lew Brown stands up for righteousness," the *St. Petersburg Times* reported at the time, "he strikes out with a force so strong and an aim so sure that escape is seldom possible, and he has never struck harder than when championing the white primary." When dealing with controversial issues, he constantly reminded the people of St. Petersburg just how far the bounds of Christian morality, good business sense, and tradition could, in his mind, be stretched. Since his newspaper also served as a voice for A. P. Avery, it played a special role in municipal affairs.[11]

Avery's chances of making money from his dealings with the city commission received a huge boost in June 1923, when the state legislature passed a law that made it easier for elected officials to provide urban services. The new act allowed municipalities to finance sewers, water lines, and paving projects by assessing adjacent land owners. Liens were imposed on the properties that stood to benefit, and special assessment bonds (SAB) were issued against those liens. The bonds were of particular importance to the myriad subdividers clamoring for public improvements, because St. Petersburg had reached its ten percent limit for bonded indebtedness early in the year. The city commission had immediately doubled the assessed value of all property to raise revenues, but this was only a stopgap measure.[12]

The city commission immediately endorsed issuing SAB on the premises that the city would continue to show unprecedented rates of growth, and that the property owners benefiting from the new infrastructure would pay off the bonds. Avery's influence-peddling also persuaded the city commissioners to sell SAB. While the American Trust Bank worked in collusion with the bond houses, the commission issued thousands of dollars worth of SAB to fund Avery's paving projects. In return for their compliance, Avery paid kickbacks to the commissioners. The system was running along smoothly until the Garvin episode, which showed Avery that he needed to bring the public works department's procedures in line with his business practices.[13]

In late July 1923, after Mayor Pulver left town for a four-week promotional junket in the Northeast, Avery, Lew Brown, and the city commission instigated a coup. The commissioners voted unanimously for Avery and Brown to co-chair a committee that would amend the city charter and limit the powers of the mayor and his staff. Although St. Petersburg lacked home rule, in 1913 the state legislature had passed a bill that allowed the city to amend the city charter through referenda, provided the city commission format remained intact. The commission set the charter for mid-August, pushing the Planning Law referendum back two weeks.

The charter committee received its strongest endorsement from St. Petersburg's staunch anti-Pulver faction, the Prohibitionists. Besides Brown, Avery, and four Prohibitionists, the group included three key members of the Avery machine: T. J. Heller, the lone realtor on the planning board, James Bussey, Avery's attorney, and W. J. Overman, the front man in Avery's paving business. On August 12, the committee completed its task, after working "night after night," Bussey declared, "without compensation or complaint endeavoring to work out a system of laws as would enable this city to keep pace with her rapid and remarkable development."[14]

Avery's design in altering the charter was to ensure that the professional staff, on whom Pulver relied to run the city, would not interfere in his dealings with the city commissioners. Under the amended charter, city department heads would report to the commission instead of the mayor, and the commission would assume the responsibility for appointing members to auxiliary boards. The charter committee also sought to undermine Pulver's position by giving the commissioners—not the voters—the right to elect the mayor.[15]

The *St. Petersburg Times* had already warned readers that the proposed amendments were a brazen attempt to institute "Tammany Hall Rule." If the mayor and the professional staff no longer had much say over spending the millions of dollars handled by city hall, the controls on corruption would be gone. When a true professional like Garvin had a reasonable amount of independence and responsibility in his job, Straub felt, he could resist the effects of influence-peddling, minimize wasteful expenditures, and give the people of St. Petersburg a better place to live. The proposed amendments to the city charter, if passed, would allow "political bosses to gain a greater clinch on power in the government of St. Petersburg," Straub wrote, "than Boss Murphy of Tammany Hall has in the government of New York."[16]

On August 15, 1923, however, the amendments passed with 55 percent of the vote. Avery had won the stronger position in city affairs that he coveted. The Planning Law was now the only obstacle between him and the city treasury. If the Planning Law passed, the city commission's questionable business practices would be scrutinized by the planning board. And Avery knew that the board would diminish—if not cut off altogether—the steady stream of money flowing from the municipal coffers into the American Trust Bank.[17]

The Planning Controversy

On August 21, 1923, eight days before the Planning Law referendum, Lew Brown issued an attack (see figure 16) that sparked an internecine political struggle. He claimed that the Planning Law imperiled St. Petersburg's version of the American Dream by threatening citizens' most sacred rights. "Have you read through this act which was slipped through the Legislature?" the *St. Petersburg Independent* asked its readers, "If you have not you had better get busy and protect your home and your liberty." "The Law of the Czars," a blaring headline read, "would be a better name for this proposed measure." Brown portrayed the Planning Law as an arbitrary measure that put "despotic power over some of the most sacred rights of citizens" into the hands of appointed officials who would control "everything affecting your home life."

Brown believed that government existed to foster the expansion of enterprise, and that giving regulatory powers to an advisory board would hinder progress. Such a transfer of power seemed especially out of place in a middle-class haven like St. Petersburg. While "despotic powers" might be necessary

THE LAW OF THE CZARS

Would Be a Better Name For This Proposed Measure Which You Are Called Upon To Vote Next Tuesday.

Have You Read This Act Which Was Slipped Through the Legislature? If You Have Not You Had Better Get Busy and Protect Your Home and Your Liberty

Figure 16 The anti-planning forces, supported by the *St. Petersburg Independent*, realized that a city plan would prevent the city from underwriting their outrageous speculations. August 1923, *St. Petersburg Independent*.

"in a big city with its tenement life," he claimed, "in beautiful, happy far-flung St. Petersburg it is neither necessary nor advisable to use the lash on the people."[18]

Brown's attacks went down especially well with St. Petersburg's realtors and subdividers. Selling real estate would be close to impossible, Brown claimed, "with an autocratic board of snoopers to tell every man just how he must build his home, how he can use it and how many people can live in a district." Forcing subdividers to follow a plan would also endanger the real estate market: "What red-blooded American citizen would want to buy real estate in St. Petersburg," Brown asked, "and submit to such dictation?" The editor doubted that any "self-respecting man or woman will want to make a home here under such surveillance and dictation." According to one realtor, the Planning Law was not a question for the voters, but the courts: "We had just about as well quit trying to sell property until the court declares null and void this proposed law of supervision and dictation."[19]

Brown's crusade gained an important ally when T. J. Heller spoke out against the Planning Law. The popular realtor, who sat on both the planning board and the charter committee, called the Planning Law "so drastic and confer[ring] such autocratic powers upon the appointed Planning Board that it is dangerous to the future welfare of the city." Heller pleaded that he was "not

75

responsible in any manner or form for having this act passed by the Legislature" and vowed to resign from the planning board if the Planning Law passed.

Heller's denunciation seemed to corroborate Brown's assertion that the Planning Law was the tool of a "vicious and dangerous political junta" aided by outside forces. In a xenophobic diatribe, Brown reminded voters that the Planning Law's "drastic powers" were "drawn by a New York lawyer [Williams]," and that Nolen had received $8,000 for drawing up a plan that "no sane person would expect to be carried out." The planning board intended to retain these outsiders, Brown warned, to "make and change rules and regulations, hold trials, keep records, and control all city development." "In short," the *St. Petersburg Independent* charged, "it creates a political junta of dictators with state law authority over the city." The prospect of a New York lawyer and a Boston planner running the Florida city's affairs was even more appalling, according to Brown, because Straub had left town before the election.[20]

Exactly why Straub chose to leave at such a crucial time is uncertain, although poor health is the most plausible reason. In the humid summer months, the bronchial condition that had threatened his life twenty years before troubled him anew. He usually escaped to the upper Midwest in the summer, but in 1923 he was scheduled to make a trip to southern California in mid-August, immediately after the original date of the referendum. Because the city commission did not change the date of the referendum until late July, there was little time for Straub to change plans.[21]

Straub, however, did not retire from the field until he had laid the groundwork for the Planning Law's defense. The *St. Petersburg Times* printed the Planning Law during the summer, and Straub wrote editorials explaining both the plan and the accompanying legislation. He made it especially clear that the Planning Law did not endow the planning board with drastic, sweeping powers. "It gives the city plan board," he wrote in June, "power only to compel the observance of city planning ordinances, after their enactment by the City Commission." He also noted that the official plan and the zoning code required public review and approval from the city commission.[22]

Besides providing a public forum for discussion of Nolen's work, Straub also kept in touch with the plan's supporters. When opposition intensified, the *St. Petersburg Times* published an editorial that Straub had written in California, while "recuperating from his daily work." The only way for the planning board to wield "any 'drastic' powers," Straub contended, was for the city commission to enact "'drastic' ordinances for the board's guidance." The Planning Law specified that elected officials, not advisory board members, were the final arbiters in the planning process. Taking the proposed legislation "for what it is, and not what the uninformed or prejudiced may say it is," Straub concluded, "there is no reason in the world why any good citizen should oppose it."[23]

Annie McRae, meanwhile, continued to work for passage of the law. On August 4, she wrote Nolen that while only a "few, small derogatory criticisms" had been leveled against the proposal, she expected much worse to come. "I want to ask you quite urgently," she wrote, "to give me some assistance in the way of suitable printed matter to bring the advantages of planning before the citizens." She would edit anything he sent her for the *St. Petersburg Times*, "whose columns are entirely open for anything I wish published." With Nolen's help, McRae vowed to make sure the Planning Law received a fair hearing: "I hope you see, Mr. Nolen, that I am writing you frankly, and that you will be quite as frank replying. I am not interested in this matter except that, as one citizen, I hope our townspeople may realize what this opportunity means to them and will have the good judgement to avail themselves to it."[24]

Nolen was attending an international planning conference in Sweden, so his young associate, Justin Hartzog, responded. He sent eight articles for McRae to use in her editorials: "The Expense of City Planning," "Cooperation Essential to City Planning," "The Relation of City Planning to the Man in the Street," "The Scope of City Planning," "The Need of a City Plan," "The Purpose of a City Plan," "Public Opinion and City Planning Progress and Legislation," and "City Planning Authorities." Within a week, Frank Williams also forwarded a report describing the origins and makeup of St. Petersburg's planning and zoning legislation.[25]

McRae countered her foes' attacks by portraying the planning referendum as a contest between pragmatic moderns and outdated reactionaries. "There are individuals who absolutely do not believe in the modern movement called city planning," McRae asserted, "just as there are those who do not believe in the new theology, or modern government methods, or that civilization has made any progress in the last few generations."[26] She cited a recent government report, which had found that more than fifteen million people in the United States were living in planned cities. Sadly, too many cities had planning forced upon them, McRae wrote, "because they found themselves mired in a swamp of perplexity from which they could only be delivered by sane zone laws." As a young city, St. Petersburg could escape the fate of other cities; but because of its rapid growth, there was little room for error. No city was growing faster than St. Petersburg, and according to McRae, if Nolen's work were rejected, "no city faces a greater confusion and disorder." She foresaw imminent disaster if some means were "not adopted to forestall the chaos which poorly planned developments are leading us into."[27]

If the proposed legislation passed, McRae believed, the planning board would be able to limit the corruption and waste that had vitiated the city-building process. With Nolen's plan in hand, the board could guide St. Petersburg's expansion in a more efficient pattern by serving as a clearinghouse when it came to spending public funds.[28] To help voters understand the origins of the Planning Law, the *St. Petersburg Times* reprinted the federal government's guidelines that Frank Williams had followed in drawing up St. Petersburg's planning legislation. McRae explained that the Planning Law resembled laws in effect in Atlanta, Washington, New York, Boston, and Philadelphia, but she wondered whether St. Petersburg would take its place among the "progressive cities of the nation or delay."[29]

Other voices spoke up as well. Garvin argued that the Planning Law offered the only means to help St. Petersburg rectify its chaotic municipal affairs. "Civilization imposes limits to property rights of the individual for the protection of the whole." Unfortunately, Garvin had learned the hard way that civilized behavior and rapacious subdividers were incompatible. "The Planning Board will need considerable moral courage," he warned, "when trying to show a prospecting subdivider the wisdom of building after a plan."[30]

On August 28, the day of the referendum, the Kiwanis Club sponsored a debate on the merits of city planning between A. P. Avery and Roy Hanna, Straub's longtime ally. Hanna argued that a comprehensive system of land-use controls provided the only method for the "intelligent guidance" of the city's expansion. Avery did not bother to show up.[31]

Although Avery never engaged in debate, his views received ample play in the *St. Petersburg Independent*. On referendum day, Brown alerted readers: "If you have not done your duty as citizens, do it now." The *Independent's* devotion to exposing the purported Machiavellian schemes of the pro-planning forces was, Brown wrote, "a matter of duty." He called on the people of St. Petersburg to protect "the future welfare of the city." "If you have not yet voted, do your duty before the day's sun has set."[32]

Voters followed Brown's directive and sent the Planning Law down to a crushing defeat. Out of 1,072 ballots, the Planning Law received only 138 (12.9 percent). The *St. Petersburg Independent* thanked voters for their "noble" performance. "There can be no mistaking the fact that the people of this city," Brown wrote, "can recognize a dangerous political scheme even when it is well disguised." To Brown, the result of the referendum proved that "autocratic and arbitrary rule" was "contrary to the free-spirited sentiment of the Sunshine City."[33] It also guaranteed that the city commission would continue to line Avery's pockets.

After surveying the wreckage, planning advocates were able to salvage some hope. Despite the reversal, "those seeking some measure to control unscrupulous builders and developers and to provide some machinery to beautify the city and its natural environs," McRae wrote, "were not totally disheartened." She attributed the loss to her opponents' "personal prejudices and ignorance," not to any fundamental error in the Planning Law. She recommended that the *St. Petersburg Times* initiate a new campaign of "reconciliation and education" to prepare citizens for the eventual adoption of a city plan.[34]

Straub had a more difficult time reconciling himself to the outcome. The travel-weary editor returned within a week after the election. The vote, he sadly noted, "was the loss of the city and it was a serious loss," because St. Petersburg's chaotic growth demanded "intelligent and systematic control and guidance." Those responsible for the Planning Law's defeat had won a Pyrrhic victory, postponing the inevitable to their own detriment. Eventually St. Petersburg would have to "meet and solve," Straub predicted, "the more important civic problems the city planning law would have enabled it to undertake now."[35]

Despite the loss of this golden opportunity, experience had taught the crusading editor that to achieve anything worthwhile meant working through opposition, delays, and setbacks. Straub had encountered this cycle of events in his recent trip to Los Angeles: "Los Angeles grew into a sizeable city before 'finding herself' and she is afflicted with many ugly mistakes St. Petersburg can avoid."[36] Despite the Planning Law's defeat, St. Petersburg could still escape the problems that plagued Los Angeles—if citizens reformed the city-building process. But before too much time passed, the people of St. Petersburg must, Straub wrote, "turn their thoughts from groundless alarms to the inception and the encouragement of plans that will hasten the day of the great city."[37]

While Straub continued to write about the urgent need for planning, the idea remained foreign to most. Although some of the city's leading citizens were in favor of it, the planning campaign never gained broad community support. As Pulver explained to Nolen, "The planning proposition goes over heads of the people." Pulver urged Nolen not to take the loss personally; the referendum disaster was typical of citizens' response to progressive initiatives. Pointing to himself as an example, Pulver lamented, "I am on my third recall. . . by the same bunch fostered by Brown and their political henchmen."[38]

The enthusiasm for the Nolen plan evaporated once realtors and subdividers realized that a comprehensive plan meant a regulated real estate market. Turning against the Planning Law, they became its most vocal critics, and their power in city affairs ensured the initiative's defeat.[39] While members of St. Petersburg's various civic clubs deliberated "gravely upon an unending number of transitory, incidental, and trivial matters," Straub wrote, they shut "their eyes to the basic fundamental conditions and problems." This was especially difficult for Straub to accept, because the Rotary Club had first placed city planning on the public agenda in 1921. In 1923, however, the Rotarians did not even address the issue.[40] The Chamber of Commerce showed "no more interest in the whole matter," the *St. Petersburg Times* reported, "than [in] shooting a rocket to the moon."[41]

The planning board's inability to publish Nolen's plan hurt the Planning Law's chances in the referendum. Without a document to study—a document whose publication should have been funded by the city commission or the Chamber of Commerce—it was hardly surprising that the townspeople "fell so readily," Straub wrote, "for the atrociously false political campaign."[42]

Even if the plan had been published, it probably would not have convinced enough voters. Brown's demagoguery was tailored to his audience, which was bedazzled by new riches. The huge profits they were reaping from land sales made the dream of an unregulated, ever-expanding city perfectly credible to many. Adopting a plan to deal with dangers in the distant future offered nothing to speculators making easy money in the here and now. When the majority is content with the status quo, Americans typically refuse to face problems with alarming long-term consequences.[43]

During the boom years, St. Petersburg's developers and promoters were loud in their praise of the promises of growth, prosperity, and profit—all of which they believed would be unending. With thousands of dollars being made buying and selling vacant land, only a courageous soul would advocate regulation. "The subdividers and promoters had more or less power and authority," Jonsberg, the planning board chairman, wrote Nolen, "which would have had a serious influence in any attempt which I might make to put the plan through in its entirety."[44] In St. Petersburg, supporting the Planning Law constituted heresy: "I would have been deemed a traitor to both city and state had I in any way indicated my position on the matter."[45]

The Expansive City

City planning ran counter to the assumptions on which St. Petersburg's new prosperity was based, namely, that property rights were sacrosanct, that land served the individual owner's economic interests, and that government existed to further—not inhibit—free enterprise. Most citizens were too busy angling for returns on their investments to care much about corruption or extravagant government expenditures. Unhampered by planning regulations, speculators heaped up riches, denying that there were limits to growth. The city's horde of realtors and subdividers believed that the real estate boom marked the beginning of everlasting prosperity, and that St. Petersburg would inevitably become one of the world's great resorts. For those who were uncertain about the future, it was comforting to know that "the so-called 'boom,'" as one journalist, Charles D. Fox, wrote, "will last forever, for there can be no let-up to the development of a state which offers so much to so many classes of people."[46] The future was bound to be prosperous, so there was no reason to plan: One only needed to believe. "St. Petersburg is the tale of a magic Utopia," one booster claimed, "a city of magic growth and immeasurable richness of future. The Florida foundations were already there. . . . Faith was the only requirement."[47]

Well-advertised building projects helped further the utopian vision of St. Petersburg. In 1923 the city's first million-dollar hotel, the Vinoy, opened to an astounded audience. This exclusive establishment occupied twelve acres of waterfront property in the heart of downtown. The Vinoy's lavish architecture included Moorish arches, tiled cupolas, and Georgian ballrooms, and the hotel was host to such varied celebrities as Calvin Coolidge, Babe Ruth, and H. L. Mencken.[48] The response to the Vinoy's opening seemed to justify St. Petersburg's almost mystical financial optimism: "What does this era of millions mean to St. Petersburg? Simply St. Petersburg is no longer a gamble, a speculation or a vision unrealized. Today St. Petersburg is a reality and the reality is dreaming a new dream with an almost certainty of realization."[49]

Although substantial building took place in downtown St. Petersburg, the real estate boom as a whole rested on a fragile foundation of promotion, speculation, and myth. Speculation fueled real estate sales; the belief in an unending boom fueled speculation. The boom was "unexpected and unrelated to anything," John Rothchild writes, "an Orphic delirium that swept across the state, entrancing the people, forcing them to speculate wildly in real estate and to buy swampland."[50] Neither good sense nor large amounts of cash in hand were prerequisites for buying land. Thousands across the state mortgaged the future to profit in the present. Investors approached "speculative mysticism" as they ignored reality and bought property solely in the belief that its value was predestined to increase. "Money was so easy to come by" for the St. Petersburg developer Walter Fuller and other investors, "that no one saved . . . everybody was spending—why worry?" "It became an accepted fact that all one had to do to make money was to buy land . . . and you could double your money in a year."[51]

Florida laws encouraged speculation, and buying and selling land, with its get-rich-quick allure, dominated state affairs. During the 1920s, enough land was subdivided in Florida to rehouse the entire population of the United States. This occurred at least in part because title searches and the recording of deeds were considered formalities and often postponed. In addition, option buying, through "binders," fueled tremendous increases in the price of land. A binder—five percent of the selling price—held a piece of property for thirty days, with no restrictions on the number of times it might be resold. In a month, dozens of transactions might take place on a single binder, yielding a profit to each investor. Although little cash changed hands, such deals produced a speculative profit that inflated property values far beyond what the market could actually bear.[52]

The realty business was a game of financial legerdemain. Most investors were not interested in developing land, but in turning it over for quick profit. Investors purchased binders for immediate sale; the last buyer was responsible for future payments. People rushed to profit now by ignoring tomorrow in a gamble that almost everyone in St. Petersburg seemed willing to take.

In 1925, six thousand real estate agents were registered in St. Petersburg. Binder holders, or "binder boys," waited in droves at train stations, ready to sell their services. An Illinois journalist wrote that everyone "want[ed] to get in the game and buy something and take a chance on the future, along with other boosters." Even retirees became "inoculated and succumb[ed] to the urge for activity."[53] Buying and selling went on at such a frantic pace that, "salesmen nearly ran over each other in their mad efforts to sell lots." According to Walter Fuller, "The Boom was not an urge to retire to a pleasant cottage or bask in luxurious villas or seaside hotels. It was a greedy delirium to acquire riches overnight without benefit or effort, brains or services rendered."[54]

Throughout the state journalists, public officials, and business leaders worked to transform the speculation into reality.[55] St. Petersburg's Chamber of Commerce assured newcomers that they would experience the "promise of prosperity and growth."[56] One booster claimed that the dream of the Sunshine City was "coming true because the city of sunshine and birds and flowers has chosen to be clean of heart."[57] Perriton Maxwell was even more effusive, linking Florida's newfound prosperity to the myth of Aryan superiority: "The movement is no boom; never forget that. It is no bubble, to swell and gleam for an instant and then burst and vanish. It is a manifestation, a recurrence of the racial instinct to migrate, to penetrate new frontiers. Mountains and rivers and endless prairies never have halted the migrations of the Aryan races in the past . . . and will not halt this latest migration."[58]

St. Petersburg's boosters preached a civic religion that proclaimed the wonders of Florida generally—and their hometown specifically. But unlike true religions, this one had no eschatological aspect: With the riches funneling into

St. Petersburg, the city's boosters were already experiencing heaven on earth. All they needed to make their heaven last was to lead others there.[59]

Like other communities committed to boosting, St. Petersburg based its important communal decisions more on wishful thinking than on reality—and more on conviction than on reason.[60] The diligence with which St. Petersburg was boosted as the "Sunshine City," the "Tourist Metropolis," or "Florida's Best City" was an attempt on the part of the business community to attract investors and make money. But individuals' fervor and unquestioning commitment to their city showed that more was at stake here than profit. Local enthusiasts, like Lew Brown, historian Ray Arsenault writes, "devoted their lives to the cause of boosterism."[61] If you were a St. Petersburg booster, Brown would remind his readers, "You will have to be up before 7 a.m. and here is your program for the rest of the week . . ."[62]

Citizens' perseverance in boosting St. Petersburg brought the real estate market into the city's public, private, and religious institutions. No matter the setting, the message was always the same: Growth and expansion were absolute goods, because they generated prosperity. Religious leaders equated a church's physical expansion with its spiritual growth. Under pretext of providing winter tourists with a place to worship, churches went far beyond their means in building impressive new structures.[63]

Fearing that his congregation was sliding into apostasy, because it lacked a commanding edifice, the Reverend W. A. Hobson, the minister of Grace Baptist Church, the city's largest, exhorted his congregation to display its faith by building a larger temple. Hobson, who was president of the Florida Baptist Convention, used the Old Testament to legitimize his call for city building and preached a message of fire and brimstone. He took Isaiah 54:2 as his text: "Enlarge the place of thy tent, and let them stretch forth the curtains of thine habitations; spare not, lengthen thy cords, and strengthen thy stakes." Hobson announced that the church had not kept pace with the city's growth. Grace Baptist was "out of harmony with its environment" and faced "the necessity of readjustment."[64]

Hobson pleaded with the faithful to contribute to the building fund in order to keep from backsliding. "A backward church had no place in a progressive city; unless it is awakened and becomes alert it will be eliminated by the momentum of progress." Institutions, he believed, were the expressions of ideals, and he warned parishioners that if they fell behind the "progressive movements in the growth of the city," their church would become "an incubus on the community and a burden to the commonwealth." To prevent this catastrophe, Hobson invoked "sound business judgment and a spiritual vision." In his peroration, he echoed the boosters' theme: "Since this church was erected St. Petersburg has grown by leaps and bounds and property values have multiplied into the millions. No man need come to this land of Flowers, this paradise of leisure, of beauty, of natural resources, and financial opportunity and go away any poorer in health and wealth."[65]

Hobson's homage to the sales pitch exemplified the kind of faith that bound the people of St. Petersburg. Although he paid lip service to ideals, what Hobson really wanted was a large, modern church building. Such a building would prove beyond a doubt that Grace Baptist Church was a dynamic and progressive force in St. Petersburg. The physical building—quite aside from any question of what went on inside it—would affirm the sacrifice made by the Reverend W. A. Hobson and his flock to St. Petersburg's most cherished belief.

The people of St. Petersburg were rarely affronted by such blatant appeals. Instead, they felt that their desire to build a new Eden bound them together. The community's unprecedented growth had created a void between tradition and modernity. The community's continual self-glorification depicted the land boom as the outcome of a rational series of events that would lead to an even more prosperous future. However hollow St. Petersburg's zealous boosting may appear now, such behavior was hardly out of the ordinary. During the 1920s Americans went to great lengths to recapture the sense of community that mass culture was systematically destroying.[66]

During the 1920s, Americans enjoyed the rewards of prosperity, but they were searching for more. As the role of church, school, and family in forming values weakened, individuals increasingly turned to the mass media, consumerism, and boosterism for emotional nurture. Whether in St. Petersburg or in *Middletown* (1929), a seminal study of Muncie, Indiana, during the 1920s, people were trying to cope with a new set of values. In both places, compulsive club-joining, boosterism, and an insistence on conformity marked attempts to establish an equilibrium between the communal rites of the past and the combination of freedom and homogeneity that defines modern life.[67]

In *Middletown*, Robert and Helen Lynd described an "increasing sense of strain and perplexity" as the populace saw their "ideals and behavior patterns collapse."[68] Unlike their counterparts in Indiana, the people of St. Petersburg seemed immune to this modern uncertainty. The communal perspective in St. Petersburg was one of irrepressible self-confidence. Whether it was because of the voluminous advertising in the city's newspapers, the threefold population increase in five years, the plethora of million-dollar real estate deals, or Mayor Frank P. Pulver parading down New York's Broadway during midwinter dressed in white from straw hat to vanilla oxfords, it seemed that the Sunshine City had solved the cultural dilemma of the 1920s. In an anxiety-ridden age, St. Petersburg claimed that it was an outpost of tranquility, a place where people knew "the *Secret* of getting the most out of life." Life was "more than drudgery and existence," the Chamber of Commerce contended. "Here men have learned how to combine healthful living conditions with rare advantages for material advancement and mental and spiritual enrichment."[69]

Blessed by Providence and the powers of nature, the people of St. Petersburg believed they were chosen people. They could, as they thought, hold to their laissez-faire beliefs and still enjoy a life of wealth and leisure. A city of dreams in the heart of Eden did not need to plan for the future; its destiny was certain. A prosperous future merely depended on "the touch," as one subdivider put it, "of the magic wand of capitalism and enterprise."[70]

5

The End of a Dream, the Institution of Planning

The child of St. Petersburg remembers a wilderness of scrub pine and palmetto brush at the edge of town. There were rusted fire hydrants, ornate streetlights overgrown with vines, old brick streets half sunk in sandy soil, some railroad tracks, as if the area had been prepared for civilization and then abandoned quickly, as the Maya had abandoned their temples. This was not a ruin of the Spaniards, but of the earliest developers.

John Rothchild, 1985

William Straub refused to be deterred by the disastrous results of the Planning Law referendum. In the *St. Petersburg Times*, he ran a series of editorials extolling the virtues of city planning, on subjects ranging from women's important role in the process to how a comprehensive plan would enhance property values. Other editorials illustrated the pitfalls and nuisances that could have been avoided with a city plan. Streets failed to intersect, roads were paved at different grades, important natural features were lost, and two houses were built on one lot—and these were just some of the problems besetting the city.[1]

Straub described the planning referendum as "a public calamity, the most unintelligent vote ever known in St. Petersburg." The Department of Public Works, proceeding according to no plan, was plagued by cost overruns, delays, and inefficiencies. The disbursement of public funds was speculative at best and corrupt at worst. In 1924 alone, the sale of SAB (Special Assessment Bonds) nearly doubled the bonded public debt, which went from $3.8 million to $7.5 million. Straub feared that the city would bankrupt itself unless a plan was adopted.[2]

Planning was, to Straub, the only means to bring order to St. Petersburg's chaotic finances. Aesthetics was no longer his watchword; instead, the incentive became good business sense. "City planning," he wrote, carried a "degree of commercial success and profit that makes it in reality a 'business proposition.'"[3] Slowly, this pragmatic approach began to draw supporters.

The work of Frank Jonsberg, the former chairman of the planning board, aided Straub's endeavor. In August 1924, Straub persuaded the Chamber of Commerce to form a city planning committee. The group elected Jonsberg chairman and Walter Fuller vice chairman, and the two worked diligently to educate the community about the merits of planning.

By November the new committee had begun to have some success. Election Day brought in new city commissioners who were ready to revisit the planning issue. Although Pulver was no longer mayor (Brown's third recall was at last successful), the city commissioners who had thwarted him either declined to run or lost. In December the new commission appointed Commissioners Reed and Snyder to study the feasibility of implementing a city plan. They returned a favorable verdict, and in May 1925 the city commission appointed Straub to lobby the state legislature for another planning act.[4]

By 1924 Florida had awakened to the idea of city planning. After Sarasota, Clearwater, Jacksonville, St. Augustine, Gainesville, and Fort Myers had signed contracts with his firm, Nolen opened a branch office in Jacksonville.[5] These municipal governments hired Nolen because their planning commissions lacked both expertise and resources. And without a general state enabling act, each city had to get its own planning law from the legislature. This process proved especially troublesome, so Straub helped out by forming the Florida City Planning Association. The group elected him chairman of the legislative committee, and he coordinated the drafting of a general state planning act that went to the legislature in 1925. Rural legislators killed the initiative in committee, but Straub immediately organized committees to write bills for each city interested in planning—including St. Petersburg. All of the measures passed.[6]

St. Petersburg's new legislation, like the 1923 Planning Law, allowed the planning board to design a comprehensive plan for the "conservation and preservation of the public, health, safety and general welfare." An amendment stated that the city could hire consultants as needed. In contrast to the 1923 legislation, which had to be put to a referendum, the new act could be ratified by a majority vote of the city commission. In June the city commission voted unanimously for the act, and a month later it appointed a five-member planning board that included Jonsberg, Straub, and Fuller. At the planning board's first meeting the members voted to rehire John Nolen.[7]

In August 1925, John Nolen received the following telegram from Straub: "Political problems smoothed out and administration behind us. Public interest at this time requires your personal presence."[8] Nolen signed a $6,500 contract to draw up a comprehensive plan and a zoning ordinance. At the same time, he informed the planning board that he could not devote his personal

:ntion to St. Petersburg, because his firm held contracts with more than thirty municipalities across the state.[9] Nolen was also president of the American City Planning Institute (ACPI), a position that came to occupy a good portion of his time.[10]

Justin Hartzog, a junior planner in the Nolen firm, received the St. Petersburg assignment. After discussions with the planning board, Hartzog agreed to update Nolen's earlier plan. On August 21, 1925, Hartzog wrote Nolen that "work was progressing" and that he was "receiving cooperation from practically everyone in St. Petersburg." After the 1925 elections, however, this spirit of harmony died. One of the new commissioners, Scott Serviss, wanted to break with Nolen because he feared that adopting a plan would depress the real estate market. He asserted that planning hardly constituted a science. With the city's rapid growth, "If we make a plan today," he reasoned, "it will be no good tomorrow."[11]

Serviss was voicing the sentiments of A. P. Avery. "Our friend [Avery]," Straub wrote Nolen, "is of course putting everything in our way he can and has one member of the city commission with him who causes endless delays."[12] Avery vowed that he would remove from office any commissioner who voted to execute the agreement with Nolen.[13]

Cowed by Avery's threats, the city commission pressed the planning board to ask for a less ambitious plan than Nolen's. Shortly after the November election, the planning board informed Hartzog that he should not update Nolen's earlier plan. Instead, they requested that he draw up a plan with "simpler proportions," analyzing no more than the land within the existing city boundaries. In addition, the board wanted Hartzog's analysis to focus only on the physical mistakes that impaired city building.[14]

Before the city commission's capitulation to Avery, Nolen had intended to exhibit Hartzog's plan at the National Planning Conference, scheduled in St. Petersburg for spring 1926. Nolen decided to bring the nation's planners to the Sunshine City, he wrote Straub, "because of the leadership St. Petersburg has among Florida cities in city planning matters."[15] Not only was he seeking to stimulate interest in planning in St. Petersburg and throughout Florida; he also wanted to announce his new vision for the state.[16]

The 1926 National Conference on City Planning

Nolen realized, as city planning historian Mel Scott wrote, "that if ever a state needed help in avoiding mistakes and profiting by the experience of areas with some history of planning, it was Florida."[17] Instead of serving as a model for urban America, Florida had become an epitome of bad taste. Without a system of land-use controls, a crowd of disconnected subdivisions cluttered the landscape, and the state's natural resources had suffered from wholesale destruction. After working in Florida for four years, Nolen believed that Florida needed to install a comprehensive system of planning more than any other state.[18]

In late March 1926, two hundred planners arrived in St. Petersburg—including Nolen, Olmsted, Unwin, Harland Bartholomew (a leader in the new field of traffic engineering), and Robert Whitnall (the chief planner for Los Angeles). St. Petersburg had changed dramatically since Nolen's first visit four years earlier. The population had doubled, to 40,000, and although countless lots were being sold in the hinterlands, the most intense building had been downtown.[19] The Snell Arcade, Perry Snell's monument to the Mediterranean Revival movement, anchored the developing skyline. St. Petersburg had also expanded into Tampa Bay after voters approved a million-dollar bond to build the giant pier of Lew Brown's dream, now approaching completion. At the head of the pier stood the Casino, a two-story architectural wonder distinguished by a large central atrium and an open-air ballroom. The Casino, together with the Soreno and Vinoy Hotels, gave the St. Petersburg waterfront an elegance unimaginable a decade earlier. A monumental skyline, two grand hotels, a booming real estate market, and an unmatched spirit of boosterism furnished an interesting backdrop for a meeting of America's city planners.[20]

Frank Jonsberg opened the proceedings with a warm welcome. For years he had revered city planners "for the way in which with a few lines of pen and a few deft strokes of a brush they can transform a 'just-growed' Topsy town into a superlative quintessence of metropolitan perfection." Local planning commissions, however, remained responsible for "effecting the miracle as best they can." While they were armed with a plan, they lacked "the blandishments of counsel and advice of city planners." He urged his listeners to help their clients learn the trick of striking a compromise between those looking to the past and "visionaries who cherished fondly fluttering hopes of a civic perfection that could only be attainable through Divine inspiration." In their task, planners needed to proceed "if not with wisdom, at least with common sense."

Jonsberg also furnished a few hints on how to deal with the locals. He warned anyone considering the purchase of "one of our wonderful sand lots, teeming as they are with humus, nitrates, phosphates and red bugs," that St. Petersburg's realtors were unequaled in their powers of persuasion. For those "walking in the darkness of ignorance regarding lots there is always a real estate man ready to take him by the hand and lead him into the light of understanding." "Like the lion and the lamb, they will lie down together—and in a little while one of them will get up and go to work again."[21]

Olmsted spoke on the planning of resort communities, calling on planners to assess carefully the relationship between the natural environment and tourism. He recounted how many once fashionable resort cities "were strangled by the results of their own popularity." Their pleasing character stimulated a growth "so rapid and so unregulated that it ran wild destroying the qualities that originally made the resorts attractive." Olmsted stressed preserving unique natural features "for the maintenance of pleasurable qualities." While providing open space and public landscaping would create beauty, the planner's real task was to create a good working relationship with the private sector. Olmsted encouraged planning commissions to oversee the approval of building plans through property covenants. Such covenants would ensure that both the developer and the public agreed to incorporate beauty in new projects. Olmsted also thought that covenants would benefit the public by preventing the issuance of zoning variances.[22]

In his presidential address, "New Communities to Meet New Conditions," Nolen delivered the outline for his forthcoming treatise, *New Towns for Old*. Because America lacked any meaningful urban models, he wanted the United States to construct planned new towns similar to English garden cities. "The old simplicity and charm of American villages and towns have largely disappeared," he told his colleagues, "but a new form of urban beauty has not yet taken its place." The construction of new towns could also guide America by making certain that modern city-building techniques respected the beauty of the landscape. Despite Florida's many faults, Nolen still clung to the hope that the state could serve as a showcase for urban planning.[23]

The new era of leisure had pushed Florida's economy to record heights, but the accompanying wave of urban expansion did not have to ravage the landscape. The success of Coral Gables was an excellent example, Nolen noted, "that beauty draws more than oxen." George Merrick had proven that strict architectural controls and site planning could create pleasing living environments—and healthy profits. While many subdivisions offered facades that simulated the feeling of Coral Gables, few developers followed a plan. Nolen proposed that local and state officials should work with the private sector to build an interconnected system of new towns. Florida could channel its growth into "an harmonious expression of new city ideals" by designing urban environments that reflected "topographical and climatic conditions."

But before such an enterprise could proceed, the state government needed to regulate the location of future towns and cities. To Nolen, "the uncontrolled growth of cities is the problem that gives gravest concern today." He wanted the legislature to adopt a plan for the state that would set guidelines for regional and city plans. With the aid of the state, local governments could then guide their own growth, and the private sector could invest in building new towns.[24]

Mrs. Robert Seymour fleshed out Nolen's proposal in her address, "A State Plan for Florida." Mrs. Seymour, a resident of Miami, had worked with both John Nolen and Patrick Geddes. In 1923, after having been elected president of Florida's Federation of Women's Clubs, she organized a conservation program to promote state-mandated planning at the county level. She wanted county seats to serve as centers for a radial system of parks and highways that local planning commissions would design. Such a radial system could connect the state. Once this process was initiated, she felt citizens would find innovative ways to enhance their locality's "heritage, landscape, and character." Playing to her audience, she claimed that Florida was "a place that cries aloud for engineers and artists and landscape architects who will work together." She challenged the convention to pass a resolution calling for mandatory planning in Florida. If "we have the recognition," she concluded, "then we can go to our men of wealth in our organizations and get support."[25]

Gordon Whitnall, the director of the Los Angeles Planning Commission, commented that "through the idealism that has been expressed by Mrs. Seymour," Florida held the "germ of an idea which must come to fruition."[26] Seymour, however, failed to get the endorsement she wanted. Instead a general resolution was passed encouraging all states interested in planning to consult the standard planning and zoning enabling act prepared by the U.S. Department of Commerce.[27]

While a directive to promote a special agenda for Florida never passed, the conference did help to lessen St. Petersburg's antipathy toward planning.[28] The conference had covered a range of issues that might help "the rapidly growing cities of Florida avoid the mistakes and profit by the city planning experiences of municipalities elsewhere."[29] This assemblage of "erudite, aloof, exalted, campus-looking personages," as one reporter described the planners, looked quite respectable, and hardly seemed the type to perpetrate any rabid governmental excesses—in spite of Lew Brown's claim to the contrary.[30]

The developer Walter P. Fuller, the planning board's effusive vice chairman, also used the conference to help calm fears. Fuller, a local hero and former star athlete at the University of North Carolina, was trusted by many realtors. In a special meeting with the Realty Board, he assured those assembled that the planning board did not possess any "mysterious power." As an advisory board, it could only review land-use issues and make recommendations. According to Fuller, his board wanted to prevent the numerous "physical mistakes that impaired the welfare of both builders and the community." At his urging, the Realty Board passed a resolution supporting the planning board.[31]

With the publicity gained from the National Planning Conference and the support of the Realty Board, St. Petersburg finally seemed ready to experiment with city planning. But all talk of planning was abandoned when Florida's great real estate boom collapsed.

The Bust

By 1924, the heavy speculation in Florida real estate had drawn the attention of the leaders of America's financial institutions. Eastern and Midwestern bankers became concerned when depositors started withdrawing their savings to buy land in Florida. Although prominent banks in Ohio issued dire warnings about the dangers of "wildcat land speculation," customers continued to channel their funds into Florida real estate. In Cleveland, after banks reported that clients had transferred over $80 million to Florida, the director of the state's Department of Commerce, Cyrus Locher, went south to investigate. On his return, he advised outlawing the sale of Florida property in Ohio. He alleged that Florida's development was a farce: "They are only building a few houses and a few roads and the whole population seems to be engaged in subdividing land into lots and selling them." Shortly thereafter, Ohio enacted "blue sky" laws, which prohibited certain firms from selling Florida real estate in Ohio.[32]

By mid-1925, the national press had begun a campaign of Florida-bashing. Journalists and businessmen on both coasts—and in the middle of the country as well—produced a steady stream of criticism. Some of their accusations were legitimate. Investigations by the National Better Business Bureau turned up a number of fraudulent land schemes and illegalities in the sale of bonds. But Los Angeles journalists' claims that life in Florida was only a pale imitation of the good life enjoyed along the Pacific Coast were born of jealousy, not concern.[33] Regardless of the motives behind it, however, anti-Florida rhetoric appealed to a public tired of hearing about the state's wonders. People stood back to await Florida's downfall.[34]

Governor John W. Martin tried to reverse the anti-Florida trend by calling a meeting in New York to discuss the "Truth about Florida" with America's leading publishers. An impressive entourage of the state's city builders and land barons, including George Merrick, Blanton Collier, and Paris Singer, accompanied the governor. Afterward Martin called the meeting an unqualified success and encouraged similar endeavors to counteract "scurrilous propaganda."[35]

Figure 17 Even when the boom turned to bust, the people of St. Petersburg believed a lecherous Uncle Sam would always court the beautiful Miss Florida. Note the flower denoting Miss Florida and the "1926 Building Program" in the swirl of her skirts. March 1926, *St. Petersburg Times*.

Florida's editors, bankers, realtors, and public officials hastened to assure America that the state's economy was still strong. Although the frenzied pace of buying and selling land was undoubtedly slowing, the state's growing municipalities, they said, had laid the foundation for long-term prosperity.[36] Now that modern technology had put Florida in touch with the rest of the nation, the state had begun "sowing the seed," the New South journalist Richard Edmonds wrote, "for a great harvest in the future."[37]

93

This campaign to maintain Florida's image was not limited to oratory. The state moved to end fraudulent speculation by licensing realtors and restricted the sale of the binders that had helped fuel the real estate frenzy. The state cut the life span of a binder from thirty to ten days, increased their cost, and required public officials rather than investors to update title abstracts. A Better Business Bureau was set up to field complaints and track false advertising in out-of-state newspapers. The state also started to regulate prices of hotel rooms, which fluctuated wildly during the winter season. These efforts proved quite successful, and by early 1926 Florida was receiving considerably less bad press. But, at the same time, real estate sales remained sluggish.[38]

In late summer and autumn 1925, a series of setbacks had a crushing effect on the state's economy. The East Coast Line dramatically cut service in August to repair damaged track, and only food, livestock, and perishables were allowed into Florida. By late October, every rail line in the state had followed the East Coast Line's example. Builders, unable to secure necessary materials, had to make immediate layoffs. Many projects were left unfinished; others never even got started. When the slowdown ended the following April, Florida's building industry was in a severe depression.[39]

The threat of investigation by the Internal Revenue Service also discouraged speculation in land. During late summer 1926, rumors began circulating that agents planned to audit returns showing profits from real estate. The possibility of a tax reduction in 1927 also pushed some investors to push property sales to the new year. After the stock market dipped in February and March, speculation in Florida real estate dropped precipitously, and by July the great Florida land boom had ended. "The world's greatest poker game, played with building lots instead of chips," Stella Crosley wrote in *The Nation*, "is over."[40]

While the rest of America accepted the demise of Florida's real estate market, the people of St. Petersburg could not. A. P. Avery even assured citizens that St. Petersburg was embarking on a new and more orderly period of expansion and prosperity. "St. Petersburg," he told the community in March 1926, "is rushing into its greatest period of abundance." The "boom hysteria" was over; the city's financial institutions would continue to exhibit the "sound and conservative judgment," he maintained, "that had built St. Petersburg."[41]

In mid-March 1926, the Realty Board announced that St. Petersburg was still safe for investors. According to the board, realtors' interest in community affairs outweighed their desire to make a sale. As proof, they were buying property in order to spark a new era of "prosperity and stable investment."[42] According to the board's president, N. G. Pearce, the market was entering an even more prosperous phase, as the closing of less reputable operations gave "real buyers" better opportunities "to make real profits."[43]

Throughout 1926, the city's newspapers gave running accounts of the record activity in private and public building. Headlines announcing big real estate deals made it seem that the market was as healthy as ever, but this was an illusion. Investors who had bought real estate between 1922 and 1924 made their final payments in 1926. All these final payments created a flood of conveyances—and a spurious impression of vitality. "The distressed purchaser knew in his heart he was sunk," Walter Fuller wrote, "but hoped a brave front would bring a buyer."[44] Properties were not now being sold to eager northern speculators, but to local citizens who purchased them at record high prices. These investments demonstrated the triumph of faith over logic. As Fuller admitted, "We became the suckers."[45]

The vast public works program rested on an equally shaky foundation. Since the majority of municipal projects were financed through SAB, the millions of dollars going into paving, street lights, and sewers in no way reflected the city's economic health. Improvements continued regardless of the property owner's ability to pay, because municipal officials had signed contracts with bond houses and with Avery's bank.[46] Despite a mushrooming public debt, realtors depicted the municipal improvements as a sign of St. Petersburg's economic vitality. In spring 1926, realtors used the 122 miles of new streets under construction and the $25 million building program to assure investors "that every dollar here is worth 100 cents and that the growth of the city has only fairly begun."[47] Throughout 1926 and into 1927, the city commission spent millions of dollars building public improvements in outlying areas. By the end of 1927, the city had a road system capable of serving a metropolis six times its size.[48]

This tremendous feat in city building rested on the premise that an influx of tax-paying property owners would come to St. Petersburg, build homes, and pay off the municipal debt. The construction of sewers, roads, and sidewalks in the hinterlands was also promoted by a very few, who became very rich. In mid-1927, "when the economy was as dead as a salted mackerel," according to Fuller, Avery started paving streets to open up thousands of lots for development. This scheme was "about as useful as a pair of skates would be to a legless man," Fuller wrote.[49]

Despite all the optimistic predictions, in late spring 1927, St. Petersburg was a harbinger of the nation's approaching economic collapse. After mortgaging their future to build a great city, the city's inhabitants stood on the verge of ruin. In 1923 the city had a bonded indebtedness of $3.8 million; four years later, it had soared to $23.7 million—and the interest on it was a high 6 percent. SAB constituted more than $12 million of the debt, and any hope that it might be retired ended when the bottom dropped out of the real estate market. Not only had land values plummeted; the liens on the hundreds of vacant properties that benefited from the improvements were worthless. When the SAB matured, the city was stuck with these liens. During the next three years, St. Petersburg had the second highest per capita debt in the nation—Atlantic City held the dubious distinction of being first—but St. Petersburg's taxpayers were far less able to assume the burden.[50]

In the spring of 1927, an investigation by the Realty Board found city hall sunk in corruption. The board's report condemned the paving awards as "the greatest source of public waste and extravagance." The municipal government had wasted huge amounts of money on "Avery additives." It had also signally failed to coordinate the work of its departments, resulting in duplication of work and useless expenditures.[51]

After the Realty Board released its report, Straub argued that St. Petersburg's runaway debt and Avery's piracy called for major reforms. "How much longer," he asked, "are the taxpayers of St. Petersburg going to pay tribute to the paving combines?" He proposed the adoption of a new charter that would put a city manager in place. Then a professional could work with elected officials to solve the city's problems.[52]

Straub's challenge went unheeded. The people of St. Petersburg were still too dazed from the economic collapse to plan constructively. Their earlier self-confidence and assurance had been replaced by confusion and disorder. While Avery and his cronies were making the most of the situation by raiding the municipal treasury, the newly impoverished were stealing sidewalk tiles from abandoned subdivisions to make a living. Walter Fuller, who had made and lost a fortune during the boom years, survived for the summer from "the flower pots I dug up from my own abandoned nursery and sold at $2.00 a thousand."[53] On the outskirts of town, deserted homes, unfinished subdivisions, and roads leading nowhere were stark reminders of people's mindless pursuit of wealth.

Without a common goal, the community began to splinter. Most of the leading go-getters had to borrow money to get out of town. By the end of 1927, 15,000 people had fled St. Petersburg.[54] The realtors who remained were subject to almost constant ridicule. The Realty Board pleaded that they should "no longer be made the 'butt of jokes' and saddled with all blame for the ills of the county, state and city."[55] While the blame for the city's woes was fixed, civic leaders continued to flounder as they tried to stabilize affairs.

In 1927, the city's financial woes snowballed. In an effort to escape paying taxes, outlying neighborhoods decided that they wanted to invalidate St. Petersburg's annexation. Other citizens simply refused—or were unable—to pay.[56] In spite of the threat of a tax revolt, Avery's machine held its grip on city hall. After milking the city treasury for twenty years, Avery was not about to surrender without a fight.[57] But even during this inauspicious time, Frank Jonsberg was trying to convince property owners that they needed a comprehensive plan.

The Hartzog Report

After a year and a half of countless meetings, the planning board was still at an impasse. In January 1927, Jonsberg apologized to Nolen for not having sent Hartzog the data he needed to draw up a zoning plan. Practically every subdivision contained a large business section, because lots zoned for business commanded the highest prices. Although the chance that these business sections would succeed—or even be built—was almost nil, lot owners wanted to hold on to their precious commercial classification. St. Petersburg had enough commercial areas, Jonsberg wrote Nolen, "to accommodate the entire Union, including Alaska and our possessions in the South Sea Islands."[58]

In late January, Jonsberg informed Nolen that the planning board could not even reach a tentative agreement with landowners. Jonsberg wanted to ignore the zoning issue and just present the city plan for adoption. Although he regretted having to make such a decision, Nolen concurred: "The Zone Plan can wait," he informed Jonsberg.[59] But after conferring with Whitnall, the Los Angeles planner, Nolen wrote to Jonsberg again in March. Nolen now believed that, unless many of the city's proposed business sites were eliminated, the plan would offer little. "I don't know how far you and I," he confided, "can save the situation."[60]

In early April 1927, Jonsberg received a forty-page report, a platting ordinance, a minimum housing code, and a land-use map from Hartzog. A zoning ordinance was also included in case the commercial zoning issue was resolved. This plan paled in comparison to Nolen's 1923 work, but the planning board had asked for a less ambitious work, and Hartzog complied. It was a superficial endeavor that offered sound advice but little vision. Even the plan's title was changed to indicate the shift in emphasis. *St. Petersburg Today, St. Petersburg Tomorrow* had given way to *A Report on City Planning Proposals for St. Petersburg, Florida.*[61] Hartzog recommended that it was time for a "firm belief in sound public finance and timely action." His report provided solutions either to solve or to prevent problems, and afforded the opportunity "for the public to take an account of stock, to unhurriedly and wisely plan ahead, to acquire the land necessary for public improvements and municipal projects, and to begin with confidence the systematic execution of the city planning proposals."

Hartzog concentrated on solving existing problems and improving the city's layout. He proposed removing eyesores like the downtown railroad and undertaking new civic projects, including an expanded airport and a new civic center. He also included the code for minimum housing standards and a platting ordinance to improve building practices. Traffic planning was a major priority, and Hartzog set up a road system with three classifications: main arteries, intermediate thoroughfares, and local streets. The system would funnel traffic from narrow local streets into the wider intermediate and arterial thoroughfares. The secondary thoroughfares were undivided roads between 80 and 100 feet wide; arteries were divided roads between 100 and 120 feet wide, including a planted median. Hartzog recommended that the city concentrate commercial properties in shopping centers on principal arteries, locate apartments on secondary roads, and place single-family houses along the tertiary streets.

The beaches created particular problems for transportation. The 1927 plan differed from its predecessor, which had recommended preserving the barrier islands for public use. Hartzog found that the "great difficulty of the beaches" lay in their inaccessibility. To remedy this situation, he recommended constructing a new causeway and running an electric trolley to the beaches. The report, however, failed to mention the most appropriate land uses along the Gulf, an area still largely undeveloped.

Hartzog reiterated Nolen's earlier recommendation to create a comprehensive park system. Given St. Petersburg's reliance on tourism, "Much controversy and waste of enthusiasm and energy can be avoided," he wrote, "if a policy of park acquisition and maintenance is adopted." In determining the best use for the city's land, the preservation of "an interesting bit of woodland, lake, or lake country" was often the "most economic means." Hartzog felt that the city needed at least two large parks, at Saw Grass Lake and Papy's Bayou, and a parkway system to connect them to the waterfront. A parkway system could be built without significant expense if the city commission gained title or easements to the floodplains surrounding drainage canals and creeks. Hartzog also proposed a "bulkhead line" specifying the boundaries for coastal fills. This boundary would limit dredge-and-fill operations to areas contiguous to the existing coastline. If reclamation were not confined, it would cause "an unhappy situation on the shore line through the excessive and illogical building out into the water."

One portion of the plan received much more attention than its predecessor—citizen participation. Although St. Petersburg was in possession of the necessary enabling legislation, the city commission would not adopt Hartzog's report until the planning board convinced skeptics that the new plan would not hinder property investments. But Jonsberg had already been trying to reach a consensus with property owners contesting land-use designations for more than a year, without success. Hartzog recommended that the city hire a full-time planner. Otherwise, "the plan is likely to be pigeon-holed, and the time and money put into the first degree stages of the work wasted."[62]

Building a New Consensus

Nolen asked Jonsberg to have the Hartzog report printed so that he could exhibit it at the National Planning Conference in Washington. He wanted St. Petersburg's plan to back up the regional plan his office had drawn up for Tampa Bay. Such a study had been "needed for some time, because growth has been taking place in an unguided manner." Nolen had undertaken this work on his own, and he thought that the region's cities would support it. Nolen also wanted Jonsberg to critique this project before the Washington meeting.[63]

The beleaguered Jonsberg had no time to spend on another planning project. The city commission owed Nolen's firm $1,000, and it refused to release funds for printing the plan, especially as, at this low point in the city's history, the public was hostile to almost any government action. "We are all familiar with the political situation in St. Petersburg and are particularly anxious," Jonsberg wrote Nolen in June, "to avoid furnishing any ammo for any possible enemy of the city plan to use for the possible destruction of all our work by an appeal to the thoughtless voter along the lines of 'economy.'" Lew Brown had taken special offense because he believed that "'Mr. Nolen was trying to make a job for himself for life.'"[64]

The planning board decided to manage the planning process on its own. While he understood Nolen's desire to see the plan implemented, "We who are in the first line trenches and continually on the defensive," Jonsberg explained, "feel that we are right in our contention that the best way to escape trouble is to side step it whenever possible."[65] Nolen appreciated Jonsberg's honesty and he thought that "a frank statement of the necessity for city planning" would appeal to residents' common sense. In July 1927, Hartzog contacted Jonsberg and was shocked to find that further agitation over politics and retrenchments had jeopardized the plan. "It seems like a perilous time to submit any new ideas, but we have perfect confidence in your diplomatic skill to guide the planning program through successfully."[66]

In mid-August, Nolen returned from an extended visit to England and the Mediterranean coast with a new outlook on the situation in St. Petersburg. "All the world wants more comfort and beauty and pleasure," he wrote Jonsberg, "and an escape from the harshness of modern cities and cold climates." Nolen assured his friend that St. Petersburg could "help supply what the world

99

wants, and could profit greatly by it." After having revisited the English garden cities and the French Riviera, Nolen was distressed to see St. Petersburg squandering its potential. "City planning has got to be prosecuted by the people of the city and the whole city government with more vigor and generosity." It might be "alright [sic] to pray for guidance, but we must do more." " 'Trust the Lord,' " Nolen advised his friend, "but don't fool with him."[67]

Jonsberg replied at once. He had taken Nolen's advice to heart, but he could not act on it at this time. "Our citizens and city commission are faced with so many concerns and perplexities," he wrote, that, "for me to attempt to project our city plan into this atmosphere would spell disaster." Once the city had acquired a degree of stability, he promised to pursue a more aggressive policy. He reassured Nolen that the city would adopt a plan— "provided we do not become too urgent."[68]

Although it was a painfully slow process, Jonsberg felt that the people of St. Petersburg were finally seeing the need for city planning. "You may think that I am slow in putting forward our city plan but there were reasons which I hardly dare[d] give utterance to sooner."[69] During the furor over the first plan, Jonsberg feared that he would have been permanently ostracized if he had strongly supported Nolen's work. Now, however, the "overlords of the Boom" were subjected to ridicule, and the time was ripe for a plan. "The vaporings of such of these men as are left among us could have no possible effect," Jonsberg noted, "and to my mind this relieves me of the more serious antagonistic aspect which I felt we had to combat."[70]

While Jonsberg was writing to Nolen, Straub was describing the new disposition of the populace in his newspaper. The demise of the "orgy of unrestrained greed and speculation" had brought, he wrote, a "new spirit of thoughtful restraint." Citizens seemed to realize that fantasy could not build a city. "It would be well for St. Petersburg folks to forget for a few years their dreams" and discard their "fictitious values based upon speculative greed." Straub claimed that those not willing to disown the "Golden Calf," were "traitors to the community."[71] To build a stable foundation for the future, residents would have to acquire a "respect for those things of life which are not bartered for by money."[72]

Straub's idealism had a strong appeal, because the bill for the city commission's profligate spending had at length come due. By the end of 1928 St. Petersburg's bonded debt had reached $28 million, and the city had suffered its first bank closing—with more to come. Audits found that various banks had had questionable dealings with the city commission, and people's trust in their municipal government decreased daily. The growing financial distress illustrated "the utter folly of neighborhood and crony government," Fuller wrote, "by a hit and miss group of councilmen."[73]

As the struggle over governmental reform continued, Nolen became more and more bewildered. He returned from Europe, anxious to revisit St. Petersburg—yet the city seemed so backward. He wrote Jonsberg, "Whenever we think of the planning work done for St. Petersburg, we always think of the understanding of yourself, Walter Fuller and several others; but at once comes the reaction that there are hundreds of others who don't have that understanding. . . . That situation disturbs us. Can't something be done about it?"[74]

St. Petersburg reached a turning point in spring 1929. On March 31, the city commission unanimously adopted Hartzog's plan, but without a zoning ordinance the plan was no more than good intentions.[75] Although the Nolen firm had sent the planning board a zoning ordinance, any hopes of passing it vanished when A. P. Avery announced his candidacy for the city commission. If elected, Avery could be expected "to thwart and kill the plan."[76]

Avery's candidacy—he had not run for office for thirteen years—was a last-ditch attempt to hold onto power. "I do not need a platform," he claimed, "the people know that I stand for the best interest of St. Petersburg first, last and always." He announced that he would straighten out civic affairs and return St. Petersburg "to economical and sane growth."[77] The *St. Petersburg Independent* was quick to sound the praises of its favorite son: "The election of A. P. Avery will insure a sound and efficient administration, an improved moral condition that will not permit freedom to con men, booze-dealers and other criminal characters and also insure the open transaction of the people's business so the people may know what is being done."[78]

The *St. Petersburg Times* responded by attacking Avery's candidacy as a "return to the old story of political machinations in city hall."[79] Although Avery breezed into office, he no longer had enough political clout to rescind the city plan, and shortly after the election, his bank folded. When the auditors finished their report in August 1929, Avery's public career was at an end. The audit showed that the bank lacked sufficient collateral to cover its loans, and that its owner had been falsifying records for years.[80]

With the express purpose of recalling Avery from office, two LaFollette Progressives, F. S. Hammond and S. V. McCleary, formed the Progressive Club. Hammond, once an Avery supporter, was dumbfounded by what had happened. "Mr. Avery fooled me," he stated, "Mr. Avery's the only man who ever fooled me." Avery's efforts to tie up the recall election in court only prolonged his sentencing. A new era was dawning. "As soon as we get rid of Avery," McCleary announced at a Progressive Club rally on the day of the recall election:

"We want to take hold of the political situation in the city and clean it up. We are tired of ring rule and we want you people to rid the city of this rule and in voting out A. P. Avery today you are destroying the head of the ring who has ruled for more than a quarter of a century."[81]

On December 30, 1929, Avery was recalled from office. He showed little remorse; in fact, the longtime power broker seemed glad that it was over. "He had nothing to worry about," the St. Petersburg Independent reported, "since 'he had not spent a nickel' on election day in any attempt to get out a vote for himself." With his thrifty career in politics over, Avery moved to Panama City, where he soon regained his Midas touch and made a small fortune in real estate.[82]

Avery may have managed to prosper, but St. Petersburg went into default when it failed to meet bond obligations in May 1930. With Avery gone, and the city finances in ruin, the city commission established a committee to reorganize the municipal government. The group, led by Straub, finally drafted the new charter, instituting a city council/city manager form of government, that he had been asking for for years. The state legislature endorsed the bill in spring 1931, and the city's voters approved it in July.

Wilbur Cotton, the new city manager, came in under almost the worst imaginable circumstances. In 1925, St. Petersburg had had ten banks with over $46 million in deposits, but by June 1932 there was a single bank—with $116,749.[83] Cotton was dumbstruck by what the bonds had financed: "The city had been expanded in area so that the present city could easily care for a population ten times its present size of 40,000. Many improvements cost more than the reasonable value of all the properties that benefited from these investments."[84]

Nolen, meanwhile, was baffled by the city's failure to print the planning report. Planning would never get anywhere if it could not even take this first step. St. Petersburg had "halted at the brink twice," he wrote Jonsberg. "Let's go over it now if we can."[85] On May 31, 1930, the day St. Petersburg defaulted on its loans, Jonsberg informed Nolen that the city was on the verge of collapse. With St. Petersburg's dismal financial situation, "it would be inadvisable to spend money or give any opportunity for argument among the thousands of distressed citizens who are walking around with a chip on their shoulders."[86]

In 1931, both the economy and the chances of city planning seemed to have died in St. Petersburg. No zoning ordinance was adopted, and the planning board had ceased meeting. Without a planner or an actively engaged planning board, the city plan, as Hartzog had predicted, was pigeonholed indefinitely.[87]

The New Deal: Catalyst for Planning

The New Deal revived city planning in St. Petersburg. The federal government's use of planning to solve social ills—ranging from public housing to land conservation—gave the profession a new respectability. Nolen felt that planning "advanced more rapidly in importance in the United States in the two years from the spring of 1933 to the spring of 1935, than in two decades prior to 1933."[88] In early 1933 St. Petersburg's planning board began to meet again, and in July the city council finally adopted the zoning ordinance prepared by the Nolen firm in 1927. The city plan was overloaded with commercial areas, but since it reflected the desires of the most vocal property owners, only one person objected when the city council moved to accept the measure.[89]

Although St. Petersburg's plan lacked balance, it did give municipal officials some leverage when they applied for federal funds. The New Deal programs were largely unconcerned with reforming the economic or physical makeup of urban America, but they did reward cities that had comprehensive plans tied to capital budgets. In addition, business leaders found that more federal grant money came to their cities when they worked in concert with municipal officials and planners.[90]

With the aid of their new plan, St. Petersburg received a generous cut of federally funded projects. Throughout the depression, the Pinellas economy was heavily dependent on jobs created by such federal programs as the Works Progress Administration and Public Works Administration. Between 1933 and 1941 the federal government allocated over $10 million for St. Petersburg, an unusually high figure for a city of its size.[91]

In the mid-1930s, the city began work on the projects Hartzog had enumerated. The railroad terminal was removed from downtown; a new airfield was built; and a comprehensive drainage system was started. The city also adopted a platting ordinance, and Hartzog's recommendation for minimum housing standards led to St. Petersburg's first building code.[92]

In 1935 the Florida legislature established a state planning board and passed a bill that allowed counties to form their own advisory planning boards. Under this act, the Pinellas Planning Board was formed; Straub was elected chairman. Although no powers were vested in it, the Pinellas Planning Board followed St. Petersburg's example and made such public projects as erosion control on the beaches and the expansion of sewer and water lines a priority. As these projects were funded, the region's economy slowly recovered. Pinellas residents began to appreciate the government's expanded role.[93]

St. Petersburg weathered the Great Depression better than most cities. Although conditions were far from ideal, the town was relatively well off, and the plant closings, droughts, bitter winters, and labor unrest that plagued other cities were largely absent. While the rest of the nation experienced the severe chill of winter during the mid-1930s, Florida's unusually mild weather spurred tourists to go south.[94]

St. Petersburg began to move toward financial stability after the state legislature passed the Murphy Act in 1935. This bill sought to lighten the debt burden of municipalities, handing properties whose owners were delinquent in paying taxes over to the state for sale at public auction. The proceeds were used to pay off municipal debts. Although the real estate market was still too flat for the state to hope to sell these lands, city officials finally had the means to solve the debt problem. St. Petersburg's economy turned a corner between 1935 and 1940. Housing starts and tax revenues showed a steady increase. In 1937, the city was no longer a defaulter, and by 1940 its debt had dropped to $19 million.[95]

In 1936, an upsurge in tourism and the building industry made zoning once more a point of controversy. In response to the improving economy, almost a hundred residential property owners filed to have their lands rezoned for commercial use. After the planning board and the city council turned down some of these requests, the Realty Board pushed for a revision of the city plan. Straub immediately replied that the abundance of vacant land marked for business left "no market or little value in any of [these properties]."[96] Straub felt citizens should work to beautify the city, not turn it into one huge business district. During the boom years many natural assets had been "despoiled by private interests and lost to the public and there are not so many now," he lamented. Despite these irretrievable losses, the city had done nothing to prevent similar abuses in the future. For example, aside from the downtown waterfront, St. Petersburg owned no shoreline parks or sizable nature preserves.[97]

Straub had suffered a series of strokes. He realized that his role in civic affairs had almost run its course. In one of his last editorials, he regretted that John Nolen's original vision for St. Petersburg had fallen by the wayside. If "someone like John Nolen" returned to St. Petersburg, Straub urged, organizations should meet him "and learn something from him about a new meaning of those saddest of all words—'It might have been.'"[98]

In fall 1936, John Nolen made his own last public presentation, delivering a speech in Miami on the benefits of regional planning in south Florida. As usual, he received positive reviews but little follow-up, and in February 1937 he passed away.[99] Two years later, Straub died as well. These two pioneer planners left the lasting legacy of a more rational procedure for city building in St.

Petersburg and throughout Florida. Their efforts, though often treated with contempt in their time, were not forgotten. St. Petersburg's waterfront park bears Straub's name, and a park in Venice is home to a plaque honoring Nolen.

At the time of their deaths, Nolen and Straub's ideal of a resort city that combined natural beauty and economic opportunity was a fading memory. But St. Petersburg had at least adopted a plan, and there was reason for optimism in this city that had teetered on the brink of catastrophe. Unlike most Americans, the people of St. Petersburg had the chance to build a model city, but they turned away from this vision in a frenzy of speculation and banal boosting. The people of St. Petersburg squandered their opportunities because they failed to understand the nature of true liberty. Liberty without virtue or common sense is a recipe for disaster, for it is ludicrous to assume that people will sacrifice for a common goal when they are locked into the licentious pursuit of happiness. Although greed did not destroy the promise of building a new Eden, the people of St. Petersburg had only taken a small step toward that elusive goal.

6

The Bartholomew Plan: A Formula for Efficiency

This research has as its purpose the determination of the requirements
of the American city as to land areas used for various purposes, ratios
of these areas to a given population unit, and analogous statistical information that will be an aid to more scientific zoning practice.

Harland Bartholomew, 1932

Planners are the cause of our urban and suburban ills. Once they threw
out the body of knowledge that was their heritage of 3,000 years, they
were left with nothing but statistics.

Andres Duany, 1989

By fall 1938, the municipal government's finances had finally stabilized. The
city debt was still heavy, almost $20 million, but it no longer had to default on
payments. Population had grown by 20,000 since 1930, and the economy was
advancing at a slow but steady rate. Once the real estate market began to show
signs of life, investors overwhelmed the planning board with petitions to have
properties rezoned. With Straub dead and Walter Fuller in the state legislature,
there was no member of the board who could discern where the comprehensive plan stopped and the zoning code took over. The board amended the land-
use plan at the whim of property owners, and the planning process soon fell
into disarray. Between 1934 and 1938, the planning board considered 800
cases; it granted the exceptions requested 90 percent of the time. Many of
these changes pushed residential properties into business categories—in a city
already grossly overzoned for commercial uses. As a result, the zoning map bore
little relation to existing uses.[1]

The city council dismissed the members of the planning board and established a blue-ribbon committee to find a solution to the "planning crisis." The
committee recommended that the city council establish a new planning
board and give it a "broad scope of authority."[2] The planning board was not,
however, given any additional powers, although on October 5, 1938, Mayor

Vernon Agee appointed a new five-member group that would "make for an aggressive and efficient board."[3]

The realtor John Wallace, brother of the New Dealer Henry Wallace, headed the new planning board, and Walter Fuller was vice chairman. Wallace belonged to a new generation of leadership that promoted planning as an important tool for meeting the demands of growth. At the opening meeting, he announced that St. Petersburg needed to join the "ranks of the intelligently planned American cities." Unlike earlier planning boards, the board he chaired enjoyed the support and cooperation of civic leaders. This was a definite improvement, but Wallace and his colleagues were "feeling [their] way in the dark." Although they had a copy of Nolen's first plan and a land-use map, the Hartzog report and the minutes of previous planning boards' meetings were missing. Despite these impediments, the board persevered in its quest to set guidelines for, as the St. Petersburg Times put it, "the ideal plan."[4]

The planning board soon realized the gargantuan nature of its task. The existing plan was a disaster, but the board had neither the expertise nor the resources to replan the city. In early 1940, the city council hired the firm of Harland Bartholomew and Associates to design a new comprehensive city plan. Ronald E. Riley, an associate of Bartholomew's since 1929, headed the project team.

In the early 1940s, Harland Bartholomew specialized in analyzing the financial consequences of unbalanced urban growth. His firm concentrated on designing plans that stressed the efficient provision of urban services while maintaining the integrity of older urban centers. "His intent was that city planning be used to contain," Christopher Silver writes in his analysis of Bartholomew's work in Richmond, "rather than unleash the forces of urban growth."[5]

The Bartholomew Plan

In October 1943, the St. Petersburg Planning Board received a 300-page plan from the Bartholomew firm.[6] The work started from the premise that a more efficient infrastructure would improve the city's economic health and, in turn, make it a more appealing place for tourists. The planners compared St. Petersburg to a machine, the car, that could be regulated to run at prime efficiency. "No matter how well or carefully the auto is driven it will not give maximum pleasure or economy if the motor and chassis are obsolete and in poor condition." With its $19 million of bonded debt and overextended services, St. Petersburg was considerably more like a dilapidated jalopy than a well-tended luxury automobile. The city needed "a sound, adequate physical structure" to spur economic activity and once again run at full speed. Unless changes were made, the economy would stagnate, and St. Petersburg would never be "a desirable place in which to live."

The planners thought the municipal government could provide urban services more efficiently—and at the same time increase the tax base—by concentrating new development around a central urban core. The recent trend had been for the population to scatter away from the downtown area. If this continued, public improvements would increasingly be made at the expense of the city's older districts. With 78 percent of the city's fifty-three square miles vacant, the community's fiscal health remained in jeopardy, because only one section of the city—the area between 16th Street and Tampa Bay and North and South 22nd Avenue—contained the "proper balance" of building density (eight units per acre) and city services. Furnishing services to the rest of St. Petersburg would be prohibitively expensive. "A more compact development must be provided for the future," the consultants warned. Otherwise the continued dispersal of growth would drive up tax rates, impair the provision of municipal services, and cause the decline of older districts.

The Bartholomew planners limited future development to a 17,500-acre, or about twenty-seven-square-mile, area to solve St. Petersburg's infrastructure problem. The urban boundary's configuration (figure 18) took into account both existing improvements (paved streets, sewers, and water lines) and the demand for future urban services, based on a projected population of 120,000. St. Petersburg's population had almost tripled during the 1920s—from 14,237 to 40,083—but in the 1930s it grew by only 50 percent. (The entire country experienced its slowest urban growth rate of the twentieth century during these years.) Extrapolating from these trends, the consultants predicted that St. Petersburg's growth rate would continue to decrease, and that by 1960, the population would stabilize at 120,000. A community of this size, according to the firm's standards, should occupy 17,500 acres; the city's remaining 16,000 acres would "never be needed for urban purposes."

To keep development within the prescribed urban zone, municipal agencies would have to clamp down on the extension of utilities. Because the existing infrastructure would meet projected growth demands for another two decades, Bartholomew and Associates felt that the city could take a hard line on this policy. Property owners would undoubtedly demand water and sewer connections, "but if these are firmly resisted, new development will gradually locate within the proper sections."

Land lying outside the urban zone was designated rural, with no more than one residential unit per three acres. The plan called for a series of "farm-

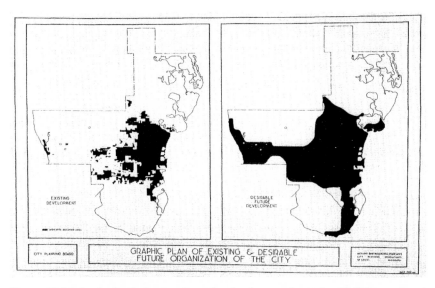

Figure 18 Under the Bartholomew plan, urban land use was limited to 17,500 acres, based on an analysis showing that St. Petersburg's population would never pass 120,000. Courtesy of the St. Petersburg Department of Planning.

ettes"—with truck gardens and citrus groves—that would form a greenbelt around the city. Land speculators might demand rezonings, but because the new plan provided "a reasonable use for property owners in this district," the city would have the support of the law.

The planners also recommended that the city council lower the assessed valuations for rural land; with fewer tax dollars at stake, there would be less pressure to run services into this area. In addition, these lands were hardly lucrative investments. Almost all of the city's 16,500 tax-delinquent parcels were in the rural district; many of these properties had reverted to state hands after passage of the Murphy Act in 1935.[7] The city council could either buy this land at a discounted rate or establish a partnership with the state to lease it to farming or lumber interests.

Of course, if the municipal government wanted to restrict property rights in half the city, it needed to enhance opportunities for development within the urban zone. The first priority was additional park land. The city's ratio of 0.42 acres of park land per 100 inhabitants was well below the national standard of one acre. While the existing 120 acres of parks met most adult recreational needs, adequate play areas for children were sorely needed, and apart from the municipal waterfront, there were no large expanses of open space.

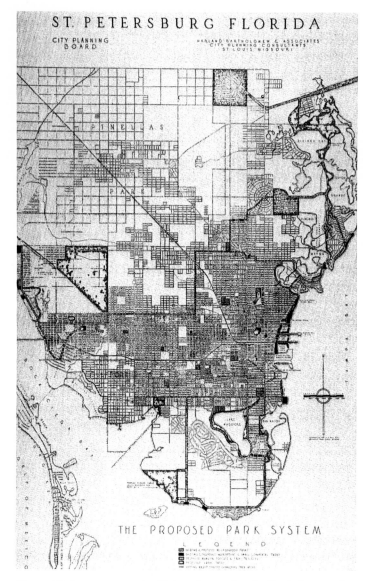

Figure 19 In contrast to the Nolen plan, under the Bartholomew plan parks did not follow the natural contours of the land but were rigidly geometrical. Courtesy of the St. Petersburg Department of Planning.

Bartholomew's firm prepared a park plan (figure 19) that would add another 240 acres to the existing system. Despite the lack of large parks, the planners thought that the close proximity of the beaches precluded the need to establish nature preserves. Instead, they placed twenty neighborhood parks throughout the city, within a half-mile walk of all residences, to provide a mixture of recreational uses and open space. The plan also included two community parks previously proposed by Nolen. One would encircle Lake Maggiore, while the other covered forty-seven acres on the southeast shore of Boca Ciega Bay.

The park plan also set aside 2,300 acres in four "forest preserves" that contained mostly poorly drained pine flatwoods. Although these sites were mostly inaccessible and offered little in the way of scenery or recreational value, they were cheap, ridden with tax-delinquent properties, and good for logging. In addition, the proposed preserves lay on the periphery of the city and were prime locations for a city dump. The four parcels were: Maximo Point on the city's extreme southwest corner (this was also the location for Van Bibber's Health City); Toytown, on the north side of St. Petersburg; the long-forgotten Florida Riviera development to the northeast of the city; and a 1,085-acre site on the city's northwest border.

The Bartholomew Formula

Harland Bartholomew (1889–1989) reached the top of his profession by promoting city planning as a scientific field of study that used economic and statistical analyses to provide practical solutions.[8] In an era when the "word 'planner' conjured visions of a long-haired, dreary-eyed, visionary who never had to 'meet a payroll,' Bartholomew presented the image of a serious and practical man of experience who would give you realistic advice on 'how to get great things done.'"[9] Unlike Nolen and Olmsted, Bartholomew never found European planning philosophies or design concepts to his liking. Instead, his pragmatic approach to planning reflected a purely American experience.[10] In his quest to solve the United States' urban problems, Bartholomew had no patience with plans based on utopian notions or aesthetic forms. When the 1909 Planning Conference emphasized "the economic rather than the aesthetic," Bartholomew wrote, it "marked an important turning point in planning."[11]

After studying civil engineering for two years at Rutgers University, Bartholomew encountered two divergent views of city planning on his first job in 1912. The young assistant engineer worked under George Ford and E. P. Goodrich. Ford wanted the Newark City Planning Commission to concentrate on housing and "the aesthetic aspects of city planning," Bartholomew wrote, "whereas Mr. Goodrich's interest ran to streets, traffic and transportation."[12] Ford worried that planners were developing such a fixation on efficiency that they were reducing the city to a "soulless machine,"[13] but his plan for Newark was judged unrealistic, and the planning commission dismissed him. Bartholomew stepped into the breach and completed the project according to Goodrich's specifications. From this experience, the young consultant learned that traffic engineers could produce quantitative data that would make city planning acceptable to its many doubters. Over the next decade, Bartholomew emerged as one of the profession's most successful practitioners, because he could sell planning as a scientific procedure for managing a city's complex urban infrastructure with machinelike efficiency.[14]

Like Nolen and Olmsted, Bartholomew condemned the intense speculation that was driving the expansion of America's cities. The nation's urban ills, he wrote in 1932, stemmed from "a deep-seated malady whose origin can be found in excessive real-estate speculation." Bartholomew's prescription, however, separated him from planners who emphasized the environment and aesthetics in their work. His plans rested on the presentation of precise analytical data to verify what he called "scientific zoning practice." Bartholomew's understanding of zoning, the editors at Harvard University Press wrote, helped make the planning profession more "rationalized and related to sound economic policy."[15]

Bartholomew's firm began work by surveying existing land uses. After breaking down the survey information into acreage-to-population ratios, the staff compared these data with national averages. From this analysis it was possible to create a "satisfactory norm for the future growth of the city." By incorporating national standards into local plans, Bartholomew's firm provided municipal governments with a reasonable assessment of the land required for a particular zoning category. Whether a city needed more parks or fewer commercial designations, a bevy of statistical standards allowed planners to foster "the development of comprehensively conceived and economically organized cities."[16]

Bartholomew also believed that zoning ordinances based on functional standards would carry more weight in court. If planners were able to assign numbers to "the actual urban requirements," land speculators and their attorneys would have more difficulty setting aside a plan. When deliberating over the enforcement of land use controls, judges who had a quantified, systematic planning method before them would find it easier to rule consistently.[17]

Bartholomew considered the environment and the promotion of an urban aesthetic secondary. While cities needed beautification, he believed that a preoccupation with aesthetics doomed the planning effort. "The value of landscape and architectural features is admitted," Bartholomew wrote in 1914, "yet they must not be made the sole consideration, for we are living in an age of commercialism and it is feared we know too little of the value of art."[18] For a society that idolized engineering and efficiency, Bartholomew's plans were a rational, if not always comprehensive, solution to the problems of urbanization.[19]

The Failure of the Bartholomew Plan

St. Petersburg presented a new challenge to the Bartholomew firm. Perhaps no city in the nation had suffered more from a lack of planning than St. Petersburg. The size of its debt and its unpaid taxes were symptoms of this malaise. Bartholomew and Associates proposed a logical way to solve the city's financial problems: channeling development around the urban core. Critics of the plan, however, argued that the firm's efficiency model, appropriate for industrial cities, needed adjustment for a resort city like St. Petersburg. During the winter, tourists inundated the city, and they wanted to spend time outdoors. Yet the plan was relatively unconcerned with protecting the peninsula's natural features—its calling card for tourism.

Although the Pinellas Peninsula was hardly virgin territory in 1940, it was still one of the most unusual and biologically diverse natural environments in the United States. The region had experienced only limited building since the 1920s, and the landscape contained a mixture of natural areas, cultivated land, and distinctive communities.[20] The surrounding bays were clear and teeming with marine life, which attracted both commercial and sport fishermen. For the most part, buildings were concentrated on higher, more stable land, and the system of inland wetlands was largely intact (see figure 20). William Straub's description of Pinellas, written ten years before, was still true: "The ogres of destruction have not yet come into our garden. It stands here with open gates, an Eden guarded by no fearsome angel with flaming sword. What shall remain of it is merely the guess of the pen that writes these lines. Greed, the neglect of beauty, the ravage of useless fire—all these are to come and press down heavily upon the loveliness of this day."[21]

The Bartholomew planners, instead of addressing the ideals Straub and Nolen had found so compelling, dismissed Nolen's work as "the optimistic opinions of what the ideal city should be." Instead of wasting their time on utopian forms, the team designed a more efficient city based on a "thorough analysis of facts." "To intelligently plan," their work read, "it is essential to know approximately how many people will need improvements and where

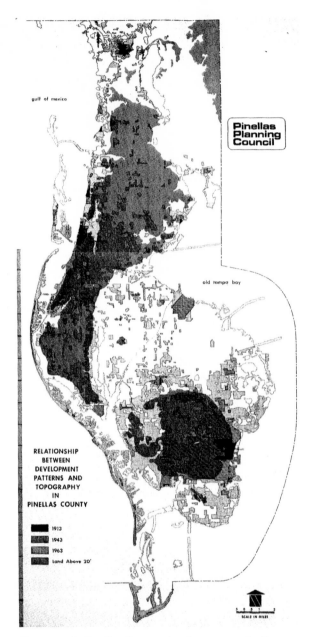

Figure 20 In Pinellas County, development gradually over-
took the wetlands. As these were drained for construction,
the peninsula's environmental problems accelerated at an
alarming rate. Courtesy of Pinellas County Department of
Planning.

they will live." Of course, if their population projections were flawed, or their quantitative techniques failed to appraise the land adequately, their plan was useless.

Walter Fuller, the planning board's vice chairman, took a keen interest in the Bartholomew plan. While its length "discouraged anybody from reading it," he managed to find some "sound, hard-hitting points." But before any public discussion could take place, the *St. Petersburg Independent* blasted the work as a waste of the city's scant resources. After the *St. Petersburg Times* devoted only a short paragraph to the plan, Fuller wrote to its publisher, Nelson Poynter, who was working in Washington.[22]

As a New Deal Democrat in a conservative town, Poynter used the *St. Petersburg Times* to prod residents with provocative editorials and proposals for reform. Like Straub, Poynter grew especially passionate on the topic of protecting Pinellas's "natural gifts" from haphazard development and wasteful commercial practices.[23] In October 1943, Poynter had paid Fuller $750 to write a proposal that the city council could use to acquire tax-delinquent properties from the state. With these properties, the city could establish a system of parks and small farms on the outskirts of St. Petersburg.[24] Two weeks later, Fuller apologized to Poynter for not having written earlier. He had reviewed the Bartholomew plan, "things are now crystallizing in my own mind and making sense." Despite the preponderance of "lofty and double-jointed words," Fuller informed Poynter, "there's gold in them thar 276 pages."[25]

Fuller felt that the Bartholomew firm's assessment of the city's past mistakes, financial difficulties, and overextended infrastructure could help the *St. Petersburg Times* encourage "a wide and deep educational campaign." The plan held a wealth of facts, but Fuller disagreed "completely with the philosophy of the report"—and also with its population projections. Fuller sent Poynter and the other planning board members a twenty-page critique of the Bartholomew plan.

The planners' assumption that St. Petersburg's population would follow a declining national trend especially baffled Fuller. With the advent of Social Security and the eventual return of military personnel (120,000 soldiers had trained in Pinellas and a million in Florida) to civilian life, he doubted that the city would "gradually and painfully increase to a city of 100,000 as the statistical planners say." He thought that St. Petersburg could anticipate the arrival of 100,000 new residents over the next decade. As Fuller wrote, the new immigrants would be looking for "the spirit of Florida living—the outdoors." In their assumption that St. Petersburg would be like the "average commercial city," the planners had missed this point.

The Bartholomew planners also failed to realize that St. Petersburg "was in the entertainment business," and that the city needed to attract wealth, not manufacture it. If St. Petersburg imitated the design of cities "built before horse cars, much less automobiles and airplanes, then it has thrown away all that it professes to be," Fuller wrote, "a place where life can be enjoyed all year in the open." The consultants compounded this mistake by their failure to recognize the economic value of "beauty and nature" and St. Petersburg's "almost exaggerated need of public lands." Fuller wanted to raise the city park standard from 0.42 acres to 1.5 acres per 100 residents. The city and the county could reach this goal, if they pooled their funds and bought inexpensive, bankrupt properties. Such land could then be reforested to create a string of scenic wildlife refuges that would offer hiking, camping, and improved flood control. Fuller also wanted the city to acquire sites on the beaches and make them the cornerstone of an expanded park system. But before St. Petersburg could even think of a plan that would "beautifully house 150,000 people," civic leaders needed "to shatter the spirit of defeatism and acceptance of smallness and mediocrity."

The Bartholomew plan's mechanical prose and limited vision offered little inspiration; it sought only "to coax another 60,000 people into this area" and retire the municipal debt. Fuller wanted a plan with greater vision. Some planning issues, such as the acquisition of park sites, affected the entire peninsula. Fuller also encouraged the county commission to adopt a plan that set a high priority on public investment and instituted a system of unified land-use controls. "Such a bold and revolutionary approach . . . will never happen, unless a small group of men, with sufficient and enlightened self interest does the preliminary study and missionary work."[26]

Poynter agreed with Fuller's assessment and immediately wrote, "We must get out the heavy artillery to get the sights of the whole town lifted." He agreed that the population projections were ludicrous. The city's future population growth had "no more to do with the population curve of the United States than that of an oil-boom town." Poynter also believed that the principal issue facing St. Petersburg was how to plan adequately for the crush of postwar immigrants.[27] In the next two weeks, the St. Petersburg Times ran two articles summarizing the plan, and on Sunday, November 28, 1943, Fuller consolidated his report into a full-page editorial.

In his piece for the St. Petersburg Times, Fuller exposed the Bartholomew plan's chief flaw: "It does not sufficiently visualize a major replanning and rebuilding of this community as an ideal tourist and residential Florida City." After discussing how to accomplish this task, Fuller challenged readers to move beyond the consultants' narrow vision and invest in a "bold over-all Plan" that required moving beyond the "restricted mental horizons of the past." Citizens would have to "unite, plan boldly, and act with vigor."

Fuller's plea fell on deaf ears. Although the city council adopted the Bartholomew plan in late 1944, the concept of a county plan never moved beyond the pages of the *St. Petersburg Times*. The city council asked the planning board to use the new plan to rezone the city after the war, but even before the war ended the plan's credibility was next to nil. A mid-decade census revealed that, in contrast to the Bartholomew firm's prediction, St. Petersburg's population had grown 40 percent in five years. This surge in population, coupled with wartime restrictions, made it impossible to provide enough housing. The shortage intensified when postwar immigrants flocked to the city. Developers demanded that the state return tax-delinquent properties to private ownership. Tallahassee quickly complied, and the pressure of land sales forced the planning board to jettison any notion of confining new building to the urban core.

In 1946 and 1947, the state sold off thousands of parcels to builders and speculators at bargain rates. Auctioneers held sales on the steps of city hall and the county courthouse, where canny investors could pick up lots in posh neighborhoods for only ten dollars. The sale of abandoned properties helped St. Petersburg pay off its bonded debt in 1947.[28]

In 1950, St. Petersburg's population passed 100,000; in the next two years, it rocketed over the Bartholomew firm's anticipated cap of 120,000. By 1960 St. Petersburg had 181,200 inhabitants. The population had almost doubled in ten years—and tripled in twenty. Since the Bartholomew plan had assumed a declining population rate, it offered little guidance for municipal officials facing the demands of growth. To make matters worse, the Bartholomew staff had made no adequate provision either for changing the plan or rezoning the city. Although the plan contained a recommendation for hiring planning staff, the consultants had assured city officials that the plan would require only few and simple changes. The planning board quickly learned that without experienced staff to revise the plan, informed decisions about land use were impossible.[29]

Although the land-use plan proved unworkable, the planners' analysis of the city's traffic system provided the basis for restructuring the transit system. In 1947, the city council voted to phase out the thirty miles of trolley lines on the recommendation that a bus system would be more cost-effective. The last trolley line ended service on May 7, 1949. Three years later, the city hired Walter Drucker to serve as St. Petersburg's first full-time traffic engineer. The city already had a more than adequate supply of streets, which allowed Drucker to concentrate on expanding parking and road capacities according to Bartholomew and Associates' specifications. City hall devoted its resources to projects that would enhance auto mobility, but as the pace of building continued at breakneck speed throughout the 1950s, many other planning problems were becoming acute.[30]

St. Petersburg's Postwar Expansion: Planned Sprawl

The postwar building boom was entirely different from the speculative whirlwind that had swept through the city in the 1920s.[31] As Fuller and Poynter had predicted, returning soldiers, retirees, and those just seeking the Florida lifestyle came in droves to St. Petersburg. Subdivisions that had lain dormant for two decades sprang to life, and a suburban landscape splayed across the peninsula (figure 21). Between 1940 and 1960, the number of housing units in Pinellas County increased by more than 400 percent, jumping from 40,525 to 165,823. Three-fourths of all units were built in the 1950s, and 37,636 (40.4 percent) of the 93,141 new units were built in St. Petersburg.[32]

Figure 21 After World War II, subdivisions blanketed the landscape with their efficient, yet monotonous, form. Courtesy of the St. Petersburg Historical Museum.

The thousands of people moving to St. Petersburg found the American Dream in its affordable housing, sunshine, and good jobs. By the mid-1950s, an aggressive campaign to attract industry to Pinellas had garnered four giants of the defense industry, Honeywell, Electronic Communications, General Electric, and Sperry Rand. These firms, with their heavy payrolls, well-educated employees, and contracts for businesses, brought a new and different kind of life to the city's economy. Manufacturing as a percentage of county employment jumped from 2 percent in 1940 to 14 percent in 1960. As a result of diversification, St. Petersburg began—at least economically—to resemble the typical American city.[33]

The 1960 census revealed the remarkable transformation that St. Petersburg and Florida had undergone since the turn of the century. In 1900, St. Petersburg was a small unincorporated village, and Florida was one of the poorest and most isolated states in the Union. By 1960, the median family income of $4,700 was the highest in the South and stood at 92 percent of the national average. Although St. Petersburg's median family income was only $4,200, this was due in part to the high number of single retirees. In 1960, 27.4 percent of the population was over sixty-five. Although St. Petersburg residents had less disposable income, they did have more invested income. The median value of a house in St. Petersburg was $12,000, compared to a state figure of $11,800, and a national one of $11,900. As tourism moved increasingly to the beaches, the city was becoming more suburban and more stable. Almost 75 percent of the city's residences were owner-occupied. The national average was only 61.9 percent.[34]

While St. Petersburg was becoming more prosperous, its landscape was losing its uniqueness. The suburban subdivision epitomized middle-class life both in St. Petersburg and in the United States at large. The eclectic mixture of prewar housing styles gave way to vast tracts of nearly identical houses. Air conditioners, pesticides, heavy machinery, and concrete blocks all contributed in their different ways to the mass production of single-story homes with small windows and attached garages. Only pink flamingos and blue porpoises differentiated the thousands of new white and pastel block homes. Builders could put in air conditioners, which counted as a luxury, then cut costs and save time by reducing the size of windows and porches. And, as elsewhere across America, people moved from their porches to sit in front of their televisions, seemingly finding the new mass medium a satisfactory replacement for the neighborliness of the past.[35]

Suburban expansion also mercilessly reconfigured the landscape. Before grading and road construction, developers stripped sites of all vegetation. They filled wetlands and shunted streams into culverts to increase the number of building lots. The city offered some parks, but developers seldom dedicated land for recreation or open space. By the time the first residents arrived, their only clues to the original landscape came from the subdivisions' names: "Orange Estates," "Oakview Estates" "Eaglecrest," "Pelican Creek." While the larger front yards were excellent places for children's games and casual meetings, the opportunity to explore "Old Florida" was quickly disappearing. Before the war forests covered 95,000 acres on the peninsula; by 1959, there were only 57,000 acres left. Over the same period, citrus acreage dropped by 50 percent.[36]

By 1960, a standardized suburban fabric covered the Pinellas landscape. Each municipality merged into the next without noticeable landmarks or hints of different street layouts, architectural types, or land-use patterns. The new subdivisions provided more living space, greenery, and convenience for auto users than their prewar counterparts, but they drained the landscape of vitality and distinctiveness. Auto use was on the rise, and homeowners' frequent trips took them past an unending string of commercial strip centers and run-on subdivisions. From the car, the landscape was little more than a blur— except for the blaring signs.[37]

The sprawl also abetted traffic congestion. Before World War II, building densities, which averaged about eight units per acre, supported a transportation system that allowed residents to choose between a trolley, a car, a bus, or walking (figure 22). In the postwar era, because more and more people owned cars, developers could build subdivisions at lower densities (four to six units per acre) on cheaper, outlying land. In these settings home buyers could indulge their desire for more space. As new residents thronged to tract housing, mass transit use plummeted. The new subdivisions were too sparsely settled to support a bus system. Walking was no longer preferred nor practical. The subdivisions' wide streets, minimal street plantings, and lack of sidewalks were for the driver, not the pedestrian.[38] But whether they were commuting to work, driving to the beach, or dropping children off at school, residents soon realized that south Pinellas's roadways were the most congested in Florida.[39]

In 1955 U.S. 19, a four-lane highway running the length of the county, was completed, but it gave little relief from the chronic traffic congestion. To generate more tax revenues, the St. Petersburg Planning Board allowed a continuous belt of land along the highway to be zoned commercial. Soon a multitude of signs, motels, restaurants, and strip shopping centers cluttered the highway. In addition, a series of busy connectors from the new subdivisions dumped thousands of drivers onto Pinellas's only north-south arterial road. The proliferation of crossings and business access points made more traffic lights necessary, and by 1960, U.S. 19 was a tangle of stop-and-go traffic.[40]

Figure 22 Prewar development followed trolley lines as well as new roads. Courtesy of the St. Petersburg Historical Museum.

As the building boom spread across Pinellas, the quality of the natural environment suffered. Before World War II, mules and labor crews had to clear land, and building could take place only at higher elevations (see figure 20).[41] But the bulldozer and sophisticated machinery for draining wetlands allowed developers to open up land once impossible to build on. The building industry was a dynamic force in the local economy, but development also inflicted a heavy cost. The draining of the peninsula's interior wetlands exposed residents to greater risk during the tropical storm season. Marshes and swamps act like sponges; they soak up large amounts of rainfall, then slowly release the water, protecting surrounding lands from flooding. In Florida, if 10 percent of the landscape is wetland, flooding is reduced by 60 percent; with 20 percent coverage, it drops off by 90 percent. Besides regulating the quantity of water flowing through a system, wetlands also improve water quality. These swampy areas filter pollutants from agricultural and urban runoff and keep the underlying aquifer or the surrounding bays clean.[42]

But even building on the uplands affected the surrounding wetlands. The nonporous surfaces that had replaced the vegetation accelerated the rate of stormwater flow into the low-lying swampland during the rainy season. The reduction of rainwater seeping through the uplands' sandy soil also created problems during the dry months. As the groundwater level dropped, saltwater moved into the aquifer. The wetlands could not get enough groundwater recharge, and hundreds of acres dried out. As the pressure to develop increased, the alteration of the "hydrologic regime" intensified. Environmental problems reached an unforeseen extent.[43]

The Tyrone Boulevard area is typical of the marginal lands developed during the 1950s. Before the war, the land in this section of northwest St. Petersburg (between 66th and 58th Streets North and 38th Avenues and Tyrone Boulevard) was mostly wet and vacant. By 1960 the area contained the city's largest shopping mall and a series of subdivisions that brought thousands of additional cars to the primary roadways. When the rains came, stormwaters that these low-lying lands had once captured flowed into Boca Ciega Bay. The stormwater carried pollutants from roads, parking lots, and driveways, as well as fertilizers, insecticides, herbicides, and pesticides from suburban lawns. Partially treated sewage from the new subdivisions also oozed into Boca Ciega Bay. As the once clear lagoon turned a murky green, residents could see the once hidden costs of development.[44]

As the quality of the environment declined and commuting times increased, there was a call for better planning. While conservationists protested the loss of natural areas, the executives of large national corporations, which had invested millions in the region, wanted to make sure that St. Petersburg offered an appropriate quality of life. C. W. Skinner, a Honeywell executive, stated in 1956, "We are very concerned whether this community is going to be able to grow gracefully and beautifully with well-planned neighborhoods, streets, schools, businesses, recreational areas; or whether the extremely rapid rate of growth which appears to be coming over the horizon is going to result in the community ending up by being a congested mess of hodge-podge buildings; roads and streets; poorly planned commercial areas; inescapable traffic congestion."[45]

In 1955, in response to the mounting problems, the city council hired its first full-time planner, John Harvey. After reviewing the existing city plan, Harvey thought he had read a "horror story." There was enough land zoned for shopping centers to serve a city of 300,000. This seemed especially inappropriate since many districts zoned commercial and industrial remained empty. Harvey wanted to initiate the rezoning process, which had languished for a decade, but he had neither the resources nor the experience to confront St. Petersburg's most powerful stakeholders. At Harvey's urgent plea, the city council hired Fred Bair, Florida's most accomplished planning consultant, and in 1956, the two took on the unenviable task of trying to regulate the city's leading industry.[46]

Since the war, St. Petersburg's economic base had shifted from tourism to city building. The numerous firms (contracting, development, real estate, engineering, architecture, legal, and mortgage and lending) and public utilities that profited from the hectic pace of construction and house sales had a strong hold on both the local economy and civic affairs.[47] The most vocal opposition to Harvey's undertaking came from the commercial realtors, the group with the most to lose. Walter Ramseur, a spokesman for the Chamber of Commerce and the Realty Board, argued that the rezoning process should promote, rather than limit, commercial and industrial enterprise. He complained that, while realtors in other cities were extremely prosperous, the "average real estate man in St. Petersburg is barely eking out an existence due to the restrictive zoning of the city." Ramseur found this especially disturbing because, in his view, his profession had done more than any other business to build St. Petersburg and make it "known throughout the United States." Yet the city's leading entrepreneurs were now trapped "in a zoning straitjacket" and enduring "severe financial distress." The planning board could rectify this problem and bolster the city's tax rolls, Ramseur claimed, if outlying agricultural and single-family residential areas were rezoned for business and industrial uses.[48]

Fred Bair wrote off these assertions as a "fascinating romance," replete with "erroneous conclusions and mistaken facts." In a city overrun with vacant commercial properties, Bair chided Ramseur for claiming that businesses would appear just because a parcel of land received a commercial zoning designation. "If zoning would create what it permits, the logical course would be to go whole-hog," Bair concluded, "and zone the entire city for oil wells or uranium extraction, thus raining prosperity on everybody."[49]

Rezoning the city proved to be a three-year ordeal. Harvey, Bair, and the planning board held numerous meetings with property owners before reaching any consensus. Even though the planning board shifted commercial designations interspersed throughout residential districts to major shopping and business districts, it was unable to reduce the amount of land zoned for commercial building. In 1960, commercial properties covered three percent of the city, and industrial uses one percent. The new zoning map set aside eight percent of the city's land for commercial uses—twice the national average—and four percent for industrial development. The surplus in these categories was offset by a deficit in parkland. More than anything else, this discrepancy between St. Petersburg's land classification scheme and national planning standards reflected the degree to which commercial realtors dictated public policy.[50]

Between 1954 and 1958, however, the long-running feud over zoning paled in comparison to another conflict pitting regulators against speculators: turning water into land. The extensive dredging and filling of Boca Ciega Bay for new homesites pushed one citizen to declare that, if local officials kept

Figure 23 The dredging of Boca Ciega Bay by the "Progress Boys" created waterfront homes—and ecological disaster. Courtesy of the *St. Petersburg Times*.

"explaining away the dangers of dredge and fill, St. Petersburg will become an inland city." In 1957, after surveying the countless fills in Boca Ciega Bay, Governor LeRoy Collins commented, "Pretty soon we are going to have to drill to find water there."[51]

As the giant dredges filled Boca Ciega Bay's vast meadows of turtle grass with mud and sand, the dark side of progress became all too evident (figure 23). "We have been chopping down the trees, filling up bays, that gleam just never died in the 'Progress Boys' eyes," one resident wrote in 1957. "Why must we destroy these very assets that are the siren call to the fine people who choose our environment?"[52] Representatives of conservation groups and homeowners' associations were appalled to find that the existing city plan did not address the dredge-and-fill issue. "The problem with the Bartholomew Plan," John Harvey claimed, "was that it was too practical of a plan."[53] The failure of the Bartholomew firm to identify a strategy for regulating coastal building, a task the Nolen firm had performed thirty years before, left municipal officials with a perplexing problem. While the dredge-and-fill projects yielded huge profits for developers, they were threatening the public welfare. The degradation of Boca Ciega Bay sparked a movement not only to protect St. Petersburg's most important natural resource, but to restrict the property rights of the city's most powerful caste.

7

Beyond Limits: The Death of Boca Ciega Bay

> There is no shortage of land to cause the panic to dredge bays and
> bayous. What is needed is good city planning. It is not good business
> to not plan and spoil our most important assets.
>
> *St. Petersburg Times,* 1957

> The whole Bay has been raped.
>
> Dorothy Sample, 1984

Bartholomew and Associates' failure to include a plan for protecting St. Petersburg's coastal environment contributed to the indiscriminate dredging and filling of Boca Ciega Bay, a beautiful coastal lagoon that contained one of Florida's most abundant fisheries. The lagoon's condition provoked a twenty-year-long political controversy. Elected officials, courts, and agencies from the local to the federal level were entangled in legalities and politics as they tried to find a solution agreeable to both developers and conservation groups. The effort to protect Boca Ciega Bay also forced municipal officials to reevaluate the planning process. It was obvious that the giant machines rearranging the landscape were diminishing the bay's aesthetic appeal, but a study by state biologists revealed that dredging and filling were also destroying the marine ecosystem. This study, which introduced ecology into the decision-making process in 1956, ensured that city building in St. Petersburg—and the rest of Florida—would never be the same.

Ecology, the Subversive Science

By the mid-1950s, grassroots opposition to projects that threatened America's scenic natural areas had become increasingly vocal. Although movements against overdevelopment were spontaneous and often occurred without a central organization or a coordinated plan of action, they expressed a strong common desire. Whether they were fighting dams in the Southwest, clear-cutting in the Northwest, or dredging projects in Florida, conservationists battled for a new set of public priorities. Previously Americans had viewed the natural world as a commodity to exploit as efficiently as possible. Now they wanted protection for the scenic lands and waters that played such an integral role in their quality of life.[1] When its leaders, reasoning from that nascent science, ecology, challenged traditional notions of property rights and progress, the budding environmental movement introduced a radical concept into the mainstream of American thought.[2]

Although the roots of ecology go back to the work of eighteenth-century naturalists, it did not become a serious field of study until the postwar years. A major breakthrough had occurred in the 1930s, when the botanist Frederick Clements demonstrated that natural systems, or ecosystems, evolve. Clements found that ecological communities originate during the "pioneer stage," when plants first take hold on virgin soil. Eventually they reach a climax, or mature juncture, where a stable, self-sustaining ecosystem exists. The barrier islands off the Pinellas coast exemplified Clements's pioneer-to-climax model. Over time, this watery habitat evolved from sandbars into a stable, yet fragile, fabric of land that supported a wide diversity of terrestrial plants and marine life. According to Clements, such a system maintained an ideal balance with the forces of nature and could continually reproduce itself—unless altered by climatic changes or invading organisms.

By the 1950s ecology had moved beyond Clements's prototype of the stable climax community. Although this model remained important, ecologists found the study of ecosystems more pertinent. By analyzing the relationship between flora and fauna in a continuous range of environments, ecologists could explain both the self-regulating aspects of a natural system and the changes that alter that system. When concerned citizens began to find their surroundings degraded, ecology—because it stressed the interconnectedness of humans and their environment—furnished the ideal source of information.

The term *subversive science* defined ecology once activists started using its theories to challenge the idea of progress. The ecological hypothesis—that natural communities evolve towards an efficient point of equilibrium—goes against the capitalist ethos of endless growth and ever increasing consumption. By bringing ecology into the debate about the preservation of natural resources, conservationists moved beyond questions of aesthetics. By 1970, ecologists were contending that maintaining the health of the ecosystem was crucial to sustaining human life. A society predicated on growth and consumption could be at least as destructive as it was creative.[3] Boca Ciega Bay proved to be an important test case for a nation wrestling with the issue of environmental protection.

Boca Ciega Bay: Destruction, Profits, and Controversy

By the mid-1950s, Boca Ciega Bay was hardly a pristine body of water. During the depression, the U.S. Army Corps of Engineers had tied the coastal lagoon into the Intercoastal Waterway by dredging a fifteen-foot-deep channel. The Corps deposited the bay bottom in large piles that formed "spoil islands." Several hundred acres of bountiful marine habitat were covered with dredged mud and sand, and the grasses that had held the sandy bottom material could not grow in the deep channels, which led to increased levels of turbidity. The flow of partially treated sewage and the stormwater runoff inadvertently generated by the new developments also lowered the bay's water quality.

Despite these problems, Boca Ciega Bay managed to remain one of the state's most prolific marine systems. Mangroves dotted its shores, and vast expanses of turtle grass covered the southern half of the bay. The largest concentration of turtle grass, and one of Tampa Bay's most fertile fisheries, lay off Cat's Blank Point in southwest St. Petersburg. In 1953, in excess of four million pounds of fish were taken in Pinellas—more than any other county in Florida. Forty percent of this haul came from Boca Ciega Bay. Hundreds of tourists and residents enjoyed shellfishing along the mudflats, and there was also a viable shrimping industry.[4]

In 1953 Albert Furen, a local developer who owned six acres of shoreline property at Cat's Blank Point, purchased the rights to fill 504 acres of bay bottom adjoining his holdings (figure 24) from the Trustees for the Internal Improvement Fund (TIIF). The TIIF, a commission chaired by the governor and comprising the state's independently elected cabinet members, was established in 1850 after the federal government deeded to Florida all unowned public lands "wet and unfit for cultivation." From its inception, the TIIF served as a primary revenue-generating source for the state, and it rarely restricted the sale of Florida's land and water.[5]

After World War II, developers dredged indiscriminately, filling Florida's bays to meet the heavy demand for waterfront homes. In the early 1950s, conservation groups from coastal communities called on the state to restrict these projects, which were fouling some of the nation's most beautiful and productive waters.[6] During the 1953 gubernatorial campaign, LeRoy Collins promised to address this and many other issues. After his election, Collins came into the national spotlight when he attempted to break segregation's hold on Florida, but he did not forget his promise to the conservationists.[7]

Collins enjoined a two-year moratorium on the TIIF's sale of submerged lands to give the state time to develop a program for regulating coastal building. He also issued a new policy that required investors seeking to buy

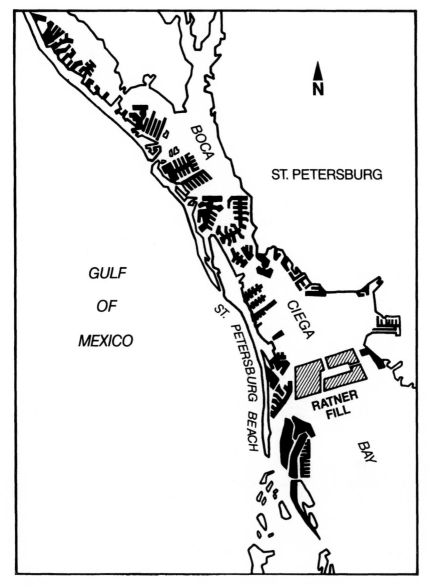

Figure 24 Approximately 25 percent of Boca Ciega Bay was either dredged or filled by 1970.

submerged land from the TIIF to furnish environmental-impact studies for their proposed projects. Collins also established the State Land Use and Control Committee (SLUC) to explore ways to regulate dredge-and-fill operations in Florida waters.[8] Furen's fill soon became a focal point for the Collins administration. As Ney Landrum, one of the governor's aides, declared, "Things were entirely out of control in Pinellas and something had to be done."[9]

In Pinellas, where "dredges were as routine as seagulls," elected officials openly abetted dredging operations.[10] The county commissioners had never opposed a single fill proposal, and it seemed probable that the St. Petersburg City Council would extend city services to Furen's project. If Furen went on with his fill, the Collins administration feared, the impact on Boca Ciega Bay would be devastating. The fill would also set an alarming precedent, because the huge project was "not related in a bonafide manner" to Furen's six-acre shoreline holding. If they supported the Furen project, the governor warned members of both the St. Petersburg City Council and the Pinellas County Commission, the state would intervene.[11]

In December 1956, the St. Petersburg City Council voted four to three to negotiate with Furen about providing city services; the following March, the county commission gave its initial approval on the Furen fill. Collins backed up his threat by sending a condemnation act to the legislature. If passed, it would return Furen's submerged lands to the state. When the governor found that the large Pinellas delegation would block his draft act, he had the state attorney general, Robert Ervin, retain Tampa attorney Thomas Shackleford on behalf of the governor and the Florida State Board of Conservation. Shackleford's role was to request a rehearing if the county commission gave final approval to the Furen project. In April, Ervin warned the commissioners that if they sanctioned the fill and refused to reopen the case with the state, Shackleford would file suit in circuit court.[12]

The Collins administration's effort to regulate dredge-and-fill operations received strong support from Nelson Poynter, publisher of the *St. Petersburg Times*. In increasingly Republican Pinellas County, Poynter gave Collins's Democratic administration outspoken support, especially on this issue. Poynter's generous 1953 campaign contributions to Collins heavily influenced the decision to call a moratorium on the sale of submerged land. Poynter felt that Pinellas's "sparkling waters" represented gifts of nature that needed protection from developers like Furen.[13] "Furen and his partisans equate progress with quick profit," one editorial read. "Opponents think progress has a much wider and infinitely deeper meaning—Growth can be benign or cancerous."[14]

While the *St. Petersburg Times* had always advocated the conservation of natural resources, it became a fervent supporter of Florida's ecology movement

Figure 25 While best known for his stand against segregation, Governor LeRoy Collins also championed Florida's early environmental legislation. Courtesy of the University of South Florida Special Collections.

after Poynter struck up a friendship with the naturalist Rachel Carson. Carson, whose book *Silent Spring* (1962) awakened the nation to environmental dangers, came to Tampa Bay in the mid-1950s to study marine ecology. Her ideas soon caught Poynter's attention. Carson's predictions about the consequences of human alteration of natural systems made Poynter intensify his campaign against dredge-and-fill. In 1955, the *St. Petersburg Times* published a series of articles describing how filling portions of Boca Ciega Bay for development would upset the ecological balance of the entire estuarine system. Poynter wanted the state to analyze the potential ecological ravages of additional dredge-and-fill projects in Boca Ciega Bay before the TIIF lifted its moratorium. He also urged the city council and the county commission to incorporate the results of such a study into a plan for regulating coastal development.[15]

In 1956, a *St. Petersburg Times* editorial claimed that the destruction of Boca Ciega Bay was especially "distressing for citizens interested in good planning and preserving natural resources" because it pointed up the failure of the city's "ill-conceived planning philosophy." Bartholomew and Associates had omitted "human motivation" from their plan. People flocked to the Pinellas area for its beautiful waters; yet the planners had failed to set the guidelines that could preserve these natural resources. Local politicians chose to ignore this argument, but the plight of Boca Ciega Bay drew attention from outside the region.[16]

Ecology and Planning

By 1955, the U.S. Fish and Wildlife Service (USFWS) was reporting that Boca Ciega's "priceless assets" were in peril. Given "the serious threat of impending dredging projects and the need for a *comprehensive plan* [emphasis added] to insure preservation of these resources," the USFWS urged, "a prompt and intensive study of this problem is warranted." The agency recommended that the Florida State Board of Conservation undertake the study, because regulating fill projects fell under the state's jurisdiction.[17]

The board immediately commissioned Robert Hutton, a marine biologist, to study the effects of dredging and filling on Boca Ciega Bay. Hutton, a former professor of marine biology at the University of Miami, oversaw the project; Ken Woodburn, the state's first ecologist, did much of the fieldwork. Five years earlier, the state had established a marine laboratory in St. Petersburg, and the research team had already analyzed portions of the bay. Between September 25, 1955, and January 1, 1956, Woodburn and Hutton carried out studies at fifteen sites throughout the bay. They recorded hydrological changes, analyzed bottom samples, and accumulated a mass of biological data from examining mangroves, sea grasses, algae, plankton, bacteria, echinoderms, fish, mollusks, and shrimp. Hutton also used the work of Robert Ingle, who had studied the effects of dredging in other southern states, for comparative analysis.

In late 1956, Hutton completed his report, *The Ecology of Boca Ciega Bay, with Special Reference to Dredging and Filling Operations*. This study was the first ecological analysis that the state had sponsored to assess the impact of development. Hutton concluded that Boca Ciega Bay would suffer irreparable damage if the Furen project proceeded. Continuing to dredge and fill would heavily curtail commercial fishing because vast expanses of turtle grass, the bay's "keystone species," would be sacrificed for waterfront homes.[18] Ecologists determine the health of natural systems by analyzing keystone species, which perform vital functions in the system and affect many other organisms. Turtle grass was essential to Boca Ciega Bay. Without it the estuary's interrelated web of land and marine life would collapse.

Besides providing a nursery for marine life, the root structure of the turtle grass kept the sandy soils at the bottom of the bay from dispersing. Further dredging projects would kill some turtle grass and cover the bay bottom with silt, choking a good portion of what remained. Turtle grass was the catalyst for the organic decomposition of waste. It could not survive in the deeper, dredged portions of the bay. Without this vital species, the ecosystem's ability to recycle waste would be impaired, and the bay's water quality would drop exponentially. Where dredging had already occurred, Hutton found that sulfate-producing bacteria had created a rank black ooze that covered the bottom of the bay. Unless dredge-and-fill operations ceased, the bacteria that infested this anaerobic mud would spread throughout the bay.

Dredge-and-fill operations like Furen's would only intensify the growing public health risk. While these projects were an inexpensive way for developers to create waterfront real estate, the public had to bear the cost of, as Woodburn put it, "permanent pollution." The destructive potential of the Furen project "should be weighed," Hutton concluded, "against expected benefits of the project before dredging is permitted to proceed."[19]

In March 1957, Hutton's findings played an important role in the framing of the "Bulkhead Law," the SLUC's proposal to regulate dredge-and-fill operations. The idea was hardly new (the Nolen firm had presented a similar proposal), but the time had now come to deal with the nearly intractable problem. Every deed to waterfront real estate in Florida carried a riparian provision that allowed landowners to extend existing lot lines into the water as far as the bulkhead, which was usually set at the edge of navigable channels. Property owners could fill the area between the coast and the bulkhead line with material excavated from the adjacent bay bottoms.[20] The Bulkhead Law would preserve waterfront property owners' access to existing channels, but all fill projects would have to meet minimum standards of health, safety, and welfare. The SLUC defined welfare as the "conservation of wildlife, prevention of erosion, and damage of natural beauty." Its definition of health included the "prevention of pollution." The Bulkhead Law also granted all cities and counties the authority to regulate fills through zoning. In addition to the Bulkhead Law, Collins requested legislation to regain the bottom lands that Furen held either by buying them or by exercising the right of eminent domain.[21]

In 1957, in a special address before the opening session of the state legislature, Collins alerted Floridians to the pillaging of the state's most magnificent bays. Local officials had not only abused the public trust; they "actually encouraged the misuse of Florida's natural resources." Since county and municipal governments appeared unwilling to protect Florida's waters, Collins announced that the state would regulate waterfront development.[22]

While the governor's conservation agenda was taking shape, Lee Ratner, a multimillionaire developer from Chicago, bought out Furen. Ratner claimed that his project would fill a gap in St. Petersburg's housing market by creating an exclusive setting for northern businessmen. "It has been proven that buyers of this type tend to bring their business enterprises to Florida," he said. Ratner's attorney, Leonard Bursten, a young lawyer who had started his career as an investigator for Senator Joseph McCarthy, promised that his client would negotiate with all governmental agencies to improve the design of the project.[23]

Lee Ratner had millions of dollars, but a less than sterling reputation. Earlier in the decade, he had used advertisements in northern papers to sell thousands of acres of unseen land near Fort Myers. Many of the buyers, novice investors, found that their "fabulous, improved lots," were instead watery plots in an impassable cypress swamp. Ratner's fraudulent scheme forced the state legislature to call a special session to discuss regulating land sales.[24]

Ratner was the slick postwar developer personified.[25] Besides his heavy use of advertising and other marketing ploys, he had an entourage of lawyers and consultants run through Florida's weak but growing list of regulations. Well-placed political contributions and questionable ethics completed a scheme of operation seen all too often in the Sunshine State. During the 1950s, elected officials seldom worried if developers misled them. For "the good ol' boy crowd," these entrepreneurs were simply trying to advance commerce and prosperity. It was just a matter of time before local officials began, John Rothchild writes, "codifying the promotional slogans into the county zoning."[26]

On April 11, 1957, the Pinellas County Commission approved the Ratner Fill, as the project was now called. At the end of the meeting, Shackleford handed the commissioners a petition for a rehearing and warned them that he would pursue the issue in court. Bursten claimed that the effort to block the project was "just because the people in Tallahassee disliked his client." He described the TIIF as a "bunch of bleeding hearts," and he cast doubt on the honesty of Hutton and Woodburn. Following in the steps of his former employer, Joe McCarthy, Bursten derided Hutton as a paid lackey who had "deliberately set out to wreck my client's plans." The aggressive young lawyer made a parting shot at Floyd Brown, the representative of the Alliance for the Conservation of Natural Resources (ACNR): "Instead of 20,000 members he is supposed to represent, the number had dwindled to a death march of a handful."

Mrs. Robert Davis, an ACNR officer and president of the St. Petersburg Garden Club, immediately challenged Bursten. "If you want us to bring 1,000 members up here to protest this fill, we'll do it." Since the city council had voted to work with Furen in December, the ACNR had sent more than 2,000 letters of protest. Floyd Brown also informed Shackleford that the ACNR would join the state board of conservation as a plaintiff if the state went to court against Ratner.[27]

Davis, Brown, a high school science teacher, and Mary Bigelow had formed the ACNR in 1954. Bigelow devoted the most time to the organization. She had visited St. Petersburg in the early 1940s and had become enchanted with the region's natural beauty. In 1951 she moved to St. Petersburg. Three years later, she awoke one morning to the dull roar of a dredge. Incensed that her waterfront vista was being transformed into a subdivision, she organized the ACNR by gathering members from eight civic organizations. Between 1954 and 1958, she traveled to Tallahassee numerous times to testify before the TIIF as the ACNR's representative.[28]

On April 23, 1957, Bigelow was in Tallahassee when Ratner's lawyers and William Windom, St. Petersburg's city manager, appeared before Governor Collins and the rest of the TIIF board. Windom explained that Ratner would modify his project in exchange for the deeds to an additional section of the bay. When Windom admitted, despite Bursten's vehement objection (when Windom made his statement Bursten leaped up to and almost over the bar separating the audience from the TIIF), that Ratner intended to fill more than the area granted under the existing deed, Collins shook his head in disbelief. When the governor spoke, he chastised Windom for representing Ratner and endorsing a project "contrary to the interests of the city." He also informed Windom that the state would continue its effort to stop Ratner's project: "We have not counted ourselves out of the picture, even if you have." Windom apologized for having given the impression that the city wanted Collins to change his stance.

Gerald Gould, the lawyer in charge of marketing the project, appeared next before the TIIF board. Gould complained that the state government had placed private citizens in jeopardy because agencies were "constantly changing their positions." The previous administration had already deeded the lands his client held, and Gould argued that the state's efforts to regulate development were inconsistent with his client's legal standing. He also stated that he had a letter binding Florida's chief executive to "our legal position and moral position." Collins bristled as he told Gould, "I don't know who had told you what, but I do think I have a pretty good knowledge of what has been said at this table which is the official place that governs our conduct."

The governor countered that the previous administration's decision represented "a considerable stretching of state policy." Then he asked Gould to produce his letter. The counselor haltingly admitted, "I'm not sure just where that letter is." The governor warned him to be more careful in what he said, and

Gould managed to stammer, "I'll try to get that letter." Collins suspended the discussion when Gould claimed that the governor had made certain promises to Ratner. Collins had never spoken with Ratner, he informed Gould, and the state would do whatever it could to stop his client's project. After the governor's declaration, Gould backed away from the stand, slumped down next to Bursten, and began murmuring into his briefcase.[29]

Collins's stand ushered in a new era (figure 26). Even a multimillion-dollar project funded by northern capital was no longer an unquestioned good. While turning productive estuaries into subdivisions added to the local tax rolls, destroying Florida's natural resources compromised the public welfare. Collins represented a growing constituency that had come to see that the benefits of protecting an important natural system outweighed the profits from private development.

In June, despite opposition from the entire Pinellas delegation, the legislature passed an amended version of the Bulkhead Law. The bill's chief supporters came from coastal communities that feared their bays would suffer the same fate as Boca Ciega Bay unless the state took action. When Representative Thomas Carey of St. Petersburg tried to exempt Pinellas from the regulations, a Fort Myers representative noted that in "Pinellas you are filling everything around there except the Sunshine Parkway" (the bridge between Bradenton and St. Petersburg). Carey countered that although the fish faced relocation, "We are putting people where we are filling." Later Carey tried to shuttle the bill into committee, in hope that it would die a slow death. This motion lost after a representative from Bradenton, William Grimes, made the comment that if "we study this bill all summer isn't it possible Manatee County bays might end up as bad as Pinellas County bays?" Carey also failed to get a special exemption for the Ratner Fill, setting the stage for an important test of the state's new legislation.[30]

While the Bulkhead Law represented an important step in the effort to regulate coastal development, it did little to alter existing building practices. The bill encouraged cities and counties to establish bulkhead lines, but it did not give any specific guidelines. In addition, the state legislature failed to provide funding for the technical assistance needed to design bulkhead lines properly. While the act gave the TIIF the right to withdraw lands from sale if the "conservation of natural resources were [sic] imperiled," there was no definition of what constituted peril. This flaw became only too apparent at the rehearing.[31]

In December 1957, the county commission reopened proceedings on the Ratner proposal with expert testimony from Ratner's consultants.[32] James B. Lackey, a marine biology professor from the University of Florida, testified that his employer's project would "encourage fish and marine life." Deep channels

The Sheriff Of Blunder Bay

Figure 26 Governor LeRoy Collins's fight against the Ratner Fill marked the beginning of a new era in Florida. Development, even in the form of a multimillion-dollar project funded by northern capital, was no longer seen as an unquestioned good. Jim Ivey, April 1957, *St. Petersburg Times*.

on each side of the project would flush water into the most polluted section of the bay (north of the project), which would improve water circulation, disperse bacterial pollutants, and even regenerate the dying scallop population. John Dequine, a fish biologist for the Southern Fish Culture Company, backed up Lackey's testimony and added that fishing opportunities would actually improve. The dredging operation would create deeper pools where fish would congregate, and the angle of the fabricated underwater slopes would also help to attract fish. "The heights of sophistry were reached," according to Ken

Woodburn, "when one consultant testified that sea grass beds were of little consequence to fish populations in Boca Ciega because fish came and went with the tides."[33] Perhaps even more bizarre was the testimony of Dequine's employer, J. Hardin Peterson, a former U.S. Representative and Furen's attorney. He claimed that the project would greatly benefit St. Petersburg because it would buffer the mainland during a hurricane. "I would suggest," commented John Orr, the lawyer representing the ACNR, "this human buffer they are going to put out there certainly won't be in the real estate ads."[34]

Robert Hutton, the author of *The Ecology of Boca Ciega Bay*, testified for the state. But before he could refute Ratner's consultants, he endured hours of interrogation by Bursten. Bursten first tried to discredit *The Ecology of Boca Ciega Bay* by challenging Hutton's scientific credibility. After questioning the scientist three separate times about his "compensation from the state," the lawyer tried to prove that Hutton was incapable of understanding the Ratner Plan. Hutton finally received a respite when the state's attorney gained the floor.

When asked what effect Ratner's project would have on the bay, Hutton reiterated his premise that the destruction of turtle grass beds would devastate the bay's marine system. Besides filling 500 acres of prime fishing grounds, the dredging operations would deepen the shallow water surrounding the huge fill to a depth of between seven and twenty-five feet. Turtle grass thrived in depths of two to four feet, and Hutton had never found it in water deeper than six and a half feet. He pointed out that eliminating an estimated thousand acres of turtle grass would increase the siltation problem, lower the water quality, and accelerate the spread of anaerobic muck across the bottom of the bay. He also doubted that trading boat channels for grass flats would enhance fishing. "In my opinion," he concluded, "the elimination of Cats Blank Point would materially and adversely harm marine life."

The Demise of Boca Ciega

The Pinellas County Commission ignored Hutton's testimony and voted unanimously for Ratner to proceed. This was hardly surprising, especially after the county administrator, Dewey Morris, warned the ACNR to drop its opposition because the Ratner Fill would come "hell or high water."[35] The anti-fill forces received more bad news when the ACNR and Shackleford challenged the commission's decision in the local circuit court and lost. Judge S. H. Harris ruled that the TIIF's original sale to Furen was consistent with sound governing policy "and that public policy [was] irreversible."[36]

The Collins administration contested the ruling, appealing jointly with the

ACNR and the TIIF. In addition, the ACNR, the TIIF, and John Brantley, a St. Petersburg council member, challenged Ratner's title in a separate case. The coalition gained a very minor victory when Attorney General Ervin ruled that the TIIF could not grant title to submerged land off Cats Blank Point because St. Petersburg, not the state, held the rights to this domain.

On January 8, 1959, when the court challenges were still pending, Ratner's lawyers tried to force Collins's hand. A year had passed since the county commission had issued Ratner's dredging permit, and if the operation did not begin within the year, the permit would lapse. Bursten informed Ervin that, unless the Collins administration agreed to a compromise, his client would begin dredging. Collins responded to Bursten's threat by having the circuit court issue a restraining order against Ratner's project. He also informed Bursten that his administration would "resist to the fullest extent we can under the law and under legal obligations we have in the premises."[37]

A month later the state court of appeals affirmed the lower court's ruling on the Ratner project. The ACNR and Ervin immediately petitioned the state supreme court. The petitioners claimed that the TIIF had exceeded its powers by selling lands outside its jurisdiction. The Florida Supreme Court denied this motion and ruled that it would not hear complaints against the actions of a state agency. With no legal means of redress, the Collins administration had little choice but to cut a deal. Ratner agreed to a slight modification of the project, decreasing its size from 515 to 445 acres. He also donated some land to Presbyterian (now Eckerd) College and dedicated a right-of-way for the Bayway, a toll road that would link the south beach communities to St. Petersburg.[38]

In 1961, Ratner's firm completed its dredging operation. While this project alone did not ruin the bay, its location and size ensured that the bay could never be restored to its former health. By 1964, this once shallow coastal lagoon, with its vast meadows of turtle grass, had been transformed into a channelized cesspool. Fills occupied 12.5 percent of the bay's 20,000 acres, while dredging operations had altered another 5,000 acres to build the fills. The "suburbanization" of the bay left the water discolored, stagnant, and laden with pollutants. As a layer of anaerobic muck replaced the sand of the bay bottom, commercial fishing interests, which brought in a yearly haul worth $1.4 million, saw their catches plummet. By the late 1960s, Boca Ciega was Florida's most polluted bay, and fishing boats had to go into the Gulf of Mexico.[39]

The first move to halt development in Boca Ciega Bay came in 1966, when the wealthy investor and environmentalist Nathaniel Reed joined Claude Kirk's Republican campaign for governor. In a surprise victory, Kirk returned the governor's office to the Republican Party for the first time in almost a century. One of Kirk's first appointments went to Reed, who accepted the post of "environmental advisor" and immediately set out to limit dredge-and-fill operations. During the 1967 legislative session, Kirk and Reed teamed with Representative Tom Randell of Fort Myers to secure passage of the Randell Act, which required developers seeking dredge-and-fill permits to furnish a detailed environmental-impact study that met specific state guidelines. Reed also persuaded Kirk to oppose any applications that significantly altered coastal habitats. Before the Randell Act passed, Florida approved an average of 2,000 fill projects a year. By 1970 that number had shrunk to 200.[40]

In 1969, Florida's bays received additional protection when Kirk signed the Aquatic Preserve Bill into law. Representative Dorothy Sample, a Republican attorney from St. Petersburg, spurred a bipartisan effort that prohibited dredging in designated preserves. She also convinced her colleagues to make Boca Ciega Bay Florida's first aquatic preserve.[41]

During the late 1960s, new federal statutes also helped end dredge-and-fill operations in Boca Ciega Bay. In 1968 Congress passed the National Estuary Protection Act, which encouraged local municipalities to protect the biological integrity of estuaries through planning. In addition, it called for federal agencies to consider the ecological impacts fostered by development projects in coastal areas. In 1970, the federal courts first interpreted the National Estuary Protection Act in *Zabel v. Tabb*, a case involving a dredge-and-fill project in Boca Ciega Bay.[42]

In 1958, Alfred Zabel had requested a permit from the Pinellas County Commission to fill twelve acres of Boca Ciega Bay. Although it was tiny compared to the Ratner Fill, Zabel's proposal to expand his trailer park into the bay attracted fierce opposition from local homeowners. The case went to the Florida Supreme Court twice before the TIIF was forced to grant a permit in 1965. As a last—and usually pro forma—step, the project required approval from the Army Corps of Engineers.

But when the project came in for review, the Corps' Jacksonville office was inundated with protests. Colonel R. A. Tabb planned to postpone his decision until after the Corps had held a public meeting in St. Petersburg. In November 1966, more than a hundred citizens showed up to speak against the project. Only one person agreed with Zabel's attorney, Thomas Harris, who declared, "It's our land, we can do with it what we want." After the meeting, Tabb's staff consulted with other governmental agencies about the environmental impact of Zabel's project. The biologists at the Marine Research Laboratory in St. Petersburg provided the most information. Robert Ingle, a marine biologist who had worked with Hutton in the 1950s, was the director of the laboratory. In a meeting with the Corps' scientists, he restated most of Hutton's testimony from the previous decade. He also told them that the dredging and filling of Boca Ciega Bay had cost the fishing industry $1.4 million a year.[43]

In March 1967 Tabb denied Zabel's request for a permit. This was the first time the Corps had ever denied a project because of its potential to damage the environment. Harris immediately filed suit against the U.S. Army Corps of Engineers and Tabb in federal court. The Tampa circuit court ruled against the Corps because the proposed project did not impede navigation. The court took the view that protecting the environment was an ancillary issue. In 1968, however, with the passage of the National Estuary Protection Act, the Corps' responsibilities increased. The Corps had to amend its permit and include an examination of the effects of proposed work on "fish and wildlife, conservation, pollution, aesthetics, ecology and the general public interest."[44] After revising its procedure for obtaining permits, the army appealed the circuit court's ruling in *Zabel v. Tabb*. In 1970, the case went before the federal appellate court in New Orleans. It drew national attention; both developers and environmentalists waited to see if courts would uphold the National Estuary Protection Act.

In a precedent-setting decision, the court ruled that the project's destructive potential provided sufficient reason for refusing the dredging permit. The court found that, though projects like Zabel's had routinely received clearance a decade earlier, science had now clearly revealed the disastrous effects of dredge-and-fill projects on marine ecosystems. It was imperative that the government change its policies. Americans had become "aware of civilization's potential destruction," Judge John R. Brown stated, "from breathing its own polluted air and drinking its own infected water and the immeasurable loss from a silent-spring disturbance of nature's economy." Zabel appealed the decision, but the Supreme Court refused to hear the case, and a new standard was set for Boca Ciega Bay and the nation.[45]

In 1970, the federal courts also sent Leonard Bursten, Ratner's attorney during the late 1950s, to prison. Bursten had left Florida in the early 1960s to represent a group of high-rolling developers in Beverly Hills, where his intimidating tactics caught the attention of a task force investigating fraudulent real estate dealings. The Los Angles police later implicated Bursten in a scheme that involved bribing city officials, but before this case reached the courts, Bursten was sentenced to prison for tax fraud. While serving as Ratner's counselor in 1957, Bursten had earned over $160,000, none of which he reported as earned income.[46]

Boca Ciega Bay's condition, although pathetic enough, at least remained stable through the 1970s. By the end of the decade, the city's sewage plant had stopped discharging partially treated sewage into the bay. Efforts to preserve and replace such vital species as mangroves and turtle grass even brought about minor improvements, but the bay remained an environmental hazard.[47]

The U.S. Department of Commerce has featured Boca Ciega Bay in a film, *Estuarine Heritage*, that it distributes to coastal communities to warn them of unregulated development's disastrous consequences. Polluted urban bays are hardly uncommon, but no other bay in the nation has suffered such extensive damage in such a short period. Between 1940 and 1970, more than 80 percent of all Boca Ciega's marine grasses were lost, and 70 percent of the bay's nursery areas were destroyed. In 1940, Wilson Hubbard, captain of a charter boat, could fish in the bay from his fourteen-foot skiff, using only a hook and a line, and consistently pull in over a hundred pounds of speckled trout a day. "You could look right through to the bottom," he recalled, "and see the fish swimming around." In the late 1980s, Hubbard still ran charter fishing boats, but never in Boca Ciega Bay. Another commercial fisherman who had brought in giant hauls before the Ratner Fill lamented that there was nothing in the bay. "It's just so thick and heavy looking I wouldn't hardly swim in it, let alone fish it." In 1986, the county's chief health official discouraged swimming in the bay. "Why swim in it," he asked, "if you don't have to?" Shellfishing remains banned in most of the bay, and attempts to replant turtle grass have generally failed because of the poor flushing and heavy siltation.[48]

Perhaps the most poignant reminder of Boca Ciega's demise comes from Governor Collins. Shortly before his death in 1991, Florida's senior statesman despaired that his administration did not do enough to protect the state's natural resources. Although he introduced many reforms through his office, the rape of Boca Ciega Bay still haunted him—so much so that, on flights to Tampa Bay, he always faced away from the coastal lagoon off St. Petersburg. What happened there was a "monstrous desecration" that he could never bring himself to view.[49]

8

Establishing Limits: The "Quiet Revolution"

Show me a man-oriented society in which it is believed that reality exists only because man can perceive it, that the cosmos exclusively is divine and given dominion over all things, indeed that God is made in the image of man, and I will predict the nature of its cities and their landscapes. I need not look far for we have seen them—the hot-dog stands, the neon shill, the ticky-tacky houses, dysgenic city and mined landscapes. This is the image of the anthropomorphic, anthropocentric man; he seeks not unity with nature but conquest. Yet unity he finally finds, but only when his arrogance and ignorance are stilled and he lies dead under the greensward.

Ian McHarg, *Design with Nature*, 1969

The controversy surrounding Boca Ciega Bay helped put the word *ecology* in the national vocabulary. By the early 1970s, depletion of natural resources, escalating levels of pollution, and suburban sprawl were forcing Americans to address the problems they had created. The noxious results of twenty-five years' unimpeded urban expansion on the Pinellas Peninsula were apparent to all. Hazy smog and cloudy, nutrient-laden bodies of water framed a degraded landscape: roads congested with cars and billboards, deteriorating downtowns, giant malls, endless sequences of strip centers, and a clutter of suburban subdivisions. The residents of St. Petersburg joined the chorus of Floridians clamoring for stronger land-use controls. Between 1972 and 1975 the state legislature responded with a series of bills that made Florida a national leader in growth management. Planners moved from accommodating growth to restraining development that encroached on sensitive natural systems or overburdened public facilities.

Chapter 8

The Quandary of Growth

In the early 1970s, the issue of growth management dominated the public agenda throughout Florida. To address the impact of the South's growing affluence the University of South Florida hosted the Symposium on the Contemporary South in January 1972.[1] Prosperity had finally arrived, but unregulated industrial and urban development had caused a multitude of environmental and social problems.[2]

The speakers presenting their views at the symposium included John Lewis, Julian Bond, Hodding Carter, Governor Rubin Askew, and LeRoy Collins. In the last session, Collins and C. Vann Woodward, the expert on southern history, talked about the region's future. To Woodward it seemed as though Henry Grady's dream of a "New South" had finally arrived. Tampa Bay's rapidly expanding urban complex exemplified the image of a resurgent South. Yet in emulating the North's creed of growth and development, the New South faced a new set of problems that were only too obvious to those driving along Pinellas's highly commercialized thoroughfares. The full horror of a "Yankeefied South," Woodward stated, "is suggested . . . by a drive between Tampa and Clearwater."[3]

During the early 1970s, St. Petersburg embodied the fortunes of a New South city overwhelmed by growth. While the rest of the nation's economy slowed down between 1970 and 1973, in St. Petersburg, where the population increased by almost ten percent (to 235,000), government services could not keep up with the demand for new roads and urban services. To complicate matters further, a record-breaking drought wreaked havoc in southwest Florida during the same period.

The drought made the situation in St. Petersburg especially difficult. Although south Pinellas averaged more than fifty inches of rain per year, St. Petersburg's potable water had to be piped in from outside the city limits. Saltwater first intruded into the city's aquifer during the 1920s, and the city commission leased water rights from the Eldridge-Wilde wellfields in northeastern Pinellas and northwestern Hillsborough County. In the mid-1950s, the peninsula's rapid urbanization also forced the Pinellas County Water Authority to purchase lease agreements with the Eldridge-Wilde wellfields. A decade later, Pinellas authorities obtained more leases to water rights from wellfields in neighboring Pasco County, and by 1971, the 700,000 residents of Pinellas County got 43 percent of their potable water from wells outside the peninsula.[4]

The drought exposed the precarious nature of the water supply. In 1971, saltwater intruded into municipal wells in northern Pinellas; shortly thereafter, excessive water use threatened the Eldridge-Wilde wellfield with the same fate. Municipal and county officials scrambled to come up with a rationing plan, but no long-range solution emerged, and regional water supplies continued to dwindle.[5]

The region's diminishing water supply forced St. Petersburg's municipal officials to manage the city's growth in a more responsible manner. In November 1971, the city council formulated the Citizens' Goals Committee to work over a two-year period toward a series of growth management goals. The more than 200 citizens concerned in this project included environmentalists, officers of homeowners' associations, home builders, realtors, property investors, and leaders from various civic groups. The group divided into twelve subcommittees to deal with such major areas of concern as the natural environment, housing, transportation, and land use.[6]

As the drought continued through the summer of 1972, the growing number of environmental problems made planning and land-use controls a common topic. The parched conditions meant that any project demanding additional sewer or water connections aggravated the outcry for strict measures to control growth. Surveys revealed that angry citizens, who saw their quality of life eroding, wanted municipal officials to put severe limits on development. "The public did not want to hear about comprehensive plans," one reporter noted, "they wanted action."[7]

Florida's Quiet Revolution

All across Florida, elected officials, environmentalists, and citizens petitioned Tallahassee to solve the problems produced by a generation of untrammeled city building. Between 1950 and 1970 Florida's population more than doubled, jumping from 2.8 million to 6.8 million. Developers had drained wetlands and filled bays to meet the demand for new housing, amassing huge profits as they went. The drought pointed up the folly of disrupting the ecology of entire regions. In the intensely developed coastal areas, the native vegetation died out, and foreign species like the Maleleuca from Australia and the Brazilian pepper replaced them. Since these exotic trees were immune to native predators, their populations exploded. The ground beneath their tightly packed limbs became a desert.[8]

As water became scarcer, water pollution levels also mounted. The thousands of acres of cypress stands and mangroves lost to development had performed vital functions that human engineering could not replace. Besides serving as nurseries and sanctuaries for Florida's diverse wildlife, they had maintained the fragile balance between water quality and water quantity by filtering out pollutants and storing vast amounts of rainwater. With fewer wet-lands to act as filters, more pollutants found their way into Florida's waters. During the drought the problem became acute. As the levels of nutrients mounted, the available oxygen decreased. Algae blooms became common-place in the increasingly turbid bodies of green water. High concentrations of nitrogen and phosphorous also contributed to covering sandy bay and lake bottoms with layers of anaerobic muck. For many, waterfront living became a curse when the wind shifted and the stench of decay pervaded the air.[9]

The continuing dryness especially exacerbated problems in urban areas, al-ready plagued by ecological problems. In spring 1971, the St. Johns's fresh-water prairies dried out. Peat fires burned five to six feet below ground and shrouded Jacksonville, the Kennedy Space Center, and Orlando with smoke. Directly across the state, coastal cities in the Tampa Bay region fought a series of water wars against inland communities.[10]

The drought placed south Florida and the Everglades at special risk. Peat fires burning in wetland prairies throughout the spring enveloped metropoli-tan Miami in a gray haze. Water levels in the Everglades dipped to historic lows, threatening the entire region's water supply. The Everglades' countless sloughs, ponds, and wetlands were a freshwater bubble overlying a stratum of saltwater in the underground aquifer. As the Everglades' once plentiful supply of freshwater vanished, saltwater intruded more and more into the region's drinking wells.[11]

Arthur Marshall, an outspoken ecologist from the University of Miami, had been predicting such a catastrophe for years. His studies revealed that Miami's urban complex had surpassed its "carrying capacity," the ability of a regional ecosystem to support life. In 1972 he reported that south Florida's problems were ample proof that the state's urban systems needed restructuring. Unless metropolitan Miami recognized the constraints imposed by its ecosystem, the vast Everglades–Lake Okeechobee natural system was doomed. Marshall wrote, "South Florida is a classic demonstration of the facts that growth and development cannot proceed endlessly without intolerable social costs; that the constraints of ecosystems ultimately clash with the economics of city bud-gets; that a holistic interdisciplinary approach to environmental problems is essential; and that the impoverishment of our large urban areas may be the yet unrecognized environmental catastrophe many have been waiting to trigger the nation into action."[12]

After studying Marshall's report, Rubin Askew, Florida's governor from 1970 to 1978, brought Marshall on board as an adviser. Although Marshall's inabil-ity to compromise shortened his stay in Tallahassee, he did help the Askew administration craft a reform package to manage Florida's natural resources, protect ecosystems of critical concern, and plan for urban expansion. If his agenda did not pass, Askew warned the 1972 state legislature, "It is not off-beat or alarmist to say that the continued failure to control growth and development in the state will lead to economic as well as environmental disaster."[13]

Florida's coalition of environmental groups[14] backed Askew's plan, but it also received strong support from Democrat Robert Graham of Miami Lakes, who led a coalition of urban legislators seeking a remedy for their predicament. Graham had made his mark as the developer of the planned community of Miami Lakes. The success of this enterprise lent him credibility in the eyes of both developers and environmentalists. He understood the issues of private property, but still advocated planning to solve environmental problems. Working together, Graham and Askew pushed the reforms through, and in the process transformed Florida's governing system.[15]

Almost overnight Florida changed from a typical southern state devoted to boosterism and unfettered development into a national leader in growth management.[16] In 1972 the legislature passed five major acts: the Water Resources Bill, the Environmental Land and Water Management Bill, the State Comprehensive Planning Bill, the Land Conservation Bill, and the Environmental Reorganization Bill. Taken together these bills formed "Florida's quiet revolution," as Graham called it, in land use control.[17]

The Environmental Land and Water Management Bill established five water management districts to deal with Florida's water woes. The Southwest Florida Water Management District (SWFWMD) included sixteen counties around Tampa Bay. The new agency initiated work on a plan to regulate water use and warned Pinellas officials that it would, if necessary, reduce the flow of potable water into Pinellas. If this happened, the county commission would have to halt all building in order to conserve water. When the drought persisted into 1973, a prominent group of Pinellas developers threatened SWFWMD with a lawsuit if the agency moved ahead with its plans to ration water. The district's managing board, however, refused to make any adjustment that would jeopardize the region's water supply.[18]

Although the new legislation gave water management districts the power to influence local land-use planning, the State Comprehensive Planning Bill did not fare so well. Conservative rural legislators bitterly opposed any state-mandated planning that limited property rights. They managed to strike down a proposal to create a state office for comprehensive planning. Without an agency empowered to review and implement plans, the planning bill was powerless to help municipal governments manage their growth.[19]

John Harvey, St. Petersburg's planning director, felt that the failure of the State Comprehensive Planning Bill undermined St. Petersburg's effort to re-plan. If other municipalities failed to follow the city's lead, he questioned whether St. Petersburg's new agenda could succeed. In May 1973 he wrote Daniel O'Connell, "We need a State Plan and strong centralized State gover-nance of human activity to survive" (O'Connell headed the Florida Environ-mental Land Management Study Committee, a group appointed by Governor Askew in late 1972 to draw up a statewide growth policy.) Harvey warned O'Connell that Florida would "develop itself to death" unless the state adopted a long-term approach to the environmental crisis, as put forth in the Club of Rome's (an international group of distinguished businessmen, states-men, and scientists) groundbreaking work, The Limits to Growth (1972). A strong state directive for growth management was essential, he concluded, "so that . . . a Florida with 14 million by the year 2000 can be avoided."[20]

Despite the shortcomings of the State Comprehensive Planning Bill, Florida had a new look. After a few halting steps in the previous two decades, the state had finally devised a method to regulate the city-building process. "Florida is a place where, until recently, the use of land has reflected an ex-ploitative laissez-faire philosophy," Luther Carter wrote, "but this state may now be at the threshold of great changes."[21] Now that protecting the environ-ment had become almost as acceptable as making profits, those two very dif-ferent aims would drive the city-building process.

St. Petersburg: An Experiment in Growth Management

In September 1972, St. Petersburg's municipal officials faced a major test when the Joint Venture Corporation, a subsidiary of Lee Ratner's company, re-quested utility connections for a project that would house 25,000 people on Bayway Isles, the new name for Boca Ciega's largest man-made island. The ex-isting plan contained no guidelines for incorporating Bayway Isles into the city, and it was soon evident to everyone involved that St. Petersburg's plan-ning system had failed. Over the next year countless public meetings, lawsuits, and countersuits ensued as citizens' groups, public officials, and Joint Venture haggled over building densities.[22]

In July 1973, Bayway Isles came under even closer scrutiny after SWFWMD cut Pinellas's water ration by 23 percent. This cutback severely affected south-west St. Petersburg, the fastest-growing section of St. Petersburg—and the section that would give Bayway Isles urban services. The southwest sewer treatment plant "was so overloaded," according to one report, "that residents

living nearby asked the city for gas masks as defense against the fetid smell."
At a public meeting about Bayway Isles, some activists did show up wearing gas
masks. After conferring with SWFWMD, the city council halted all building
in southwest St. Petersburg until a new sewage system was ready.[23]

The city council finally worked out a compromise with the Joint Venture
Company four months later. SWFWMD's water rationing made the developers scale down their original request. Instead of building twenty-eight high-
rises with 10,000 apartments, they agreed to a more "human scale design" of
4,700 units. The developers also agreed to postpone construction until completion of the new Southwest Sewage Treatment Plant in 1975.[24]

The Joint Venture controversy forced the city to reassess its entire planning
process. The company had originally demanded that the city provide services
for 10,000 new apartments; the planning department, to the city council's indignation, could not even estimate the project's environmental impact. The
council ordered a comprehensive analysis of the Pinellas environment, which
the planning staff would combine with the work of the Citizens' Goals Committee to form a new plan. The new plan would estimate maximum development based on natural limitations, and might also "bring an end," one editor
hoped, "to the asphalting and destruction of our once lush woodlands."[25]

At the same time the city council established two new boards: an environmental development commission (EDC) and a planning commission. These
two bodies replaced the planning board, which, according to the St. Petersburg
Times, was too often "impotent in dealing with the land-boom, people-rush
growth style of St. Petersburg in the 1970s." The planning commission would
handle long-range planning issues; the EDC would review development proposals and requests for zoning variances.[26]

The EDC quickly put an end to the rubber-stamping of development proposals by requiring developers to prove that their projects would not have
adverse social, economic, or environmental impacts. The overloaded sewage
system, shrinking water supply, and crowded roads made building permits
much more difficult to obtain. The St. Petersburg Times reported: "Dozens of
times, developers, big and small, found that their vivid artist's renderings, their
slick-papered charts and plans and their expensive attorneys' best verbiage
were just not enough, and quite frequently they had no choice but to pack up
their briefcases and stride angrily out the door with a rejection slip."[27]

EDC meetings regularly erupted when developers confronted the community's new guidelines. Property investors were still encouraged to make
money—as long as their profit was not at the public's expense. "I think land is
like a stock," the EDC chairperson, Helen Thompson, argued. "They bought
it to speculate and there are no guarantees." When strip commercial projects

and proposals for intensive waterfront development came before the EDC, meetings frequently offered minor fireworks. "Occasionally, with issues like the Bayway," as a reporter noted, there were "moments of high drama." The rancorous hearings further highlighted—as if it were necessary—the existing plan's failure to guide development effectively.[28]

County officials faced their own problems in trying to deal with the tremendous pressures of growth in the region. When SWFWMD restricted the flow of water into Pinellas in July 1973, the county commission temporarily put a stop to building. The county planning staff also started assessing "a brake-the-growth-formula" to find a better way to manage development.[29] A report to the county commissioners stated, "In Pinellas County we have urbanized to the point where a project in northwest Pinellas will ultimately impact St. Petersburg and vice a versa [sic]." Since the St. Petersburg city council had already begun replanning, county officials looked to Pinellas's lead city for guidance in drawing up a growth-management plan.[30]

The county joined with St. Petersburg to establish an environmental task force consisting of planners, environmentalists, and government administrators. The goal of the task force was to assess the Pinellas environment and develop proposals for a county growth-management plan. In late 1973, the end of the drought brought a reprieve to Pinellas County. SWFWMD was able to increase the flow of water into the peninsula, and the county commission lifted the building moratorium. The county planners were granted additional time to research growth-management plans from across the country.[31] St. Petersburg, however, continued to move ahead with its growth-management agenda.

In November 1973, the Citizens' Goals Committee delivered its report to the city council. After two years of meetings, this diverse group had reached agreement on a series of growth-management goals. The committee placed special emphasis "upon maintaining satisfactory living conditions, providing for ease of movement throughout the community, maintaining a balance of economic growth and land use control, and preserving the ecology."[32]

The next phase of the planning process required the planning department to design a conceptual plan that combined the work of the Citizens' Goals Committee and the Environmental Task Force. The city council adopted an Interim Growth Policy (IGP) to guide growth in the meantime. The planning department had drafted the IGP with the goal of creating "a City for Living atmosphere."[33]

The planners proposed preserving and restoring such natural features as wetlands, mangrove estuaries, beaches, and stands of native trees to help St.

Petersburg reclaim its past climate. Fifty years earlier, water and forests had covered more land, and temperatures were less extreme. The staff also recommended setting aside as much permeable green space as possible to retain stormwater. This would mitigate flooding and allow rainwater to filter through the ground instead of pouring into the bays. With the area's mixture of sand, clay and limestone acting as a filter for more water, the threat of saltwater intrusion would decrease.[34]

The planners also proposed redirecting development patterns. John Harvey, the planning director, wrote, "Redevelopment and improvement of existing urban areas must be favored over development which will utilize the remaining open lands." For new construction on vacant land, Harvey favored pedestrian-oriented cluster developments that situated homes and apartments around large common areas. Although this urban form offered less private open space than the typical subdivision, it provided more common green space. For this policy to succeed, the city also needed to reclaim a pedestrian orientation by deemphasizing auto travel and improving the public transportation system. Besides relieving traffic congestion, a more diverse transportation system would reduce pollution and energy consumption.[35]

The IGP included directives that restricted development in areas where growth had outstripped the city's ability to provide services. The moratorium on new building in southwest St. Petersburg would stand until completion of the new sewage treatment plant, scheduled for July 1, 1975. A similar moratorium would prevent new construction in the northeastern area of the city until the new Albert Whitted Plant opened. Harvey warned the planning commission that these were only stopgap measures. If building failed to resume after a prescribed interval, the city might be violating the Fifth Amendment by having "taken" property without just compensation. To stay within legal bounds, the planning department needed to formulate a vision of the future that would allow development to proceed in the most appropriate manner.[36]

In a planning commission workshop, Harvey placed his concerns in historical context by recounting the fate of John Nolen's vision for St. Petersburg. He told his listeners, "It has taken a long time for the idea to grab hold and be accepted, and I am not sure we are to that point yet."[37] The condition of the environment and the state of Florida had, however, forced the city's hand. At the same time, Harvey worried that the EDC's desire to see an "across-the-board reduction of residential building densities" was based on an arbitrary population figure.[38] Harvey stressed that there was no legal precedent for a plan based on maintaining a desired population, and that the courts would strike down any plan that arbitrarily restricted growth. A legally defensible plan would tie capital improvements (sewers, water, roads) to a reasonable schedule. That way, the city could delay construction of projects that exceeded its current ability to provide services.

Harvey assured the planning commission that his department would provide a workable growth-management plan, once staff members had incorporated data from the Environmental Task Force's study into their work. The task force information explained "the effects of urbanization on natural systems" and suggested "directions for improved management."[39] When this information was fully integrated into the new plan, city officials would have solid legal arguments for restricting development in fragile ecological areas.[40]

The information in the Environmental Task Force report would enable planners to project a maximum population based on carrying capacity. Harvey's staff followed the planning principles set forth in Ian McHarg's landmark book, *Design with Nature*, to set building densities.[41] Although McHarg's desire to plan cities around natural constraints was hardly new, his ideas arrived at an auspicious moment. In a world finally confronting the limits to growth, planning remained the chief tool for shaping urban expansion. McHarg wrote, "There is a need for simple regulations, which ensure that society protects the values of natural processes and is itself protected. Conceivably such lands exist wherein these intrinsic values and constraints would provide the source of open space for metropolitan areas. If so, they would satisfy a double purpose ensuring the operation of vital natural processes and employing lands unsuited to development in ways that would leave them unharmed by these often violent processes. Presumably, too, development would occur in areas that were intrinsically suitable, where dangers were absent and natural processes unharmed."[42]

St. Petersburg's planners used McHarg's techniques to outline the ecological constraints on the city. They shaded each physiographic feature on a separate clear plastic sheet and then placed the profiles over a blank base map. The parts of the white underlying map that showed through represented areas most suitable for development. Overlays shading a region indicated the presence of sensitive natural features. The completed map helped planners to weigh the factors influencing various landforms and assign appropriate building densities.

Regaining a Lost Vision

In May 1974, Harvey presented the *1974 Conceptual Plan* (see figure 27) to the city council.[43] The plan presented an ideal form and served as the base for the more detailed comprehensive plan. In the *1974 Conceptual Plan*, planners

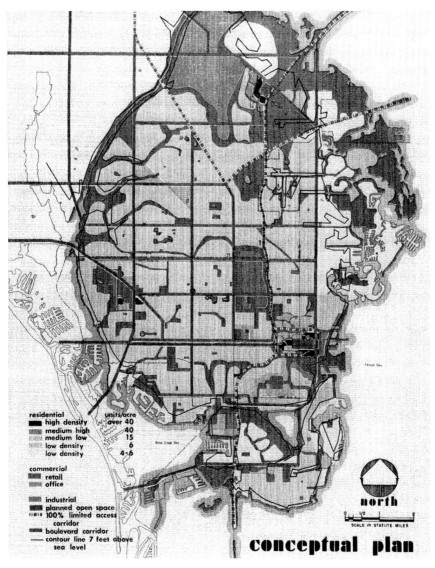

Figure 27 The "bold new concepts" that the 1974 Conceptual Plan used to develop a "man-made environment in harmony with nature" were undoubtedly bold—but hardly new. Courtesy of the St. Petersburg Department of Planning.

analyzed the lower Pinellas Peninsula as if it were virgin land, then described "the best possible urban environment" based on natural constraints. The plan presented "bold new concepts," its authors wrote, "to guide the man-made aspects of our environment and protect and enhance the parts which nature provided." The goal of promoting a "man-made environment in harmony with nature" was undoubtedly bold—but it was hardly new. John Nolen had performed the same feat fifty years earlier.

The design and methodology behind the *Conceptual Plan* and Nolen's plans (figures 27, 10, and 14) are strikingly similar. Each work analyzed the natural environment—soils, drainage, topography, and vegetation. Ecologically sensitive areas were marked for preservation or conservation, then linked with existing parks, drainage canals, creeks, permeable green spaces, and a proposed system of heavily vegetated boulevards. This network of green also provided buffers between neighborhoods and set natural boundaries for the city's expansion.

While the *Conceptual Plan* followed Nolen's general design, it furnished more precise guidelines for structuring future growth. The planning staff mapped and weighted each ecological feature to correlate building densities with the natural environment. For instance, they gave a weight of 2.0 to mangroves, deciduous forests, and poorly drained soils, while pine flatwoods and soils with medium levels of percolation were weighted at 1.0. The planning staff drew up a formula assigning lands to one of three categories: preservation (4.0 or higher), conservation (2.0–3.0) and development (below 2.0). A preservation designation precluded development, but landowners received a "transfer of development rights." The less fragile conservation areas allowed owners to build on 40 percent of their property. The development designation allowed densities ranging from 7.5 units per acre in single-family residential areas to 30.0 units per acre in the downtown district. According to the planning department's analysis, St. Petersburg could sustain a maximum population of 350,000 if property owners chose to build at maximum density levels.

The *1974 Conceptual Plan* also provided a vision of St. Petersburg fifty years into the future. Like Nolen, St. Petersburg's new generation of planners foresaw "a city very expressive of the unusual resort and residential character that is special to St. Petersburg." They centered the most intensive land uses in three "activity centers" that mixed large-scale commercial uses and high-density residential developments. Outside these areas, new residential developments, whether single homes or multifamily units, would be clustered to maximize open space. The plan also proposed recycling land, especially in the downtown area. In "a city with limited land space," the plan read, "redevelopment activity could ultimately provide as much work as new construction."

This new proposal labored under many more constraints than the Nolen plan had. In 1973 less than 20 percent of the city stood vacant; fifty years earlier nonurban uses accounted for 90 percent of the land. In addition, 95 percent of all in-town traffic used autos, sharply contrasting with the era when St. Petersburg's transportation system had both autos and trolleys. One of the new plan's principal goals was to reinstate an "integrated transportation system" by building fewer roads and making a gradual shift to public transportation, pedestrian walkways, and bikeways. Besides improving energy efficiency and lessening pollution, a "multi-modal" transportation system would allow the remaining permeable green spaces to filter the pollutant-laden runoff from city streets.

The planners proposed a system of "transportation corridors" to blend different transportation modes. The corridors would include broad, tree-lined boulevards (figure 28) and make up the "backbone of the open space system." "These boulevards will be as important for their beauty as for their function," the plan read. "They will provide welcome visual relief in the midst of an urban environment." Fifty years earlier, Nolen had recommended that a system of boulevards (figure 29) would provide "welcome breaks in the street system."[44] The primary difference between the two boulevard proposals was that Nolen encouraged the planting of native plants and trees along the corridor, while the new plan contained no landscape specifications.

St. Petersburg's planners promoted the proposed boulevards as key components in the effort to carve out identifiable neighborhoods from the city's mass of homogeneous subdivisions. The plan established fifty-two neighborhood districts, or "modular neighborhoods." Besides ringing each modular with boulevards, the planners set the following goals for each neighborhood: Increase green space, de-emphasize vehicular traffic, provide an access to a mixture of commercial uses, incorporate citizens' participation, and build a "sense of place."

The plan envisioned distinctive neighborhoods that provided places of residence, work, recreation, and commerce. Major transit connections abutting each neighborhood would lessen auto dependence. If each neighborhood had a variety of land uses, the planning staff hoped, residents would develop a new acquaintance with their local surroundings. Once the city council adopted the *1974 Conceptual Plan*, the planning staff would work with the people living in each neighborhood to assess and accentuate the area's unique characteristics.

The onerous task of rezoning the city would accompany adoption of the plan. The 1972 comprehensive plan had allowed an ultimate, "built out" population of 750,000. Even after the city council reduced building densities in 1973 and 1974, existing zoning still permitted a population of 550,000, a far

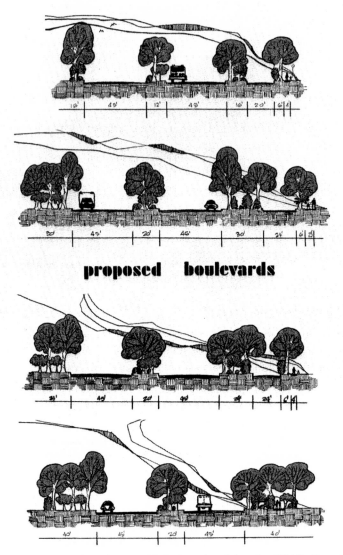

proposed   boulevards

Figure 28 The similarity between Nolen's work and this, the 1974 St. Petersburg Boulevard Plan, is striking. The principal difference was Nolen's proposal to plant native species. Courtesy of the St. Petersburg Department of Planning.

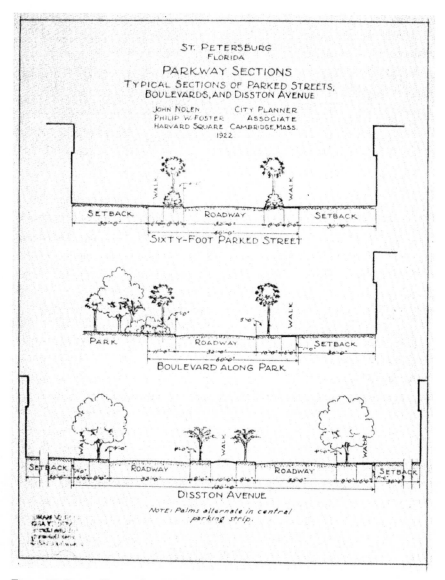

Figure 29 Pictured here is the 1923 Nolen Street Design Plan. Courtesy of the Division of Rare and Manuscript Collections, Cornell University Library.

cry from the *Conceptual Plan*'s figure of 350,000. Despite this discrepancy, the city council could move ahead because—in contrast to previous decades—there was now strong public backing for structuring growth.[45]

In fact, the support was a bit too strong. Many people believed that achieving growth management demanded draconian measures. In March 1974, when the planning commission received the *Conceptual Plan*, one city council member, Hugh Ruckdeschel, proposed a much more radical idea for meeting the demands of future growth. He wanted to cap the population at its existing level of 235,000—and give newcomers six months to leave.[46]

Ruckdeschel's proposal passed and drew national attention for the severity of its restrictions. The *New York Times* applauded the effort as "a healthy resistance to mindless expansion."[47] On its national telecast CBS News called this radical growth measure a sign of the new era in municipal government. But the city council quickly rescinded the ordinance after Ruckdeschel admitted that the move was a ploy to get the city to take the new plan seriously.[48]

Ruckdeschel's gambit illustrated Florida's new priorities. Most residents believed that the state needed to be more aggressive in restraining growth. In 1975, Patrick Caddell found in a poll that Florida was the only state where environmental concerns outweighed anxiety about the recession. Seventy-five percent of those questioned also supported stronger land-use controls to limit growth.[49]

In May 1975, the city council adopted the *Conceptual Plan* without any substantial changes or a single dissenting vote.[50] Two months later, the plan became even more significant when the legislature, acting on a report from the Environmental Land Management Study Committee, passed the Local Government Comprehensive Planning Act (LGCPA). This bill required all cities and counties to adopt comprehensive plans and submit them to the Department of Community Affairs, the new state planning agency, for approval.[51] Half a century after Nolen had introduced the idea in St. Petersburg at the National Planning Conference, Florida finally passed a state planning act. While the act gave legal standing to St. Petersburg's new urban vision, politics, not science or urban design, really drove the movement.

Concept and Reality

After the adoption of the *Conceptual Plan*, John Harvey moved on. Bruce Hahl, a Massachusetts planner, became responsible for the next phase of the planning process. Over the following two years, Hahl's staff distributed

300,000 notices and held numerous open workshops to involve the public in the design of the more detailed comprehensive plan. The media reported extensively on the team's activities. The city planning department invested hundreds of hours in research and public hearings to produce the final planning document, the comprehensive plan, which would guide development through the year 2000.[52]

The planning staff divided the city into five sectors (east, north, west, south, and in-town), then analyzed four elements: (1) land use, (2) conservation of natural resources, (3) recreation and open space, and (4) traffic circulation. The sector plans included general recommendations and design criteria for the policies and goals outlined in the *Conceptual Plan*. During the review of each sector, the city would modify its zoning ordinance and capital improvements program to reflect the plan.

The enthusiasm that greeted the *1974 Conceptual Plan* vanished when planners tried to sell their new vision. At workshop after workshop—and hearing after hearing—representatives from homeowners' associations, civic groups, environmental organizations, home builders' associations, and the realty industry battled over land-use designations. Hahl and Doug Baird, an attorney and the chairman of the planning commission, had to resolve the conflict over property rights before the plan could have a hope of being adopted. Those fighting the plan claimed that the various down-zonings—zoning land for less intensive use—abridged their constitutional rights by depriving them of the full economic use of their land. But advocates of growth management contended that property owners needed protection from the effects of those altering the landscape for economic gain. As the process moved forward, it became apparent that the idyllic lifestyle depicted in the *Conceptual Plan* represented a radical departure from the version of the American Dream being built and sold in St. Petersburg.[53]

Once Americans' sacred right to property had been invoked, the conflict soon heated up. "Who in the hell," one outraged businessman asked, "said that somebody who went to school and learned how to plan is better at planning the City of St. Petersburg than those who built it?" A small, close-knit group of developers, real estate brokers, and bankers led the assault against the plan. Despite their small number, this "high-gravity establishment," as one reporter called them, played an important role in municipal policy because its members owned most of the vacant land.[54]

William Mills, the owner of a large construction firm, and an investor, E. B. Porter, first questioned the plan. Both men sat on the board of directors of Florida Federal Savings and Loan, one of St. Petersburg's dominant financial institutions. Florida Federal had purchased land from Mills to build a branch office on the city's south side, but the planning staff down-zoned this site for residential use.

The south sector, in the planners' analysis, contained far too much commercially zoned land. A bank built on the Mills parcel would just add to the miles of commercial strip centers that lined the city's thoroughfares.[55] The planners argued that the excess of commercial lands was in no one's best interest. Store vacancies promoted blight, lowering revenues, and the proliferation of marginal uses for such land (used-car lots and secondhand stores) destroyed the appearance of an area because owners invested little in upkeep and improvements. An overabundance of commercial operations left too many competitors vying for too few consumers. With less revenue for each entrepreneur, profits and property values declined, tax revenues dropped, and the quality of life eroded.[56]

The planners advocated building commercial clusters and decreasing the land devoted to commercial strip centers. Besides making mass transit more feasible, this would foster better traffic flow, cut down on accidents, and save energy. A compact, clustered development also allowed space for green buffers and reduced the number of signs—a special need in a city overloaded with billboards and neon. If the city council wanted to realize its new vision, Hahl argued, it was essential to rezone the Mills parcel and others like it.[57]

In July 1975, Hahl informed Florida Federal that the planning commission intended to rezone the Mills property. Joseph Lettelleir, vice president of Florida Federal, promptly resigned as vice chairman of the planning commission.[58] Lettelleir had heartily endorsed the *Conceptual Plan* as a member of the planning commission, but this changed when the LGCPA made it possible for the plan's pleasing prospects and idealistic visions to gain legal standing. As the rezoning process moved forward, Lettelleir dedicated himself to eradicating the "bad parts" of the plan. After reexamining the document, he found it "stilted and one-sided," with "no sense of economics."[59]

Lettelleir's friend Charles Hicks III became the plan's most vocal critic. This second-generation real estate broker monopolized public meetings with long-winded harangues that disparaged planners for "overlooking the financial loss some people may sustain." Hicks specialized in commercial real estate, so he could lose large sums if the city down-zoned commercial properties. Hicks claimed he would relinquish his "personal property rights for the good of the community, as long as the community is willing to pay."[60]

Down-zoning also exasperated James Stephenson, the wealthy scion of a previous generation of south Pinellas developers. Stephenson, a former St. Petersburg council member, was shocked that city officials would dictate to him on questions of land use, especially after his family's forty years of service in the city. Stephenson found it absurd that officials "worry what I'm going to do with my land," he told one reporter. "All they have to do is look at what I've done."[61]

Hahl assured his critics that the city was "morally and legally bound to protect property rights." But it had no obligation "to protect the potential earning capacity of any given parcel of land."[62] While the Constitution protected landowners against government confiscation of property, it did not guarantee speculative profits. Investors who longed to turn coastal wetlands into condominiums or strip malls might even find themselves legally prevented from doing so. In *Just v. Marinette* (1972), the Wisconsin Supreme Court ruled that the owner of a swamp—who wanted to fill his property for commercial development—was entitled only to the uses of a swamp: "It seems to us that filling a swamp not otherwise commercially usable is not in and of itself an existing use, which is prevented, but rather is the preparation for some future use which is not indigenous to a swamp."[63]

St. Petersburg's growth-management agenda was not nearly so harsh as the Wisconsin ruling. The city met the legal test of reasonableness, which requires municipal governments to provide property owners with a reasonable use or an economic return on their land, by offering landowners the opportunity either to sell or to transfer their development rights to a designated parcel of property.[64] The planning staff selected conservation and preservation areas as "development right givers," while multifamily areas were "development right receivers." Investors received a 10 percent increase in building density for shifting development to multifamily areas. The mechanism for transferring development rights gave property owners the means to pursue profits, while helping to preserve environmentally sensitive lands.

These provisions meant little to those demanding the "highest and best use" of their property—which for them meant the most intensive use. The crusade against the plan "was to some extent," as the *St. Petersburg Times* reporter Dudley Clendinen wrote, "a mass exercise in miscommunication." When the planning staff held it first public meetings to review the south sector plan, Hicks sent out a 2,000-piece mailing on his own letterhead, warning property owners that their investments were in danger. He claimed that the planning department was instituting a "municipal land grab scheme" that would devalue real estate. Residents were left feeling, Hahl stated, "that we had a team of twenty bulldozers just waiting to come in and plow down their property." Shortly after the mailing, Hahl received a letter with a fake ticket for him and his family to Lowell, Massachusetts, his hometown. If it had been real, he joked, "I might have taken it."[65]

At the public meetings, Hicks, Lettelleir, and Lloyd Williams, a prominent home builder, repeatedly damned government excesses and extolled citizens' rights to private property. A coalition of those who favored growth management disputed their arguments. They pointed out that developers like James Stephenson intended to abandon the city once their ventures were played out, taking the profits and leaving the problems to the residents. For John Ritler, a livable future was worth a few sacrifices. "To bow along the way to the pressures of the moneyed community—the landed gentry," he warned the planning commission, "is an outright waste."[66]

The countless public hearings turned the conflict over planning into a war of attrition, which gave those fighting the plan an advantage. Their livelihood depended on attending planning commission hearings. Unlike their opponents, they could make it their job to attend meetings and devote time to studying technical reports. In addition, this elite group had strong ties with experienced lawyers and consultants who would plead their case. Even if they merely reiterated the alleged impositions of the plan on their clients, top attorneys from eminent firms could sway public officials.

A year of constant wrangling brought out ideologues from both ends of the political spectrum. The new plan could seem menacing even to people whose investments were not especially threatened. One ultraconservative, Earl P. Myhree, a physician, threatened to go to court if the city council approved the plan. He ranted that the endeavor was part of a conspiracy to bring in "overall 'Ism.' Socialism. Call it Communism. Whatever. We are losing our freedoms one-by-one, day-by-day."[67]

Although Myhree's right-wing fulminations were easily disposed of, they served to make Lettelleir and his allies look much more reasonable. As the review process dragged on into 1977, the city moved away from its "City for Living" stance and granted exceptions to the plan. These concessions were symbols of the city's historical weakness in prosecuting rational city building. Leading speculators reaped profits at the expense of a more balanced urban community. Once again, some of St. Petersburg's most influential citizens had sacrificed efficiency and natural harmony to the bottom line. According to the Urban Land Institute, the typical community supports one acre of commercial land for every 200 residents. In St. Petersburg, the plan adopted by the city council set a standard of one acre of commercial land for every 95 residents. With a population of 350,000, this ratio would become 1:141, still greater than the national average.[68]

The comprehensive plan adopted in October 1977 followed the outline of the *1974 Conceptual Plan*, but major compromises diminished its intended reforms. After property owners threatened legal action, the city council opened preservation lands to limited development. Owners could alter 25 percent of their designated preservation land after review by either the planning staff or the EDC. The city council also removed all restrictions on development of land designated for conservation, saying only that these "areas should be developed with caution."

By its actions, the city council made a conscious choice to trade the *Conceptual Plan's* vision of an "ecological city" for the sprawling suburban pattern typical of the modern Sunbelt city. Despite its unique environment and location, St. Petersburg was hardly a special place. Residents of St. Petersburg, like those of other Florida cities, could still revel in the sun and the sea, but the environment that had once had a diversity of plant and animal life uncommon in America was covered by ribbons of strip commercial centers and swaths of tract housing. In addition, the strand of salt marshes bordering the western part of the peninsula had vanished, and only a remnant of native forest remained. A century earlier, hardwood forests had occupied almost a quarter of south Pinellas. Now that same amount of land was covered by asphalt.[69]

Pinellas County: Following the Pattern

Although the county was less eager to plan than St. Petersburg had been, eventually residents realized that they had to bring some order to Pinellas's chaotic government. With twenty-four separate municipalities in the county, it was impossible to coordinate land-use decisions. In 1973, the state legislature established the Pinellas Planning Council to alleviate the problem by organizing local planning efforts and designing a countywide comprehensive plan.[70] But before reforms could get under way, the council needed the backing of the county commission.

Ever since Pinellas County had adopted its first plan in 1958, scandal had marred the planning process. In 1974, a detailed investigation of the county's planning practices published in the *St. Petersburg Times* exposed a web of corruption and graft. Commission members regularly ignored staff recommendations on zoning matters and voted in favor of influential developers. Hundreds of thousands of dollars changed hands for votes. As Commissioner George Brumfield explained, "That's the way the system works." In one case four of the five commissioners (Brumfield, Charles Rainey, William Dockerty, and Eddie Taylor) switched their votes in a zoning case concerning a sensitive environmental area after a friend of Commissioner Oliver McEachern gained control of the tract. As the *St. Petersburg Times* continued its probe, Pinellas residents realized that the region's growth problems were, at least in part, the fault of the county commission.[71]

The newspaper's exposé led to a grand jury investigation that revealed a level of deceit and greed fantastic even for Florida. Although Brumfield, Dockerty, and McEachern all served time in prison, no one could ascertain how many zoning changes had been sold or given away because, in the development industry, influence-peddling went far beyond the courthouse. Although many, if not most, business leaders could have testified against the commission, Jim Russell, the state's attorney, could not get a single witness to step forward. If nothing else, this failure attested to a system of ingrained deal-making that made the Pinellas case, Russell stated, "one of the greatest exposés of corruption in government that this state has ever seen."[72] After this case, few believed that the 1975 LGCPA would have any significant effect on how the county commission did business.[73]

After passage of the LGCPA, the county planning staff, like St. Petersburg's, used McHarg's overlay method and an intensive ecological study to determine land-use designations and carrying capacity for the peninsula. Their efforts resulted in a massive 400-page work, *The Conservation of Natural Resources Element of Pinellas County's General Plan*. This in-depth analysis of the Pinellas environment provided an impressive follow-up to the Environmental Task Force's examination of the ecology of the Pinellas Peninsula. Besides listing the "environmental constraints to urbanization," the report presented a number of policy directives and offered "scientific justification for all detailed recommendations." This document also contained the critical data for establishing land-use categories and carrying capacity (fixed at 1.1 million for Pinellas County). The planners' ecological concepts, however, separated them from many of the region's decision makers.[74]

After public review, the planning staff's work—altered to include the desires of the investors and realtors as well as the designs of the planner—was adopted in 1980 as the *Pinellas County Comprehensive Land Use Plan*.[75] Like St. Petersburg, Pinellas County had a surplus of commercial land and a deficit of public green space. In fact, the county ranked last among Florida's urban areas in per capita park land.[76] Despite these shortcomings, Pinellas County's growth-management plan did follow the guidelines used in such other communities as Petaluma, California, and Ramapo, New York.[77] The plan made wetlands preservation areas, for example, and gave elected officials powers to manage growth and restrict strip commercial development. But the commission's willingness to exercise these powers remained in question.

East Lake Tarpon: Changing the Pattern of Development

In 1978, planners forced a showdown between the county commission and property owners when they pushed for down-zoning in the Eldridge-Wilde wellfields and the surrounding lands in the East Lake Tarpon area. Continuing water problems had brought these lands in northeast Pinellas County under close scrutiny by both county planners and SWFWMD. Only 2,000 people lived in the 22,000 acres of pine flatwoods, swamps, and sandhills lying between Lake Tarpon and Hillsborough County. A maze of wetlands accounted for almost 40 percent of this unincorporated area, while the sandhill areas in the northeast corner of the county contained the wellfields. Although this region held most of the peninsula's remaining natural resources, during the early 1970s the county commission had zoned much of it for medium-density (fifteen units per acre) development. This translated into a future population of 218,000. Building at this intensity would not only destroy Pinellas's last pristine ecosystem, but would also place the county's water supply in jeopardy.[78]

County planners pushed to down-zone East Lake Tarpon after they found that Pinellas had imported more than half of its water (52.6 percent) from Pasco and Hillsborough Counties in 1977.[79] The Pinellas planning staff presented compelling data for cutting building densities by 70 percent in East Lake Tarpon. Despite fierce protests from landowners, the county commission voted unanimously—in accordance with the staff's report and under threat of legal action by SWFWMD—to down-zone a 10,000-acre tract.[80]

In drawing up the *Pinellas Comprehensive Land Use Plan* in 1979, planners had given special attention to the 22,689-acre East Lake Tarpon area. In addition to its special natural features, this backwater section held one-third of all the vacant land in the county. The planners concentrated their analysis on the wetland areas and the land surrounding the wellfields. They studied aerial maps and made numerous field studies to designate the boundaries of the various stands of cypress, black gum, bayhead, and hardwood swamps slated for preservation. In East Lake Tarpon, they had placed 4,375 acres of wetlands in the preservation category, which ensured that these lands would not "be developed without so altering the resource that the benefits are lost or significantly diminished."[81]

In this plan, preservation lands accounted for almost 20 percent of the East Lake Tarpon region. The higher dry land surrounding the wellfields was put in the conservation category, limiting development to one unit per acre, and the area's built-out population was lowered to 40,000. The down-zoning of East Lake Tarpon the previous year had set a precedent, and this time the planners' agenda met little resistance. Although Pinellas residents still faced critical water problems, they finally had a plan that would make the future a bit more secure.

The down-zoning of the East Lake Tarpon region marks one of the few times planners have shifted the course of city building in Pinellas. This occurred, however, only after the population had grown so large that the demand for water impinged on outside jurisdictions. Twentieth-century American settlements in scenic areas with abundant ecosystems have demonstrated a depressingly similar pattern of development.[82] Despite repeated warnings, the residents of Pinellas ignored the dictates of nature until environmental problems had reached crisis proportions. But reforms did at least curb the excesses of city building, and if regulations were first imposed out of necessity, attitudes were also changing. The environmental problems that plagued Pinellas during the 1970s convinced thousands of residents that their quality of life—and the health of future generations—demanded ethical treatment for the land. By 1980, Pinellas had the civic machinery to move in this direction. But was it too late?

9

Recycling Eden: Planning for the Next Century

We recognize the beauty, which is still hard to miss, but we also see
the filled bays, the commercial strips, the dwindling forests and the traffic and the crime and the noise and the funny yellow haze that smudges
the skyline on days with no rain. . . . The author [John MacDonald] tries
to deal with this gloom head on. . . . If the result is not a completely successful experiment, it goes off in some interesting new directions.

St. Petersburg Times, 1985

In the 1980s, after a half century of dizzying growth, St. Petersburg's population stabilized at 240,000. As the supply of vacant land dwindled, recycling
and conservation were at the top of the municipal agenda. By the early 1990s,
water, waste, and abandoned rail lines were recycled, public projects to spur
downtown redevelopment had commenced, and the county had bought endangered natural lands for preservation. Other Florida cities soon followed St.
Petersburg's lead, especially after the 1985 Florida Growth Management Act
required all municipalities and counties to draw up comprehensive plans that
complied with state directives. Although St. Petersburg had adopted a model
plan to resolve its problems, the city was hardly the prototype community John
Nolen had envisioned. Despite spending millions of dollars to rejuvenate the
downtown area, Florida's most expensive public and private partnership had
attracted more controversy than clients. At the same time, high levels of pollution, the uncertain water supply, and the perennial threat of a cataclysmic
hurricane were constant reminders of the problems that come when a city ex-
ceeds the limits of nature.

Restoring the Green Infrastructure

In accordance with LGCPA guidelines, St. Petersburg's planning department
filed a five-year review of the city's planning process in 1982. The most notable

finding was that St. Petersburg's population stood at 238,893, a gain of only one percent since 1977. Only eight percent of the city remained vacant. As there was less pressure for growth, municipal officials worked harder to structure development around the remaining natural areas.[1]

Of the 1,578 acres designated for preservation on the 1977 land use map, 530 were privately owned. Between 1977 and 1982, development took place on only thirteen of these acres. The city council had allowed the dredging of three acres; a developer who had apparently misunderstood when the new regulations went into effect built on the other ten. In 1983, the Southwest Florida Water Management District (SWFWMD) started a wetlands mitigation program to provide more protection for the remnants of this valuable natural habitat. The new regulations required developers to alleviate the impact of projects in wetlands by either enhancing, preserving, or creating more wetlands.[2]

St. Petersburg could not afford to buy land designated for preservation, but in 1980, Pinellas voters passed a referendum increasing the ad valorem tax for the purchase of "endangered lands." The measure raised $7.9 million, and a task force of environmentalists and county planners made up a prioritized list of the most important land to buy. The county acquired 1,700 acres including beachfront properties, wetlands, and lands surrounding the Eldridge-Wilde wellfield. Although the county bought no St. Petersburg properties, the task force assigned a high priority to buying the coastal mangroves in the northeast portion of the city if funding became available.

In 1986 and again in 1989 referenda supporting the acquisition of endangered land passed. The first election netted $23.9 million through an increase in ad valorem taxes. The second vote allocated $47 million for endangered natural lands (out of a total of $488 million for various projects) and raised the sales tax by a cent. This time St. Petersburg benefited, as the county commission spent $3.9 million to acquire 94 acres of mangrove habitat on Weedon Island. This purchase placed the entire 627-acre mangrove island in public hands. Besides serving as a rookery for wading birds, Weedon Island buffers northeastern St. Petersburg from hurricane storm surges.[3]

Although the county commission has the final say on land purchases, politics have not, for once, had much influence on the disbursement of public funds. Stringent guidelines for selecting properties, combined with a dearth of viable parcels, helped planners systematically assemble purchases. In 1992, county planners joined with a team from the University of South Florida's Institute for Environmental Studies to create a restoration plan for the Brooker Creek ecosystem in northeast Pinellas. The restoration plan was central to the county commission's request for a $2.7 million matching grant from the state. Besides establishing a restoration program for the ecosystem, Pinellas officials wanted to purchase thirteen inholdings in the 6,700-acre Brooker Creek Preserve, which surrounds the Eldridge-Wilde wellfields.[4]

The county commission sent its proposal to the Florida Communities Trust, which receives funding from Preservation 2000, the nation's premier land-acquisition program. In 1989, through the sale of $3.2 billion in bonds, the Florida legislature established Preservation 2000 to fund the acquisition of natural lands for ten years. The state has funneled 50 percent of Preservation 2000 funds into the Conservation and Recreation Lands Program (CARL). The CARL program concentrates on obtaining lands that are sensitive environmentally: significant wetlands, wildlife corridors, and endangered species' habitats. Pinellas's highly urbanized environment effectively precludes funding through CARL. But the Florida Communities Trust, which receives ten percent of Preservation 2000 funds, provides matching funds for the implementation of conservation policies in local growth-management plans.[5]

The Pinellas County Planning Department's fifteen-year investment in the East Lake Tarpon region played a crucial role in the decision by the Florida Communities Trust to fund the Brooker Creek project. In 1981, after the legislature allocated funds to the water management districts for acquiring "lands necessary for water management, water supply, and the conservation and protection of water resources," county planners and SWFWMD joined forces to set up the Brooker Creek Preserve.[6] To establish the preserve, SWFWMD spent $25 million on 4,000 acres; the Pinellas endangered lands program was able to set aside another 2,000 acres. The grant from the Florida Communities Trust not only allowed the county commission to buy out the remaining property owners; it also gave land managers the opportunity to restore the landscape to a more natural state.[7]

The Brooker Creek restoration plan broke new ground for environmental planning in Florida. The task force had a twofold goal for the Brooker Creek Preserve: (1) to protect Pinellas's water supply, and (2) to restore one of the region's most diverse ecosystems. Although only 100 acres of the preserve had been altered for urban uses, almost 1,000 acres had been converted to cattle pasture. In the previous half century, ranchers had drained wetlands and cleared the land to create range land. Once cattle started grazing, the quality of the environment deteriorated. The weight of the cattle compacted the soil and reduced its oxygen content. As the land lost the ability to absorb nutrients and water, its carrying capacity dropped. Undesirable "weedy" species, such as dog fennel and common ragweed, moved in. The new pasture could still support cattle, but the altered landscape hindered the movement of nutrients and species between uplands and wetlands. As ranchers continued to expand their range land, biodiversity plummeted.[8]

After taking inventory of Brooker Creek's natural resources, the task force drafted a plan to restore sections of the preserve where native species had dramatically declined and the natural habitat had become degraded. The task force wanted to return the Brooker Creek Preserve to some of its former vitality through controlled burns, the extraction of weedy and exotic species, the planting of native vegetation, and the reestablishment of wetlands.[9] In addition, the Pinellas County planners wanted to connect the peninsula's largest natural preserve to the rest of the county by way of the Pinellas Trail, Florida's most heavily used greenway.

The Pinellas Trail: Florida's "Emerald Necklace"

The Pinellas Trail, the "emerald necklace of Old Florida," as one writer calls it, is an urban greenway that will eventually stretch from St. Petersburg to northeast Pinellas, a distance of forty-seven miles. This project to recycle the old Orange Belt Railroad originated in the early 1980s, when Pinellas County planners started designing a comprehensive bikeway system. The "rails-to-trails" idea, however, did not take root until the Florida Department of Transportation (DOT) purchased a fourteen-mile stretch of the abandoned Orange Belt line in 1983. The DOT wanted this sixty-foot-wide corridor between Seminole and Dunedin eventually to serve as a light-rail line. In 1984, Dan Burden, the DOT's bikeway coordinator, suggested that a pedestrian and bike path would be a good interim use for it. The Pinellas County Bicycle Advisory Board adopted Burden's idea. Only a year later, Pinellas County planners had completed a feasibility study that addressed encroachment problems, design criteria, security issues, and cost estimates for building and maintaining the trail. The planners estimated that a ten-foot-wide, ten-mile asphalt trail would cost $657,200. They also recommended that the DOT, Pinellas County, and the Metropolitan Planning Organization (MPO) join together to fund the project. The Pinellas MPO, which is made up of elected officials appointed by the governor, was in charge of coordinating traffic planning with the DOT.

After considerable debate, the MPO delayed making a decision until its staff could conduct further studies. The MPO accepted the bicycle-and-pedestrian trail idea, but because trail users would have to cross two six-lane highways, there was a legitimate concern with safety. The MPO had its staff consider the feasibility of building a "passive recreational" facility along an additional twenty-one miles of abandoned rail right-of-way that the DOT had recently bought. (The DOT's holdings now stretched the length of the county,

The Pinellas Trail

Figure 30 Over 2 million people use the Pinellas Trail each year. This "emerald necklace of Old Florida" has become a prototype for the nation's booming greenway movement. Courtesy of the Pinellas County Commission.

from Tarpon Springs to St. Petersburg). If the light-rail project proved untenable, and the MPO's new study was favorable, construction of the bike trail could move ahead.

In spring 1988, the MPO tabled its light-rail plans. Its staff began working with Pinellas planners to design a fourteen-mile rails-to-trails project between Seminole and Dunedin. That summer the city councils of St. Petersburg, Clearwater, Seminole, Largo, Bellair, and Dunedin approved resolutions supporting a bike path along the abandoned rail corridor. In November 1988, trail activists formed a nonprofit corporation, Pinellas Trail, Inc., to raise funds and promote the greenway concept for the entire thirty-five-mile portion of the old Orange Belt line. (Greenways are linear corridors with vegetation that is more natural than the surrounding areas.)[10] Besides lobbying the county commission and raising funds, Pinellas Trail, Inc., actively marketed the vision of a greenway that would provide pedestrians and bicyclists with a protected, natural passage through the county.

In December 1988, Pinellas Trail, Inc., donated $125,000 to the county for publicizing the trail and providing support facilities. This grant enhanced the project's standing with the county commissioners. The commissioners also gravitated to the greenway concept because it seemed to be a popular issue that might translate into votes. In August 1989, the trail's supporters cleared a major hurdle when the Pinellas County Commission signed a five-year renewable lease with the DOT. The lease gave the commission responsibility for overseeing the construction of the trail planned for the thirty-five-mile railroad right-of-way. County planners started working on a plan to connect parks, schools, and commercial centers situated near the trail. A month later, the county commission appropriated $1.5 million to construct the fourteen-mile segment between Dunedin and Seminole. At the same time, Pinellas Trail, Inc., started its "A Penny for the Trail" campaign to use a portion of the proposed one-cent increase in the sales tax for the trail. In November 1989, voters adopted the measure, and the project received $5,270,000 to push the construction schedule forward and acquire an additional twelve-mile corridor along the MacKay Creek drainage system. This purchase extended the trail corridor into Pinellas's last remaining expanses of natural lands in the East Lake Tarpon area.

Once construction started in 1991, homeowners living near the rail corridor raised concerns that allowing public access to this abandoned property would increase criminal activity and lower property values. A Trail Safety and Security Task Force was established to address these issues and to serve as a liaison between police departments and trail users. Keith Bergstrom, the police chief in Tarpon Springs, headed the group, which included elected officials, concerned property owners, and greenway supporters. At the task force's request, a bicycle patrol went on duty when the first fourteen miles of the trail opened in 1991. By the end of the year, two to three thousand people a day were on the trail. Homeowners' fears dissipated when they realized that the traffic on the trail, instead of abetting crime, was a deterrent to it. "Trail-watching" became a common occupation for property owners, and gates began appearing in fences adjoining the trail. By summer 1993, homeowners' fears had so far diminished that the Security Task Force considered disbanding.[11]

Although bicycling is the most popular recreational activity in Florida, even the most avid trail enthusiasts were astounded by the Pinellas Trail's popularity. In 1992, 1.1 million people enjoyed the twenty-three-mile segment of the trail. In 1993, Pinellas Trail, Inc., had over a thousand paying members, while civic groups, churches, schools, environmental groups, running and cycling clubs, merchants' associations, and homeowners dedicated their time and money to beautify the trail and push it toward completion. In addition, almost half a million dollars in matching federal funds came from ISTEA (Intermodal Surface Transportation Efficiency Act) to construct an overpass across a major highway in St. Petersburg. The state legislature also earmarked the same amount for the Pinellas Trail from Florida's Rails-to-Trails program. By 1995 the number of users had doubled, and the trail had stretched to thirty-five miles. If funding continues on course, the project should reach completion in 1997, at a total cost of $8.7 million.[12] Ken Bryan, Florida's coordinator for the national Rails-to-Trails Conservancy (RTC), stated in *Planning* that the "Pinellas [Trail] ranks among the top five of 500 trails nationwide by virtue of its heavy usage and strong citizen support."[13]

The Pinellas Trail has also served as a spur for economic development. Its role in the resurgence of downtown Dunedin has drawn the most attention. In 1990, occupancy rates in this dying city center had dropped below 50 percent, but once the trail opened, hundreds of people traveling on it found Dunedin an ideal place to stop off. Within two years, the town had attracted a weekly farmers' market and had converted an abandoned train station into a museum. Festivals, for example, the Suncoast Mardi Gras, also moved to downtown Dunedin now that revelers were not so dependent on autos for transportation, and thus not in need of limited parking spots. By 1995 the downtown had reached full occupancy. Its small shops and restaurants now receive a steady stream of customers. Dunedin's success has not only served as a model for other communities along the trail, but has also drawn the attention of many politicians and planners from across the state.[14]

In 1992, Orange County planners envisioned a seventeen-mile greenway running on an abandoned stretch of the Orange Belt line just west of Orlando, but they were unable to obtain the consent to build it until after the Orange County Commission visited Pinellas. After walking portions of the trail and visiting Dunedin, the commission's chairperson, Linda Chapin, became a staunch supporter of the greenway proposal. The West Orange Trail opened in September 1994; the monthly number of users soon mushroomed to 30,000. Lake County's planners also brought their county commissioners to Pinellas to sell the idea of linking up with West Orange Trail and extending it across Lake County. In January 1994, the Lake County Commission appropriated $900,000 in county funds to construct a recreation/bike trail that would also use an abandoned section of the Orange Belt line. Since then, the Florida

Greenway Commission and the Florida RTC have begun planning to link Orlando with the Pinellas Trail.[15]

In January 1994, the Florida RTC chapter held its first conference in Dunedin. The president of the national RTC, Richard Burwell, opened the proceedings by proclaiming, "God Bless the Pinellas Trail." Pinellas's success offered the 150 trail advocates and greenway planners from all over Florida a blueprint for community action. Burwell announced that in 1995 the national RTC meeting would be in Pinellas because of the Pinellas Trail's "rapid development, popularity, and partnership with citizens and local governments."[16]

The Pinellas Trail has been successful because it (1) provides a link between isolated subdivisions, and (2) offers a pleasant way to explore the county. While the concept of a greenway is not new (the Olmsted Brothers had proposed an interconnected system of parkways in 1913), in Pinellas's urban environment the trail is unique because it gives people a way to see the countryside without being dependent on a car. Not only can trail users see ancient live oaks, hammocks, and tidal streams; they can also safely bike, walk, or run through one of the nation's most congested urban areas. "The Pinellas Trail," its advocates contend, "is a priceless haven in a busy, overcrowded world."[17]

Recycling Resources

While the rails-to-trails venture has been the most popular recycling project in Pinellas, the county has also been a testing ground for new advances in the recycling of other wastes. In 1977, St. Petersburg opened a new tertiary sewage complex that eradicated 90 percent of the pollutants from sewage and eliminated the effluent that once went into the surrounding bays. St. Petersburg's innovative system, the first of its kind in the nation, recycled the sewage plants' nutrient-rich effluent and used it to water public lands. During the 1980s, the system began to provide businesses and homeowners with this "gray water" as well, helping to alleviate the overall demand for water.[18]

In the late 1970s and early 1980s, the other municipalities surrounding Tampa Bay followed St. Petersburg's lead. The region made a $90 million investment in new technology to reduce sewage pollutants by 90 percent. This move not only satisfied EPA standards for fighting water pollution; when municipalities recycled their waste water, they were also freed from the necessity to make all water potable. By 1990, the Tampa Bay region led the state in the use of gray water.[19]

Even though water recycling was helping Pinellas reduce potable water consumption, a continuing drought forced SWFWMD to cut back on well pumping in July 1994. This severely affected Pinellas's supply of potable water and made new moratoriums on construction a distinct possibility. The county commission wanted SWFWMD to remedy the situation by building a pipeline between Lake Rosseau (in Citrus County) and St. Petersburg. SWFWMD, however, rejected this proposal. The agency's scientists feared that such a project would lower the water table and degrade freshwater wetlands—in a region that had already lost 35,000 acres of wetlands to overpumping. The water-rich portion of eastern Pasco County had suffered from a series of environmental problems because it had overdrawn its groundwater supply. Swamps and lakes dried up, trees died, wells pumped sand, and yards dropped into the ground. After one homeowner's yard fell like a "soufflé," she commented, "If I did this kind of damage to my neighbor's yard I'd be held criminally accountable. We realize that everybody needs water, but not at the expense of the environment."[20]

Rather than continuing to draw groundwater from inland areas, SWFWMD wanted to construct a desalination plant in St. Petersburg. The agency believed the plant would give Pinellas residents drinking water and have only a minimal ecological impact on the region. Anticipated construction costs were in excess of one billion dollars, and it would take another $70 million a year to operate the plant.[21]

Pinellas's municipal governments have had mixed success in recycling solid waste. Because there was so little vacant land, the idea of recycling solid waste took hold in Pinellas earlier than in any other major urban area in the state. In the late 1970s, a consultant's study showed that the county's overburdened landfill could never meet anticipated trash loads.[22] The county commission moved to solve the problem by constructing a massive electricity-generating incinerator that opened in 1983 (figure 31). The "Refuse to Energy Plant," located just north of St. Petersburg, burns 2,000 tons of garbage per day and generates $900,000 worth of electricity per month.[23] While the plant relieved the strain on the landfill, it has had some potentially devastating side effects. According to one study, mercury contamination in the Everglades can be traced at least in part to this incinerator. In 1990, a Florida Department of Environmental Regulation sampling found that the plant released about twenty-one pounds of mercury into the atmosphere every day. The prevailing winds carry these pollutants into the Everglades ecosystem, where they have infiltrated the food chain. Mercury levels are so high in bass that anglers are warned not to eat their catch.[24]

Figure 31 The Refuse to Energy Plant, a massive electricity-producing incinerator, burns 2,000 tons of garbage per day and generates $900,000 worth of electricity per month. Unfortunately, prevailing winds carry some of the mercury it releases into the atmosphere to the Everglades' ecosystem, which has become contaminated. Courtesy of the Pinellas County Commission.

The 1985 Growth Management Act

Despite its efforts to protect the environment, St. Petersburg could not escape the problems of growth. While the city's population stabilized in the 1980s, the surrounding urban complex continued to swell. By 1985 the population of Pinellas had passed 800,000, and 1.8 million people lived in the greater Tampa Bay area. To complicate matters, between 1974 and 1984 the amount of developed land increased at twice the rate of the population. As more newcomers crowded into waterfront condominiums, apartment complexes, and large tract developments, air and water quality continued to decline. At the same time, poorly designed and placed developments blighted the landscape and aggravated traffic problems.[25]

In the mid-1980s, yet another statewide drought exposed the weakness of the region's water supply. With less rain to recharge the aquifer, the supply of groundwater diminished, and saltwater intruded into the supply of drinking water. A lower water table also led to loss of more wetlands. The population continued to outstrip the water supply, and in 1985 SWFWMD placed St. Petersburg and the rest of Pinellas on year-round water rationing.[26]

At the same time, Tampa Bay was failing. Dredge-and-fill operations, urban runoff, human waste, and chemical dumping had all degraded this once bountiful resource. After a century of exploitation, scientists found that Tampa Bay had experienced an 81 percent loss in sea grasses and a 45 percent loss of mangrove habitat. Between 1957 and 1977, shellfish harvests dropped by two-thirds, from 20 million tons to 6.5 million tons. "Natural thresholds," scientists warned, "are being approached beyond which ecosystems fail."[27]

Air pollution also threatened the health of those living on the Suncoast. In 1983, the region failed to meet federal standards for ozone. This pollutant makes breathing more difficult, reduces endurance, helps cause disorientation, and aggravates pulmonary stress. Ozone also damages vegetation, fabrics, building materials, and rubber, and it was the principal component in the growing cloud of brown smog over Tampa Bay.[28]

In 1985, the issue of growth management dominated political agendas across Florida. Although the state was having another building boom, residents realized that the Florida lifestyle was fast eroding. The Miami Herald editor Carl Hiaasen wrote that Florida had started to resemble "Newark with palm trees."[29] "If we continue to allow our environment to be degraded," Lee Moffitt, speaker of the Florida House of Representatives, warned, "word will spread that Florida has become an environmental disaster area." The plans drawn up in the last decade, he added, amounted to little when county commissions "knuckled under whenever a developer asked for an exemption." Moffitt called for a bipartisan effort by Florida legislators to enact more stringent growth controls.[30]

During the 1980s Pinellas officials—and their counterparts throughout the state—had been willing to alter the county land-use plan to grant developers concessions. In a three-and-a-half-year stretch in the mid-1980s, the Pinellas County Commission granted 253 plan amendments for more intensive land use. Many of these projects were in already overburdened areas. "Gridlock and commercial sprawl in this county didn't just happen," the St. Petersburg Times editor Jon East wrote. "To a disquieting degree we planned them."[31]

Massive infrastructure needs also led to the outcry for growth management. Throughout the 1970s, Florida remained a "fool's paradise," growth-management expert John DeGrove wrote, "in which it was believed that growth paid for itself and that sooner or later the new growth would pay for new infrastructure." Crowded highways and schools were constant reminders not only that growth had failed to pay its way, but that it was out of control. By 1985, there was widespread support for Tallahassee to enforce a system of growth management that could balance development, the health of natural systems, and the provision of public facilities.[32]

Governor Bob Graham, Florida's longtime champion of growth management, heeded the call. He needed an issue to propel his run for the Senate in

1986, and he found the perfect vehicle. He pushed through the 1985 Growth Management Act (GMA), which revised the 1975 LGCPA. Passage of this bill gave Florida the most innovative and complex planning process in the nation.[33] While Graham received rave reviews, his successors faced the difficult task of enforcing the legislation.

The GMA granted the state additional powers to enforce and implement plans at the local level. While the LGCPA had forced local governments to plan, it had offered no guidance for designing, implementing, or funding. With no state master plan to guide local efforts, Florida was trapped in a maze of contradictory and inconsistent city plans. Under the LGCPA, the state provided little incentive to implement the planning process, and most municipalities had shelved their plans. Although the plans offered visions of a better life, they were politically untenable. The GMA sought to rectify the situation by requiring local governments to follow guidelines set down in the Comprehensive State Plan. This top-down system included review of local plans by the Department of Community Affairs (DCA), the state planning agency, to ensure compliance. If local governments failed to amend their plans, or if, after amendment, the DCA still found them in noncompliance with state directives, the Office of Budget and Planning could withhold state funds.[34]

The GMA also required local plans to meet the test of concurrency. "This element is what transforms Florida's planning act from a planning exercise," land-use lawyer Charles Simeon writes, "into a mandate for implementation."[35] Concurrency provided county and municipal officials with a tool to prevent urban sprawl and make growth pay for itself. Until public facilities for roads, sewers, water, solid waste, drainage, and parks meet adequate levels of service, as determined by the DCA, local governments cannot grant development orders.[36]

Elected officials in St. Petersburg were fortunate that the existing plan had already designated some levels of service, such as the goal to keep 50 percent of the city permeable green space. In restructuring their plan to meet the GMA mandates, the city's planning staff faced fewer impediments than most. With its limited amount of vacant land and stable population, St. Petersburg escaped the controversies over growth that slowed planning in many places.[37] The DCA found that St. Petersburg's plan not only passed state criteria; it excelled.

In April 1990, St. Petersburg received an award from the DCA for being the large city with the best plan. The state planners felt that the plan deserved special recognition for preserving natural lands and achieving the goal (first specified in the *1974 Conceptual Plan*) of keeping 50 percent of land permeable green space. The planning department had reported that permeable green space occupied 52.4 percent of the city. Projections indicated that the figure would still be above 50 percent after development of the city's 2,208 acres of vacant land.[38]

Although the DCA had recognized St. Petersburg's diligence in meeting the provisions of the GMA, people living in the city were questioning its vision for the future. Citizens generally approved of acquiring natural lands and rejuvenating the downtown area, but the price seemed outrageous.

The Redevelopment of Downtown St. Petersburg

In the mid-1980s, the city council had allocated $170 million to revitalize the downtown. The construction of a domed stadium, the renovation of the Municipal Pier and the Bayfront Center, and the Bay Plaza project represent the culmination of the growth-management process begun in the early 1970s. In 1973, the Citizens' Goals Committee had made redevelopment of the downtown a primary goal. Committee members felt that the legitimacy of the growth-management process necessitated redirecting development from environmentally sensitive areas and outlying lands into the downtown. The committee also wanted the downtown to be able to assume a larger share of the tax burden. In the early 1970s, the downtown had lost much of its vitality; by 1981, it accounted for only 3.8 percent of the city's tax base. In its 1982 "Intown Redevelopment Plan," the city council set a goal of 20 percent for the downtown. Unfortunately, the plan did not contain a comprehensive strategy to accomplish this feat.[39]

Downtown St. Petersburg had been declining as a retail destination since the mid-1960s. In the early 1980s, only one department store, Maas Brothers, remained, and its future was in jeopardy. Vacancy rates in the scattered office buildings fluctuated between 20 and 30 percent. The hotels built before World War II were sliding into disrepair and transitional uses. Yet despite being rundown and shabby, downtown St. Petersburg still projected a sense of place. In contrast to the region's giant malls, "Downtown still feels like a town center," a prestigious consultant team wrote. "With the right kind of redevelopment, downtown has the potential to become a lively, lovely and enjoyable commercial center."[40]

In 1983, the St. Petersburg City Council fully committed itself to downtown redevelopment when it voted for a $60 million bond issue. The plan was to use a third of the money to renovate the Municipal Pier, the city's most important tourist attraction, and the Bayfront Center, a cultural and entertainment complex. The remaining two-thirds would go to spur downtown redevelopment. The city council also wanted to construct a multipurpose stadium, but before going ahead with this proposal, they needed assurance that the stadium, which would cost $110 million, would bring a commensurate commitment from private investors.[41]

The city council conducted a national search to find a firm that would manage both the proposed stadium and the redevelopment of the downtown's retail core. Two developers came forward, Neil Elsey, president of Elcor Company of Phoenix, and Lynn McCarthy, president of the J. C. Nichols Company of Kansas City. Together they formed the Bay Plaza Company to capitalize on this opportunity. Elsey and McCarthy saw the stadium as a catalyst in the creation of an activity-based downtown, and they believed that the natural amenities of St. Petersburg's waterfront location would distinguish Bay Plaza's undertaking from others of its kind. "The combination of St. Petersburg's spectacular downtown waterfront location, recent development progress, easy interstate highway access, and three regional attractions (stadium, Pier, Bayfront Center) presented an opportunity unmatched," Elsey stated, "in any other major metropolitan area."[42]

In 1987, St. Petersburg and the Bay Plaza Company agreed to the most ambitious public-private partnership in Florida. Bay Plaza took responsibility for managing and marketing the pier, the Bayfront Center, and sports stadium, which would be built with city funds between 1987 and 1989. The most significant portion of the project, however, was the redevelopment plan for the downtown's nine-block commercial core. This ten-year enterprise would take place in three phases, at a cost of $200 million. The city would spend $40 million on infrastructure—parking garages, street design, park improvements, and utility relocations.[43]

The Waterfront Retail District, renamed Bay Plaza, was the focal point of the downtown revitalization strategy. Elsey wanted to raze most of the nine-block area and build 1.1 million square feet of high-quality retail shopping. Three major department stores on the order of Saks Fifth Avenue and Neiman Marcus would anchor the shopping district's dozens of smaller specialty shops, boutiques, restaurants, and cafés. According to the Bay Plaza Master Plan, "St. Petersburg, with the Bay Plaza Companies, is forming a community that holds a vision for the City's next 100 years."[44]

Without being aware of it, the Bay Plaza planners were resurrecting much of what John Nolen had proposed for Central Avenue in 1923.[45] Native plants would line the Plaza Parkway (as a portion of Central Avenue is called in the redevelopment project), which would connect the waterfront, the Bay Plaza, and the stadium. Apart from the pedestrian bridges, the street and building design for Bay Plaza is almost a copy of Nolen's original plan for Central Avenue.

Figure 32 Bay Plaza's design to rejuvenate downtown St. Petersburg followed Nolen's early lead, but the project ground to a halt when it became clear that the Tampa Bay region could not support an exclusive retail mall. Courtesy of Grubb and Ellis, Tampa, Fla.

Mediterranean architecture, open balconies, wide sidewalks, benches, green spaces, and native plants remain vital components for planners trying to promote human interaction and a sense of place in downtown St. Petersburg (figure 32).

In spring 1988, the Bay Plaza Company introduced its master plan to the public. The *St. Petersburg Times* and a citizens' group, Save Our St. Petersburg (SOS), examined the plan carefully. SOS had fifty core members; two architects, Eric Lindstrom and Tim Clemmons, and one journalist, Tim Baker, served as co-chairs. While there was general agreement that the downtown needed attention, both the newspaper and SOS questioned the project's feasibility. "The Bay Plaza would be something," a *St. Petersburg Times* editor wrote several months later, "but would it work?"[46]

In July 1988, SOS published a critique of Bay Plaza. The group favored downtown redevelopment, but a retail mall devoted to high-priced stores contradicted the city's character. St. Petersburg was a middle-income resort community, and attempting to remake the city was, SOS believed, "a radical and risky solution to the traditional urban problems of business and people moving away from the central city." "If it fails," the report went on, "the damage to the city will be severe."[47]

SOS believed that by catering solely to an exclusive clientele, Bay Plaza's venture was "more like a theme park than an urban downtown." The group recommended that the project include more offices and affordable commercial establishments to attract St. Petersburg residents. Bay Plaza's refusal to construct apartments or condominiums was another point of contention. The developers argued that "the low-income nature of downtown" made building multifamily units too risky financially. But if downtown had a "low-income nature," how could it support an exclusive mall? SOS argued further that the downtown area already contained higher-income residences at Bayfront Tower and Fareham Square, and similar units overlooking the waterfront were already planned.[48]

SOS also thought it was essential to maintain the downtown's identity. Clemmons recommended that Bay Plaza incorporate buildings of historical significance into the project, especially the Soreno Hotel, which was slated for demolition. This "million-dollar" hotel of the 1920s had shaped the city's resort character. The Vinoy Hotel aside, the Soreno was the best example of the Mediterranean Revival style that had flourished in St. Petersburg during its early boom. In 1981, the Community Development Department completed a four-year study that ranked 350 of St. Petersburg's buildings. The Soreno Hotel had the highest ranking, and the committee wanted it put on the National Register of Historic Places. SOS felt that incorporating the Soreno into Bay Plaza would ensure that the downtown embodied St. Petersburg's past as well its future.[49]

After SOS published its assessment, the *St. Petersburg Times* hired two distinguished consultants to review the Bay Plaza plan. Mary Means, the originator of the Main Street program at the National Trust for Historic Preservation, and Ronald Thomas, an expert in urban design and the author of *Taking Charge: How Communities Are Planning Their Futures*, spent a month on the project. The two gathered data, visited the site, and interviewed civic leaders, business executives, and city officials. After reviewing the project with their colleagues, Means and Thomas came to the same conclusion as SOS. "The path the city has started down with Bay Plaza is longer, is much more difficult and carries greater risk," the consultants wrote, "than either city officials or the developers have acknowledged so far."

According to Means and Thomas, the city council's $40 million commitment to the project was similar to redevelopment efforts in other urban centers. But unlike other cities, St. Petersburg would never be able to attract retailers of the caliber of Saks Fifth Avenue and Neiman Marcus, because the percentage of high-income households in the Tampa Bay area was so small. In

1987 only 13 percent of families living in the area had incomes above $50,000, compared to a national average of 21 percent. The consultants also point out, "Fully developed and built up, older cities with fixed boundaries like St. Petersburg typically lag in terms of resident income." Although downtown St. Petersburg could undoubtedly support a more viable commercial center, it was not, Means and Thomas wrote, "a Neiman Marcus kind of place."

The consultants also voiced concern over the demolition of the Soreno Hotel. As an "authentic relic" of the architectural style that Bay Plaza intended to reflect, it seemed logical to restore the Soreno to connect the new project with the past: "Under no circumstances should the building be demolished until there are guarantees that a suitable replacement will immediately rise in its place." They recommended that the city council set up an advisory committee of experienced urban designers to ensure that the Bay Plaza project maintained some semblance of continuity with St. Petersburg's history.

Means and Thomas also believed lack of citizen involvement threatened the viability of the entire undertaking. In their discussions with civic leaders, they had found that widespread agreement existed about the use of Mediterranean architecture and the protection of the waterfront. Yet they had not discovered any public initiative or debate that would turn this vague dream into reality. Baltimore's successful waterfront rejuvenation, for example, had had the support of diverse civic organizations and a business-sponsored, not-for-profit management organization. St. Petersburg's planning staff had yet to foster this type of public involvement in or commitment to the Bay Plaza project: "We found a complex climate of hope, fear, frustration, suspicion, and, most of all, confusion about the future of downtown."[50]

Robert Pittman, a longtime editor of the *St. Petersburg Times*, voiced a similar concern. Consensus building among the city's various interest groups "has been a problem for St. Petersburg as long as I can remember." The only successful endeavor on this front that he could recall was the work of the Citizens' Goals Committee, which had laid the foundation for the city's existing plan. Pittman believed that it would take the same type of long-term effort on the part of a diverse group of citizens to make Bay Plaza a reality. "The city can benefit from the expertise and knowledge of these consultants," he wrote, "but we've got to work for our own visions and decide our future ourselves."[51]

The city council ignored the recommendations from SOS and the two consultants. City staff continued to work with the Bay Plaza developers, without consulting a citizens' advisory council. The idea of forming a nonprofit management group also foundered. In 1989, construction started on the first phase of the project, an attractive five-story parking garage with 70,000 square feet of retail space on the bottom two floors. When the structure opened in late 1990, the Mediterranean design was enthusiastically received. But the building had one major problem: there were no tenants.[52]

In summer 1991, the Bay Plaza project collapsed. The existing retail space was still empty, and Elsey resigned after failing to attract any major tenants for the proposed mall. Elsey did not limit his search to the Saks Fifth Avenues of the retail world; midlevel and discount retailers declined his offers as well. In addition, St. Petersburg lost out to Miami and Denver in the competition for an expansion baseball team, and the new stadium sat empty. With the nation in recession, city officials realized that their strategy of offering massive subsidies to lure major league baseball and exclusive retailers was ill timed and ill advised.[53]

In early 1992, downtown St. Petersburg was in worse trouble than ever. Tenants were still flocking away from Bay Plaza, and Maas Brothers, long the anchor for downtown retail, had finally closed. The office vacancy rate of 35.4 percent was the highest in the state, ten points higher than second-place Miami's. As downtown properties continued to lose value, St. Petersburg faced a financial crunch. In the early 1980s, when it borrowed $60 million in long-term bonds to fund downtown projects, the city council had assumed that increased tax revenue from rising property values would cover the debt. With tax revenues declining, the city's administrators were scrambling, skimming funds from city programs to meet the mounting interest payments. By 1994, one estimate put the annual shortfall at $1.5 million.[54]

The Bay Plaza Companies went ahead and razed the Soreno, but they were unable to obtain financing, and no new building rose on the site. The destruction of the Soreno left a void in the heart of the city and seemed to symbolize the entire Bay Plaza gamble. The attempt to fit St. Petersburg's downtown into an upper-class mold had failed miserably. In March 1992, after contemplating the contrast between the scenic waterfront and the downtown's fragmented look, a Russian visitor commented that St. Petersburg looked like "a lovely lady without a smile."[55]

Hopes flickered—and were again dashed—in late 1992 when the San Francisco Giants decided not to move to St. Petersburg. Bay Plaza remained an unrealized dream, while the empty stadium was a painful token of the city's vanished hopes. The sportswriter Richard O'Brien wrote that it reminded him of "the segment in the movie *Mondo Cane* in which aborigines in New Guinea, enchanted by the big airplanes that fly overhead, clear a landing strip in the belief that it will lure the craft to their village."[56]

Missed Opportunities, Unfulfilled Dreams

In choosing to entice investors with huge outlays for dubious projects, the city council ignored simple proposals that could have yielded great returns. In 1973, the Citizens' Goals Committee advocated the creation of a multifaceted transportation system to improve St. Petersburg's quality of life. The *1974 Conceptual Plan* envisioned a system of landscaped boulevards that would allow safe and shaded access for pedestrians, bicyclists, and cars. The boulevards would also serve as the backbone of the open-space system by providing a green buffer around the city's neighborhoods. By 1982, the city council and its staff were of a different mind. While $60 million in taxpayers' money was allocated for downtown redevelopment, the planning staff declared that the boulevard concept represented an unaffordable "luxury in a time of fiscal conservation."[57]

The $40 million that subsidized Bay Plaza could have constructed between thirty and sixty miles of landscaped boulevards with bikeways.[58] Given the popularity of the Pinellas Trail, investing in beautification and bikeways would undoubtedly have been more profitable than sinking money into a grandiose downtown mall. A system of boulevards would have given pedestrians, skaters, and bicyclists safe access between subdivisions and into the downtown area. There is no reason that downtown St. Petersburg, with its public waterfront and novel sense of place, could not repeat Dunedin's success as a stopping place. A link to the downtown, moreover, would be more than an investment in infrastructure. It would be a step toward building the public support that every successful redevelopment effort needs.

The empty stadium and the Bay Plaza fiasco are all-too-familiar parts of a pattern that is as old as St. Petersburg. In the 1920s, John Nolen recommended that the city commission purchase St. Petersburg Beach for $750,000 and establish a system of interconnected nature preserves. Instead, that money went to build the Municipal Pier and fund a disastrous program of public "improvements." These past follies became especially apparent in 1985, when the county commission paid $5.9 million for only 5.3 acres of St. Petersburg Beach, the two-mile-long barrier island.[59] If the city commission had followed Nolen's recommendations, those investments might have produced exponential returns. Besides the benefits to the tourism industry and the region's quality of life, the environmental costs accompanying urbanization would have been much less. Yet St. Petersburg today, as in Nolen's time, continues on a course of luring outsiders with expensive facades, rather than cultivating its true resources.

John Nolen's plan for St. Petersburg has a timeless quality, because it rests on humanity's most inescapable relationship: our tie to the natural world. Although technology has liberated most of us from the toil of wresting a living from the environment, we ignore our dependence on the earth at our peril. In the twentieth century, the character of our relationship with our planet has changed, as Nolen recognized. Modern society can choose to consume the earth—or conserve it. Nolen's genius lay in his understanding of the dynamism of modern city building. He realized that there was an urgent need to establish collective controls in order to sustain the health of the landscape for future generations. In the case of St. Petersburg, such restraints have proved incompatible with pursuing the American way of life. For too long people have favored profit and increased convenience over such basic needs as clean air and water.

Over the last two decades, the decline of the environment globally has forced us to reexamine our relationship with the natural world. Unless city building takes place in a sustainable fashion, following the lines of nature, future generations will never enjoy a quality of life comparable to ours.[60] If we are to sustain hope for the future, we cannot ignore the past.

Seventy years ago, John Nolen offered the people of St. Petersburg the chance to build a city that would usher in a new era of urban living. They squandered the opportunity because a persuasive band of land speculators sold them on the image of a false Eden. The realtors and subdividers who mesmerized the public were brilliant in their way. They realized that, in the modern era, public relations count far more than analytical studies or facts. But once a community yields to the supremacy of public relations, reason falls away, and it becomes impossible to distinguish between fact and fantasy. Then, as was the case in St. Petersburg, tragedy awaits. "We suffer primarily not from our vices or weakness," the eminent social historian Daniel Boorstin wrote, "but our illusions."[61]

While the 1920s real estate boom is long forgotten, boosterism and speculation still drive communal decision-making throughout Florida. The cacophony of fast food establishments, billboards, parking lots, convenience stores, and harried pedestrians is a glaring reminder that we have reduced the dimensions of complex society to the point that consumption is our one common value (figure 33). In a republic founded on the ideal of citizenship, St. Petersburg's disjointed landscape reflects a culture that has equated consumerism with citizenship. The costs of an indifferent citizenry are obvious, but social scientists are only beginning to assess the damage sustained by an underclass that can neither attain nor escape the image of affluence.

Pinellas offers pockets of matchless beauty, but it is mostly a mass of undif-

Figure 33 The miles of strip commercial centers illustrate the priorities of St. Petersburg's city builders and the values of a consumer society.

ferentiated suburban sprawl. The mosaic of farmland, natural communities, and human settlements that once defined the landscape has all but vanished. Between 1956 and 1986 citrus acreage dropped from 13,540 to 394 acres, a 97.1 percent decline. During a similar period (1954 to 1988), the number of farms fell from 769 to fewer than 100, while the amount of farmland went from 60,680 to 2,877 acres. By the end of the century, planners anticipate that the peninsula will have no agricultural land. The rush of development has also pushed the forests toward extinction. Between 1959 and 1984, forest cover declined by 65.7 percent, falling from 57,949 acres to 19,862 acres.[62] Although the $50 million allocated for natural lands during the 1980s and 1990s will preserve a remnant of the forests, the county still has the least open space per capita of Florida's eight most populous counties.[63]

The most intensive development on the peninsula has occurred on the barrier islands. From Clearwater to St. Petersburg Beach, condominiums, hotels, and assorted high-rises crowd the narrow beaches. Fictional accounts, scientific studies, and computer models all offer cataclysmic projections of a hurricane descending on Pinellas's overpopulated chain of barrier islands. According to the "index of catastrophe potential" developed through computer simulation, Tampa Bay is the most vulnerable region in the nation to hurricanes (figure 34). Five billion dollars in damage to insured property is the

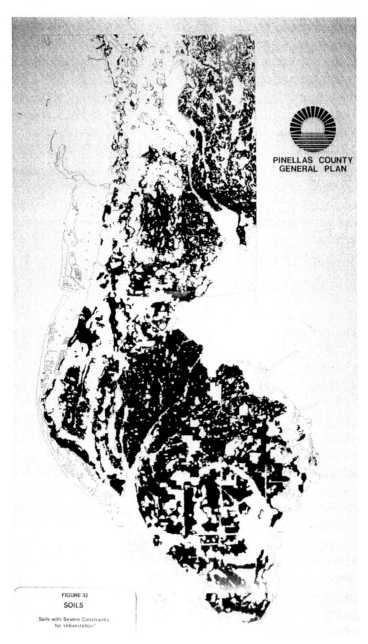

FIGURE 32
SOILS

Soils with Severe Constraints
for Urbanization

Figure 34 Black areas indicate soils with high water tables. These place severe constraints on urbanization, and during a hurricane they would experience severe flooding. Courtesy of the Pinellas County Department of Planning.

projected cost of an "average" hurricane's visit to the Tampa Bay area. Pinellas County would take 64 percent of the loss. By comparison, in 1972 Hurricane Agnes caused three billion dollars worth of damage in eighteen states. In 1985, when Hurricane Elena passed within fifty-five miles of Pinellas, it left $100 million worth of damages. Pinellas suffered greater ravages than any Panhandle county, where the storm tides were twice as high.[64]

In a state crafted by natural disasters, an innate sense of hubris united the multitudes of rootless Floridians. For some reason, Florida's residents have long believed that they are immune to natural disasters. Hurricane Andrew—and the insurance industry—have laid that myth to rest. While Pinellas did manage to escape the hurricane, homeowners felt its impact in their wallets. Andrew forced the insurance companies to confront the folly of insuring properties located on land that hurricanes periodically reconfigure. After paying out $16 billion in damages, eight companies folded, and even two of the giants, State Farm and Allstate, were badly shaken. To prevent such heavy losses in the future, insurance companies threatened to drop thousands of policyholders in Florida's heavily populated coastal communities. The state quickly moved in to fill the void by establishing a catastrophe fund and a joint underwriting association, but insurance rates continue to rise despite the state subsidy. Between 1993 and 1995, Allstate and State Farm raised their rates by 46.1 percent and 58.4 percent, respectively.[65]

If a hurricane were to strike Tampa Bay, deaths could be prevented only by a successful evacuation of the more than 100,000 residents and tourists on the barrier islands. Ben Funk, using computer estimates to support his fictional account of a hurricane's effects, wrote: "How many were killed—10,000, 30,000, 50,000? It all depended on how many ran."[66] Terrible losses await Pinellas in the future, when nature again unleashes its uncontrollable forces.

St. Petersburg and her sister Pinellas communities provided the setting for some of the late John D. MacDonald's novels. In his bestseller *Condominium* (1977), MacDonald wrote of a hurricane smashing into an overbuilt section of southwest Florida. He attempted to depict the essence of human nature and the natural world in a conversation between a construction engineer and a naive newcomer: "Opposing a big new project on one of the keys is not a popular stance in Florida these days. Even though the project will go up on fragile land? If they can get it up and sell it out before the big waves come that's all they want."[67]

MacDonald "created a heartbreakingly vivid portrait of a jungly Eden," Jonathan Raban writes, "spoiled and besmirched by human vanity and greed." His villains are never innately evil; they are only weak. Raban writes that they are "easily dazzled by easy money. They are decent Rotarians, small-town politicians and businessmen who can't resist a share of the takings when it is offered to them on a plate. . . . The irony at the heart of MacDonald's books is that these feeble, childish miscreants behave so wantonly in a setting that looks as if it really was designated to be a paradise—and could, even now, be rescued . . . just."[68]

The history of city building in St. Petersburg is the story of a people who, through folly, have lost their birthright to Eden, yet somehow have managed to keep their dreams of it alive. Although St. Petersburg is hardly the city John Nolen envisioned, there is still hope for it. It has the tools it needs to manage growth, protect the remaining natural resources, and restore others. While the water supply remains a problem, cutting the flow of sewage into Tampa Bay has helped regenerate portions of the bay. In 1994, scientists found new stands of sea grasses and a corresponding increase in marine life in those areas of the bay not scarred by dredging.[69]

St. Petersburg—and the rest of the municipalities in Florida's most urbanized county—will continue to push the natural world to its limits. Yet, at the same time, the following state, regional, and local initiatives provide a model for any metropolitan area attempting to reconcile urban expansion with environmental protection.

1. *An ecological plan.* St. Petersburg's *1974 Conceptual Plan* made use of a study of carrying capacity that set initial limits to growth based on environmental studies.
2. *A strong regional planning agency.* The planning authority given the Southwest Florida Water Management District (SWFWMD) to safeguard the region's water supply placed the protection of the system of interconnected wetlands and waterways, or "green infrastructure" on an equal footing with other infrastructure requirements.
3. *Environmental technology.* Besides securing and rationing the region's water supply, the EPA and SWFWMD worked with St. Petersburg to build a prototype waste-water treatment system to recycle gray water.
4. *Top-down state-mandated planning.* The 1985 Growth Management Act allowed the state to review plans for consistency, while the test of concurrency provided local governments with a tool to identify and preserve sensitive natural lands in a more efficient manner.
5. *Land acquisition and restoration programs.* By combining local land acquisition programs with Preservation 2000, Pinellas has managed to preserve, maintain, and even restore portions of its remaining natural systems.

6. *Greenways.* The Pinellas Trail has connected the fragmented Pinellas landscape and provided an important recreational outlet. At a time when Americans are desperate for common civic enterprises,[70] the trail has become an exemplar of building community by connecting communities.

In 1995, St. Petersburg had a stroke of good luck when major league baseball finally awarded a franchise to the city. The national pastime will undoubtedly furnish a pleasant outing for residents, and it may even elevate St. Petersburg to the status of a "major league city." Baseball, however, is no substitute for good planning. If St. Petersburg is to reach its potential, citizens must not lose sight of the vision John Nolen presented so long ago. Despite many technological advances, the formula for building livable cities has not changed since modernization first overwhelmed the nation in the 1920s. "The first step out of the present disorder," Lewis Mumford wrote in 1922, "is to ignore all fake utopias and social myths that have proved either so sterile or disastrous." Once these myths have been discarded, "We do not jump blindly into a blankness." Rather, he warned, our society must choose between designing with nature or building cities that will end in "nothing, or rather nothingness."[71]

Epilogue

The Nolen Renaissance

In fact, one of the most promising byproducts of the back-to-the-old-ways movement is the attention it has focused on such figures as Elbert Peets, Raymond Unwin and John Nolen.

Ruth Knack, 1989

In November 1990, the University of Miami's School of Architecture held a symposium on John Nolen's Florida plans. Nolen has heavily influenced the work of the symposium's hosts, Andres Duany and Elizabeth Plater-Zyberk. As principal proponents of the traditional town planning movement, Duany and Plater-Zyberk organized the symposium to explore the timeless quality of Nolen's work. Over time, planners have instituted a number of the proposals from Nolen's first Florida plan. But his recommendation to set aside a portion of the barrier islands as nature preserves, perhaps his most significant proposal, has hardly received consideration. Today the most intensely developed section of the Pinellas Peninsula occupies its most fragile landforms. Yet it is possible to catch a glimpse of Nolen's vision in the design of Seaside, Duany and Plater-Zyberk's seminal addition to American city planning.

According to Duany, "We must revert to planning approaches from the days when America was a poorer but smarter nation." By studying the works of John Nolen and Raymond Unwin, he contends, laymen can know more about urban planning than the experts.[1] Seaside has become a popular place to examine the revival of traditional town planning. Unlike the typical American suburb, in which large plots, decentralized development, and the automobile combine to isolate residents, Seaside is focused on the public realm, set to the pedestrian scale, and designed to blend with the natural landscape. Duany and Plater-Zyberk's architectural code requires homes to follow the region's vernacular tradition. During the last five years, this 280-acre new town has received more attention than any other city planning project in the nation.[2] Recently Seaside passed the most difficult test of all.

Seaside was at ground zero when Hurricane Opal ripped through the Florida Panhandle in October 1995. Although countless beachfront condominiums, hotels, and apartments near it were devastated, Seaside came through almost unscathed because it sits behind the beach dune system. This natural barrier saved the residents from everything except having sand, blown by the 110 mph gusts, filter into the pastel, clapboard homes with their tin roofs. Construction costs run 10 percent higher in Seaside than in the surrounding area, but Opal made it apparent that this investment paid a tremendous dividend. The town's landscape, most of which consists of native sandy pine and scrub oak habitat, also helped to keep Seaside safe. The native vegetation buffered the heavy winds, and the sandy soil supporting it allowed the stormwater to drain at a faster rate than in the typical suburban landscape.[3] The practical genius in Seaside's design and building reflects the adage that John Nolen delivered years before in St. Petersburg: "Well conceived ideals are more practicable than they seem."[4]

Within days of the hurricane, the town was operating at its normal pace. Although the fifteen-foot storm surge had eaten into the dunes, the boardwalks leading over the dunes were still intact, and Seaside was the only place for miles where one could escape the clutter of destruction. Three months after the hurricane, I paid my annual visit to Seaside with a class of undergraduates. With most of the coast still in a state of disrepair, Seaside offered a tranquil oasis that seemed in tune to the natural world. Couples, families, and students gathered in quiet anticipation to watch the sunsets, which were peculiarly mesmerizing. People found places on the platforms above the dunes and listened to the rhythmic pounding of the waves as they watched the sun slowly vanish beneath the horizon. "The state," one DCA official proclaimed, "is extremely fortunate to have Seaside to serve as a model for a new era of urban design in Florida."[5]

Despite Seaside's success, the project is not free from irony. Although it was designed to foster communal relations and a sense of place, it is a site to visit, not a place to live, and most inhabitants are renters. Seaside's success has also made it an exclusive place. Building lots have tripled in value since its inception. Although Seaside is successful, it is not the working model that critics would like to see. The town has become, Plater-Zyberk states, "a place of polemics."[6]

Sam Kaplan, writing in *Planning,* contends that Seaside provides a "cozy and communal feeling, albeit for persons of a particular aesthetic conceit and income bracket." He finds the traditional town design concept elitist, with "hints of a repressive, dogmatic approach to planning."[7] Similar charges come from two University of Florida professors, Ivonne Audirac and Anne

Shermyen. They view the new movement as a naive attempt to return to the preindustrial age. In the effort to reverse history, the urban designer becomes a manipulative—if not a menacing—social engineer. By limiting private spaces, people are forced into public spaces that could "turn a benign intention into a totalitarian act."[8]

These critics, however, miss one of the major points about Seaside: the environmental issues. When regulations protect endangered ecosystems, the price of land and housing goes up, reducing the amount of available and affordable private space.[9] This combination of economics and ecology has forced municipal governments and private developers to change direction. Throughout Florida, planning commissions and developers have begun to use traditional town planning concepts in an effort to satisfy the GMA and the test of concurrency.[10] At the same time, John Nolen's work has become an increasingly popular field of study for both practitioners and academics.

Seventy years after Nolen called the 1926 National Planning Conference to order in St. Petersburg, the nation's planners returned to Florida. The American Planning Association held the 1996 National Planning Conference in Orlando because it offered an ideal setting to discuss "planning in the real world, the type of suburban and growth management planning 95 percent of APA members are doing."[11] This gathering, like the one in 1926, took time to examine Nolen's ideas. In a session devoted to Nolen, academics, consultants, and public planners looked at his criteria for urban design, the livability of the communities that instituted his plans, and the relevance of his work.[12] Nolen's vision might yet come to pass, but it will "require above all," as Nolen wrote in 1923, "a cordial spirit of cooperation and a public-spirited backing of enterprises for the common good."[13]

Notes

Preface

1. Rutherford H. Platt, "The Ecological City: Introduction and Overview," in *The Ecological City: Preserving and Restoring Urban Biodiversity*, edited by Rutherford H. Platt, Rowan A. Rowntree, and Pamela C. Muick (Amherst, Mass., 1994), 9.

2. George M. Raymond, "The Role of the Physical Planner," in *Planning Theory in the 1980s*, edited by Robert Burchell and George Sternlieb (New Brunswick, N.J., 1978), 3; J. G. Fabos, *Land Use Planning* (New York, 1985), 21–25.

Introduction

1. Stanley Buder, *Visionaries and Planners: The Garden City Movement and the Modern Community* (New York, 1990), viii; J. Nicholas Entrikin, *The Betweenness of Place: Toward a Geography of Modernity* (Baltimore, 1991), 32; David Harvey, *The Condition of Postmodernity* (Cambridge, Mass., 1990), 13, 35.

2. For more on the role of utopian ideals in urban planning, see Thomas A. Reiner, *The Place of the Ideal Community in Urban Planning* (Philadelphia, 1963), 16; Michael Neuman, "Utopia, Dystopia, Diaspora," *Journal of the American Planning Association* 57 (Summer 1991): 344–47; Thomas A. Reiner, "Policy Planning: Environmental and Utopian Aspects," *Architectural Design* 45 (June 1975): 359–62; R. Fishman, *Urban Utopias in the Twentieth Century* (New York, 1977), 3–6.

3. According to Henri Lefebvre, planning involves a "struggle between individualistic and collectivist strategies." Conflicts over planning in a capitalistic society result from the "contradiction between private profit and collective need." Since land is perceived to be an economic commodity for individual use and exploitation, the only way to preserve it for the communal good is through collective controls or socialism. This seemingly irreconcilable contradiction between private profit and collective need stands at the heart of the "urban crisis" that Lefebvre claims is "the fundamental crisis of advanced capitalism" (Peter Saunders, *Social Theory and the Urban Question* [New York, 1981], 153–59). For more information on planning and contradiction, see Richard E. Foglesong, *Planning the Capitalist City* (Princeton, 1986), 233–57; David Harvey, *The Urbanization of Capital* (Baltimore, 1985), 165–84; and introduction to *Two Centuries of American City Planning*, edited by Daniel Schaffer (Baltimore, 1988), 3–8. For a historical example of the conflict between capitalistic values and ecological land planning, see Donald Worster, *Dust Bowl: The Southern Plains in the 1930s* (New York, 1979), 182–209.

4. Lewis Mumford, "The Next Twenty Years in City Planning," *Proceedings of the Nineteenth Conference on City Planning* (Washington, 1927).

Mumford propounded his theory of the relationship between unlimited urban expansion and the deterioration of culture and land in *The Culture of Cities* (1938) and *The City in History* (1961). F. Donald Hughes also provides a study of ancient civilizations that exceeded ecological limitations in *Ecology and Ancient Civilizations* (Albuquerque, N.M., 1975).

5. Albert Fein, *Frederick Law Olmsted and the American Environmental Tradition* (New York, 1972), 68. For a comprehensive examination of Nolen's life and works, see John Hancock, "John Nolen and the American City Planning Movement, 1900–1940" (Ph.D. diss., University of Pennsylvania, 1964).

6. William Wilson, *The City Beautiful Movement* (Baltimore, 1990), 20, 80–87.

7. John Nolen, *New Ideals in the Planning of Cities, Towns, and Villages* (New York, 1919), 7, 10–15, 17–18.

8. James A. Glass, "John Nolen and the Planning of New Towns" (master's thesis, Cornell University, 1984), 3; Nolen to Patrick Geddes, January 10, 1923, Box 76, Nolen Papers (NP), Cornell University Special Collections; John Hancock, "'What Is Fair Must Be Fit': Drawings and Plans by John Nolen, American City Planner," *Lotus International* 50 (1986): 30–45.

9. Walter P. Fuller, *This Was Florida's Boom* (St. Petersburg, 1954); Karl Grismer, *The Story of St. Petersburg* (St. Petersburg, 1948), 150–59; David Nolan, *Fifty Feet in Paradise: The Booming of Florida* (Orlando, 1984), 156–230; George Tindall, "The Bubble in the Sun," *American Heritage* 16 (August 1965): 76–83; James M. Ricci, "Boasters, Boosters, and Boom: Popular Images of Florida in the 1920s," *Journal of Tampa Bay History* 6 (Fall/Winter 1984): 30–55; Frederick Lewis Allen, *Only Yesterday: An Informal History of the 1920s* (New York, 1964), 225–35; John Rothchild, *Up for Grabs: A Trip through Time and Space in the Sunshine State* (New York, 1985), 75–80; Raymond Arsenault, *St. Petersburg and the Florida Dream* (Norfolk, Va., 1987), 185–251.

10. Nolan, *Fifty Feet in Paradise*, 187–88.

11. William Cronon, *Nature's Metropolis* (New York, 1991), 12.

12. John Nolen, *St. Petersburg Today, St. Petersburg Tomorrow* (St. Petersburg, 1923), NP, 11, 13, 14.

13. Donald McCoy, *Calvin Coolidge: The Quiet President* (New York, 1967), 54.

14. Maurice O'Sullivan and Jack C. Lane, eds., *The Florida Reader: Visions of Paradise from 1530 to the Present* (Sarasota, Fla., 1991).

15. Anne Shermyen, ed., *Florida Statistical Abstract* (Gainesville, 1992), 8; Bureau of the Census, *Census of the United States, 1920* (Washington, 1920); Bureau of the Census, *Census of the United States, 1990* (Washington, 1990).

16. James A. Schmid, "Wetlands in the Urban Landscape," in *The Ecological City: Preserving and Restoring Urban Biodiversity*, edited by Rutherford H. Platt, Rowan A. Rowntree, and Pamela C. Muick (Amherst, Mass., 1994), 110–11; Jan P. Lofton, "Rediscovering the Value of Wetlands," *Florida Water* 1 (Fall 1992): 16–18; A. Fernald, ed., *Water Resources Atlas of Florida* (Tallahassee, 1984), 18–19.

17. John O. Simonds, *Earthscape: A Manual of Environmental Planning and Design* (New York, 1978), 81. Also see Mark Derr, *Some Kind of Paradise: A Chronicle of Man and the Land in Florida* (New York, 1989); and Raymond F. Dasmann, *No Further Retreat* (New York, 1971).

18. *Orlando Sentinel*, October 4, 1992. For information on Florida environmental issues, see Linda Lord, ed., *Guide to Florida Environmental Issues* (Winter Park, Fla., 1993); Luther J. Carter, *The Florida Experience: Land and Water Policy in a Growth State* (Baltimore, 1974); Nelson Blake, *Land into Water, Water into Land: A History of Water Management in Florida* (Tallahassee, 1980); Ronald L. Myers and John J. Ewel, "Problems, Prospects, and Strategies for Conservation," in *Ecosystems of Florida*, edited by Ronald L. Myers and John J. Ewel (Orlando, 1990), 619–32.

19. Hancock, "John Nolen and the American City Planning Movement," 399.

20. John DeGrove, *The New Frontier for Land Policy: Planning and Growth Management in the States* (Cambridge, Mass., 1992), 7–31; John Koenig, "Down to the Wire in Florida," *Planning* 56 (October 1990): 4–11.

21. Naisbitt Group, *Pinellas County: Florida's Bellwether at the Crossroads* (St. Petersburg, 1985), 23; R. D. R. Hoffman, "St. Petersburg: The Comeback Continues," *Florida Business* (January 1990): 25; John Naisbitt and Corinne Kupers-Delinger, "Why the Future Belongs to Florida," in Florida Leadership Forum, *Progress or Decline: Issues of Growth Management* (Tallahassee, 1986).

22. Press release, Florida Department of Community Affairs, April 20, 1992.

23. Shermyen, *Florida Statistical Abstract*, 43–48; *1992 Rand McNally Commercial Atlas and Marketing Guide* (Chicago, 1992), 102, 108; Bureau of the Census, *Statistical Abstract of the United States, 1991* (Washington, 1991), 7, 36; Bradley Rice and Richard Bernard, eds., *Sunbelt Cities: Politics and Growth since World War II* (Austin, 1983), 1–30; Naisbitt, *Pinellas County: Florida's Bellwether*, 23.

24. *St. Petersburg Times*, August 18, 1985.

25. Pinellas County Planning Department (PCPD), *Conservation Element of the Pinellas County Comprehensive Plan* (Clearwater, Fla., 1989), 95–108.

26. R. R. Lewis, "Impacts of Dredging in the Tampa Bay Estuary, 1876–1976," in *Proceedings of the Second Annual Conference of the Coastal Society*, edited by E. L. Pruitt (Arlington, Va., 1977); *St. Petersburg Times*, September 1, 1964; PCPD, *The Conservation of Natural Resources Element of the Pinellas County Comprehensive Plan* (Clearwater, Fla., 1980), 105–6.

27. PCPD, *Conservation of Natural Resources Element*, 105–6.

28. PCPD, *Water Supply Element of the Pinellas County Comprehensive Plan* (Clearwater, Fla., 1978), 7–11, 23.

29. Ruth E. Knack, "Repent, Ye Sinners, Repent," *Planning* 55 (August 1989): 6; David Harvey, *The Condition of Postmodernity: An Enquiry into the Origins of Cultural Change* (Cambridge, Mass., 1990), 67.

30. David Mohney and Keller Easterling, *Seaside: Making a Town in America* (Princeton, 1991).

31. Suzanne Sutro and Ronald K. Bednar, "The Roots of Neotraditionalism: The

Planned Communities of John Nolen." Paper delivered at the Conference of American City Planning History, Richmond, Virginia, November 1991.

32. Sim Van der Ryn and Stuart Cowan, *Ecological Design* (Washington, 1996); Jay Parini, "The Greening of the Humanities," *New York Times Magazine* (October 29, 1995), 52.

33. James O'Hear III, "Man the Barricades: A Plea for Sustainable Design," in *Making Towns: Principles and Techniques*, edited by Steven Hurtt (College Park, Md., 1994), 17.

34. Gregg Easterbrook, *A Moment on the Earth: The Coming Age of Environmental Optimism* (New York, 1995), 444–45.

35. John Tibbets, "Takings Law Just Won't Die," *Planning* 62 (February 1996): 16–17.

36. Leo Marx, "The American Ideology of Space," in *Denatured Visions: Landscape and Culture in the Twentieth Century*, edited by Stuart Wrede and William H. Adams (New York, 1991), 62.

37. The concept of city building comes from the work of Harvey Molotch and his study of urban growth. Molotch found that intensifying land uses, or city building, represents the principal political and economic force in any municipality. For those benefiting from this process, the city is a "growth machine" providing income. City building is not so much a question of design as an effort to influence local governments to support growth (Harvey Molotch, "The City as a Growth Machine," *American Journal of Sociology* 82 [Summer 1976]: 309–30). For a review of growth machine theory, see Nico Calavita and Roger Caves, "Planners' Attitudes toward Growth," *Journal of the American Planning Association* 60 (Autumn 1994): 496.

38. Charles L. Harper, *Environment and Society: Human Perspectives on Environmental Issues* (New York, 1996), 294.

Chapter 1

1. *St. Petersburg Times*, February 21, 1914; Robert N. Pierce, *A Sacred Trust: Nelson Poynter and the* St. Petersburg Times (Gainesville, Fla., 1993), 26–29. *St. Petersburg Times Centennial Edition*; Walter Fuller, "The Waterfront," Walter Fuller Papers (FP), University of South Florida Special Collections (USFSC).

2. *St. Petersburg Times Centennial Edition*; Fuller, "The Waterfront."

3. *St. Petersburg Times Centennial Edition*; Fuller, "The Waterfront."

4. Walter Fuller, *St. Petersburg and Its People* (St. Petersburg, 1972), 177; St. Petersburg City Clerk's Office, City Commission File, Drawer 2. (This drawer contains notes on meetings held from 1900 to 1915.)

5. Carol A. Christensen, *The American Garden City and New Town Movement* (Ann Arbor, 1986), 29–44.

6. *St. Petersburg Times*, March 15, 1913, November 25, 1905.

7. William Straub, *History of Pinellas County* (St. Augustine, 1930), 11.

8. Pinellas County Planning Department (PCPD), *The Conservation of Natural*

Resources Element of the Pinellas County Comprehensive Plan (Clearwater, Fla., 1980), 45; Pinellas County Environmental Task Force, *Land Resources Assessment: Pinellas County, Florida* (St. Petersburg, 1974), 1.

9. PCPD, *Conservation of Natural Resources Element*, 108–9; Pinellas County Environmental Task Force, *Land Resources Assessment*, 12–13.

10. PCPD, *Conservation of Natural Resources Element*, 108–9.

11. Jeffrey Carlton, *A Guide to Common Florida Salt Marsh and Mangrove Vegetation* (St. Petersburg, 1975); R. R. Lewis and E. Estevez, *The Ecology of Tampa Bay, Florida: An Estuarine Profile* (Washington, 1988), 65–79.

12. Lewis and Estevez, *Ecology of Tampa Bay*, 61–65; Robert F. Hutton, *The Ecology of Boca Ciega Bay* (St. Petersburg, 1956), 12–18, 47–63.

13. Robert H. Simpson and Herbert Riehl, *The Hurricane and Its Impact* (Baton Rouge, 1981), 221, 244–46; PCPD, *Conservation of Natural Resources Element*, 110. During a hurricane in 1921, the storm surge not only rushed over Clearwater Beach, but returned with such force through the porous underlying rock as to create a vacuum that sucked a number of beach dwellings earthward, collapsing them from the inside (interview with Lee Marsh, Pinellas County Planning Department, Clearwater, Florida).

14. Grismer, *The Story of St. Petersburg*, 19. In 1985, when Hurricane Elena closed to within fifty-five miles of Pinellas County, tides rose six to eight feet above normal and were responsible for most of the hundred million dollars' worth of damages Pinellas residents suffered. For more information on Hurricane Elena, see the *Tampa Tribune*, September 8, 1985.

15. Frank T. Hurley Jr., *A History of Pass-à-Grille and the Gulf Beaches* (St. Petersburg, 1977), 25–27; *St. Petersburg Times*, September 7, 1958. The last major hurricane to strike Pinellas County was in 1921. Winds ranged from up to one hundred miles per hour; tides were 10.5 feet above normal in the gulf and more than six feet above average mean tide in Tampa Bay. This hurricane killed two people and caused $3,000,000 in damages in St. Petersburg. St. Petersburg's municipal pier and the two bridges that linked the beaches to the mainland were also washed away. The three largest buildings on the barrier islands suffered the same fate (Hurley, *A History of the Gulf Beaches*, 124–28; *St. Petersburg Times*, October 26–27, 1921, September 7, 1958, September 17, 1967, July 25, 1984).

16. Grismer, *The Story of St. Petersburg*, 13–16; Charlton W. Tebeau, *A History of Florida* (Coral Gables, 1972), 22–23.

17. Grismer, *The Story of St. Petersburg*, 39; Environmental Task Force, *Land Resources Assessment*, 36.

18. Grismer, *The Story of St. Petersburg*, 16–17, 29. Page S. Jackson, *An Informal History of St. Petersburg* (St. Petersburg, 1962), 31–32.

19. Grismer, *The Story of St. Petersburg*, 38.

20. Ibid.; Environmental Task Force, *Land Resources Assessment*, 36.

21. Grismer, *The Story of St. Petersburg*, 42; PCPD, *Pinellas County Historical Background* (Clearwater, Fla., 1986), 12.

22. Grismer, *The Story of St. Petersburg*, 32–42.

23. "The Healthiest Spot on Earth," *Suniland* (January 1926), USFSC.

24. Ibid.

25. Grismer, *The Story of St. Petersburg*, 74–75.

26. Ibid., 75–103.

27. July 1, 1901, May 4, 1901.

28. *St. Petersburg Times*, November 25, 1905, September 9, 1908; Arsenault, *St. Petersburg and the Florida Dream*, 89.

29. *St. Petersburg Times*, July 12, 1902.

30. Fuller, "The Waterfront;" *St. Petersburg Times*, November 22, 1902, August 1, 1908.

31. *St. Petersburg Times*, November 4, 1905.

32. Ibid., November 25, 1905.

33. Ibid., October 15, 1913.

34. Ibid., July 29 and November 11, 1905, October 15, 1913; Fuller, "The Waterfront."

35. *St. Petersburg Times*, June 25, 1904, October 13, 1913; *Miami Herald*, October 22, 1944.

36. *St. Petersburg Times*, June 25, 1904, October 13, 1913; Fuller, "The Waterfront."

37. Fuller, "The Waterfront."

38. Ibid.

39. *St. Petersburg Times*, August 4, January 12, and January 6, 1906.

40. Ibid., September 22, 1906.

41. Ibid., August 9, 1923; Fuller, "The Waterfront."

42. Fuller, "The Waterfront."

43. Fuller, "The Waterfront"; Henry C. Long, "Laying Out a Model Harbor," *Manufacturers' Record* (July 17, 1913), 55–56; *St. Petersburg Times*, May 31, 1913.

44. Fuller, "The Waterfront."

45. See William Wilson, *The City Beautiful Movement* (Baltimore, 1990); Jon A. Peterson, "The City Beautiful Movement: Forgotten Origins and Lost Meanings," *Journal of Urban History* 2 (August 1976): 415–34.

46. *St. Petersburg Times*, July 13 and 20, 1913.

47. *Miami Herald*, October 22, 1944.

48. *St. Petersburg Times Centennial Edition*.

49. Ibid., March 13, 21, 1913; Fuller, *St. Petersburg and Its People*, 254.

50. *St. Petersburg Times*, March 13, 1913.

51. Ibid., March 6, 1913.

52. Ibid., April 9, 1913.

53. Ibid., May 10, 1913.

54. Hampton Dunn, *Yesterday's St. Petersburg* (Miami, 1973), 22–23.

55. *St. Petersburg Times*, September 13, 1913. For background on Frederick Law Olmsted Jr., see Susan L. Klaus, "Efficiency, Economy, Beauty: The City Planning Reports of Frederick L. Olmsted, Jr., 1905–1915," *Journal of the American Planning Asso-*

ciation 57 (Autumn 1991): 456–70; Daniel S. Smith, "An Overview of Greenways" in *The Ecology of Greenways*, edited by Daniel S. Smith and Paul Cawood (Minneapolis, 1993) 4–5.

56. Straub, *History of Pinellas County*, 62.

57. *St. Petersburg Times*, November 24, 1913.

58. Ibid., January 6, 1914.

59. Ibid., February 10 and 17, 1914.

60. Ibid., February 21, 1914.

61. Katherine C. Ewel and Howard T. Odum, *Cypress Swamps* (Gainesville, Fla., 1984).

62. David Salvesen, *Wetlands: Mitigating and Regulating Development Impacts* (Washington, 1990), 15.

63. Dana F. White, *The Urbanists, 1865–1915* (Westport, Conn., 1989), 97; Charles E. Beveridge, "Frederick Law Olmsted's Theory of Landscape Design," *Nineteenth Century* 3 (Summer 1977): 38–43; David Schuyler, *The New Urban Landscape* (Baltimore, 1986).

64. Olmsted Brothers, *Pinellas County Park Plan* (Boston, 1913); National Association of Olmsted Parks, *Master List of Design Projects of Olmsted Firms (1866–1930)* (Boston, 1987); *St. Petersburg Times*, May 2, 1923, June 9, 1930.

65. Daniel S. Smith, "An Overview of Greenways."

66. Olmsted Brothers, *Pinellas County Park Plan*; *St. Petersburg Times*, July 25, 1914.

67. *St. Petersburg Times*, February 21, 1914.

68. Ibid., July 25, 1914.

69. *Christian Science Monitor*, February 25, 1915.

70. *St. Petersburg Times*, January 11 and October 11, 1914.

71. Luther J. Carter, *The Florida Experience: Land and Water Policy in a Growth State* (Baltimore, 1974), 43.

72. *St. Petersburg Times*, April 8, January 16, July 14, 1915.

73. Wilson, *The City Beautiful Movement*, 77; Arsenault, *St. Petersburg and the Florida Dream*, 89.

74. *St. Petersburg Times*, June 1, 1915, November 14, 1914, January 8, 1915.

75. Ibid., June 9, 1930, May 2 and April 17, 1923, November 11, 1930; Straub, *History of Pinellas County*, 62, 29.

76. *St. Petersburg Times*, November 21 and December 2, 1915.

77. Donald Worster, "Private, Public, Personal: Americans and the Land" in *The Wealth of Nature* (New York, 1993), 95–111.

Chapter 2

1. See introduction, n. 9.

2. Walter P. Fuller, *This Was Florida's Boom* (St. Petersburg, 1954), 7, 24–25.

3. John Nolen, "City Planning in Florida," NP.

4. Texas and Louisiana both passed the fiftieth percentile mark in the 1950 census.

5. Blaine Brownell, *The Urban Ethos in the South* (Baton Rouge, 1975), 1–38.

6. Stein, quoted in John Hancock, "John Nolen and the American City Planning Movement, 1900–1940" (Ph.D. diss., University of Pennsylvania, 1964), 627.

7. Henry F. May, "Shifting Perspectives of the 1920's," *Mississippi Valley Historical Review* 43 (July 1959): 405–27; Ellis W. Hawley, *The Great War and the Search for Modern Order* (New York, 1979), xv, 52–55, 70–91, 126; William Leuchtenberg, *The Perils of Prosperity* (Chicago, 1959), 242; Howard P. Segal, *Technological Utopianism in American Culture* (Chicago, 1986), 7–13, 126–28.

8. *St. Petersburg Times*, May 8, 1923.

9. Paul Berman, *All That Is Solid Melts into Air* (New York, 1982), 93–96.

10. *St. Petersburg Times*, August 9, 1921. Although Straub was not the editor of the newspaper between 1917 and late 1923, he still served as vice president and "kept a close eye on the *Times*' editorial page. In his own mind at least, Straub was always editor in fact, though not in title" (*St. Petersburg Times*, July 25, 1984). Straub regularly contributed editorials on issues—like planning—about which he had strong opinions. The relationship between Straub's correspondence with Nolen and the flamboyant editorials that usually followed also indicate Straub's hand in guiding the paper's pro-planning agenda. Edwin Naugle's (Straub's replacement) writing "displayed none of Straub's fire-eating style and he showed little taste for bitter controversy" (Robert N. Pierce, *A Sacred Trust: Nelson Poynter and the* St. Petersburg Times [Gainesville, Fla., 1993], 39).

11. Sidney Lanier, *Florida: Its Scenery, Climate, and History* (New York, 1975), 13.

12. Elliot J. Mackle Jr., "The Eden of the South: Florida's Image in American Travel Literature and Painting, 1865–1900" (Ph.D. diss., Emory University, 1977), 78–79, 88, 112.

13. Paul Gaston, *The New South Creed* (Baton Rouge, 1970), 1–42.

14. Charlton W. Tebeau, *A History of Florida* (Coral Gables, 1972), 300–305; T. D. Allman, *Miami: City of the Future* (New York, 1987), 144.

15. See Edward Said, *Orientalism* (New York, 1979), 31–73.

16. Mackle, "The Eden of the South," 103; Tebeau, *A History of Florida*, 284–87; David Nolan, *Fifty Feet in Paradise: The Booming of Florida* (Orlando, 1984), 99–111, 120–22; David L. Chandler, *The Astonishing Life and Times of Henry Flagler* (New York, 1986).

17. Mackle, "The Eden of the South," 204.

18. Ibid., 214–16; Lawrence H. Larson, *The Rise of the Urban South* (Lexington, Ky., 1985), 154–56.

19. Frederick Lewis Allen, *Only Yesterday: An Informal History of the 1920s* (New York, 1964), 227.

20. St. Petersburg Chamber of Commerce, "For Your Next Convention, 1923," Pinellas County Historical Museum (PCHM); *St. Petersburg Times*, September 30, 1923.

21. Richard Edmonds, "Florida's Future," *Suniland* (October 1925), 25.

22. Henry S. Commager, *The American Mind* (New Haven, 1940), 422; Michael R. Marrus, ed., *The Emergence of Leisure* (New York, 1974).

23. St. Petersburg Chamber of Commerce, "The Sunshine City, 1923," PCHM.

24. *St. Petersburg Times*, March 22, 1925.

25. Perriton Maxwell, writing in an editorial in *Suniland* (March 1926).

26. *St. Petersburg Times*, March 9, 1925.

27. Ibid., July 25, 1984; Fuller, *Florida's Boom*, 25.

28. Nolan, *Fifty Feet in Paradise*, 188–92.

29. *St. Petersburg Times*, February 8 and January 20, 1923.

30. Ibid., June 22, 1925.

31. Raymond Arsenault, *St. Petersburg and the Florida Dream* (Norfolk, Va., 1987), 138–39.

32. Frank Stockbridge, *Florida in the Making* (New York, 1926), 258.

33. *St. Petersburg Times*, August 16, 1927.

34. Ibid., March 22, 1925, November 3, 1926.

35. Ibid., January 14, 1923.

36. Ibid., January 1, 1925.

37. Ibid., June 16, 1925, January 26, 1923.

38. Ibid., January 10, 1923; St. Petersburg Chamber of Commerce, "Sunshine City, 1926," PCHM.

39. *St. Petersburg Times*, December 4, 1921, July 22, 1922; Fuller, *Florida's Boom*, 15.

40. Fuller, *Florida's Boom*, 63, 15.

41. Ibid., 63; *St. Petersburg Times*, July 6, 1921, April 24, 1923; E. C. Garvin to John Nolen, June 4, 1922, Box 75, NP.

42. Pierce, *A Sacred Trust: Nelson Poynter and the* St. Petersburg Times, 29.

43. St. Petersburg City Clerk's Office, City Commission File, Drawer 2; *St. Petersburg Times*, September 5, 1923.

44. Annie McRae to John Nolen, November 28, 1921; Nolen to McRae, December 3 and 6, 1921, Box 34, NP.

45. Stein, quoted in Hancock, "John Nolen and the American City Planning Movement," 420. For further reading on the RPAA, see Carl Sussman, ed., *Planning the Fourth Migration: The Neglected Vision of the RPAA* (Cambridge, Mass., 1976); Ray Lubove, *Community Planning in the 1920s: The Contribution of the Regional Planning Association of America* (Pittsburgh, 1963); Daniel Schaffer, *Garden Cities for America* (Philadelphia, 1982), 51–77. For an overview of Mumford's vision of planning in the 1920s, see John L. Thomas, "Lewis Mumford, Benton MacKaye, and the Regional Vision," in *Lewis Mumford: Public Intellectual*, edited by Thomas P. Hughes and Agatha C. Hughes (New York, 1990), 66–99.

46. Hancock, "John Nolen and the American City Planning Movement," 9–11; Paul Boyer, *Urban Masses and Moral Order in America, 1820–1920* (Cambridge, Mass., 1978), 228–30.

47. Hancock, "John Nolen and the American City Planning Movement," 9–11.

48. Edward Whiting and William Phillips, "Frederick Law Olmsted, Jr., 1870–1957: An Appreciation of the Man and His Achievements" *Landscape Architecture* 48 (April 1958): 145–48; Susan L. Klaus, "Efficiency, Economy, Beauty: The City Planning Reports of Frederick L. Olmsted, Jr., 1905–1915," *Journal of the American Planning Association* 57 (Autumn 1991): 457–58; John Hancock, "John Nolen: The Background of a Pioneer Planner," in *The American Planner*, edited by Donald Krueckeberg (New York, 1983), 43–49.

49. Cynthia L. Girling and Kenneth I. Helphand, *Yard, Street, Park: The Design of Suburban Open Space* (New York, 1994), 50–54.

50. Robert H. Wiebe, *The Search for Order, 1877–1920* (New York, 1967), 170–76; William M. Ranolle, "Professors, Reformers, Bureaucrats, and Cronies: The Players in *Euclid v. Ambler*," in *Zoning and the American Dream*, edited by Charles M. Haar and Jerold S. Kayden (Chicago, 1989), 33; Christine Boyer, *Dreaming the Rational City* (Cambridge, Mass., 1983), 60–78, 84–108, 118–26.

51. Richard Foglesong, *Planning the Capitalist City* (Princeton, 1986), 3–4; Frederick Law Olmsted Jr., "Introduction," in *City Planning*, edited by John Nolen (New York, 1916), 2.

52. William Wilson, *The City Beautiful Movement* (Baltimore, 1990), 290.

53. Nolen to Patrick Geddes, January 17, 1915, Box 95, NP.

54. John Nolen, "The Place of the Beautiful in the City Plan," *Proceedings of the Fourteenth National Conference on City Planning* (Springfield, Mass., 1922) 133–45.

55. Nolen, "City Planning," 155.

56. Olmsted, "Introduction," 5.

57. David Harvey, "On Planning the Ideology of Planning," in *Planning Theory in the 1980s*, edited by R. W. Burchell and G. Sternlieb (New Brunswick, N.J., 1978), 228; Foglesong, *Planning the Capitalist City*, 168–79.

58. For an account of early planners' difficulties in relating the comprehensive plan to zoning, see Mel Scott, *American City Planning since 1890* (Berkeley, 1969), 144–45; Foglesong, *Planning the Capitalist City*, 225–29; Boyer, *Dreaming the Rational City*, 126–30, 171.

59. Boyer, *Dreaming the Rational City*, 131–36; Hancock, "John Nolen and the City Planning Movement," 163; Olmsted, "Introduction," 3.

60. Robert H. Wiebe, *The Search for Order*, 170–76; Foglesong, *Planning the Capitalist City*, 217–29; Boyer, *Dreaming the Rational City*, 131–36, 153–69.

61. Nolen, quoted in Hancock, "John Nolen and the City Planning Movement," 231.

62. Hancock, "John Nolen and the City Planning Movement," 227.

63. Nolen was instrumental in the passage of the Wisconsin Planning Enabling Act of 1909, the first state enabling act. See Brian F. O'Connell and Dan Dyke, "The Wisconsin Planning Enabling Act of 1909," *Planning History Present* 6 (1992): 1–6.

64. Ray Lubove, *The Urban Community: Housing and Planning in the Progressive Era* (Englewood Cliffs, N.J., 1967), 13–14; John Nolen, "Planning Problems of Industrial

Cities," *Proceedings of the Eleventh National Conference on City Planning* (Chicago, 1919), 30–31; John Nolen, *New Ideals in the Planning of Cities, Towns, and Villages* (New York, 1919), 6, 138.

65. Hancock, "John Nolen and the City Planning Movement," 231, 295, 19–21, 418–31.

66. Ibid., 299, 239–40, 618.

67. Raymond Unwin, "The Overgrown City," *Survey* 49 (October 15, 1922): 85–86; Lubove, *Community Planning in the 1920s*, 49; Walter L. Creese, ed., *The Legacy of Raymond Unwin: A Human Pattern for Living* (Cambridge, Mass., 1967), 109–11.

68. Stanley Buder, *Visionaries and Planners: The Garden City Movement and the Modern Community* (New York, 1990), 87; Peter Calthorpe, "A Short History of Twentieth Century New Towns," in *Sustainable Communities*, edited by Sim Van der Ryn and Peter Calthorpe (San Francisco, 1991), 195.

69. Nolen, *New Ideals in the Planning of Cities, Towns, and Villages*, 40.

70. Ibid., 11.

71. Ibid., 7, 11, 14.

72. Ibid., 10.

73. Ibid., 40–43, 29–30, 53, 90.

74. Ibid., 10.

75. Ibid., 16–18.

76. Ibid., 17–18, 23.

77. Ibid., 16.

78. Ibid., 17–18.

79. James A. Glass, "John Nolen and the Planning of New Towns," (master's thesis, Cornell University, 1984), 3.

80. John Nolen to Patrick Geddes, January 10, 1923, Box 76, NP.

81. John Nolen to Frank Williams, February 8, 1922, Box 76, NP.

82. John Nolen to Frank Williams, March 22, 1922, Box 99, NP.

Chapter 3

1. John Nolen to Lewis Mumford, January 11, 1923, Box 76, NP.

2. John Nolen, *St. Petersburg Today, St. Petersburg Tomorrow* (St. Petersburg, 1923), 11; Lewis Mumford, *The Story of Utopias* (New York, 1922), 267–68.

3. Nolen, *St. Petersburg Today, St. Petersburg Tomorrow*, 11–12.

4. Ibid., 4.

5. Raymond Arsenault, *St. Petersburg and the Florida Dream* (Norfolk, Va., 1987), 202.

6. Louise Weaver, "Florida Vernacular Architecture," St. Petersburg Historical Museum Exhibit (January 21, 1993).

7. *St. Petersburg Times*, March 3, 1922.

8. Nolen, *St. Petersburg Today. St. Petersburg Tomorrow*, 4. For an idea of what the Pinellas landscape looked like in the 1920s see William Straub, *The History of Pinellas*

County (St. Augustine, 1930), 14–15. In 1927 there were over 700,000 citrus trees, which perfumed the air each spring (17).

9. *St. Petersburg Times,* March 4, 1922.

10. Ibid., March 7, 9, 1922; Nolen to J. P. Lynch, April 13, 1923, Box 75, NP.

11. John Nolen, "City Planning in Florida," NP.

12. John Nolen, *Replanning Small Cities* (New York, 1912), 2.

13. NP includes a collection of research materials Nolen used.

14. Nolen to Lew Brown, July 29, 1923, NP.

15. *St. Petersburg Times,* January 23, 1915.

16. Garvin to Nolen, June 4, 1922, Box 75, NP.

17. *St. Petersburg Times,* December 4, 1921; April 4, 1923.

18. Nolen to Straub, July 27, 1922, Box 75, NP; *St. Petersburg Times,* July 22, 1922.

19. *St. Petersburg Times,* July 20, 1913.

20. Ibid., June 10, 1923; Arsenault, *St. Petersburg and the Florida Dream,* 199–200; Karl Grismer, *The Story of St. Petersburg* (St. Petersburg, 1948), 148–49.

21. *St. Petersburg Times,* April 1, March 27, and April 24, 1923.

22. James A. Glass, "John Nolen and the Planning of New Towns," (master's thesis, Cornell University, 1984), 402–3; John Hancock, "John Nolen and the American City Planning Movement, 1900–1940" (Ph.D. diss., University of Pennsylvania, 1964), 295–96; Margaret Wolf, *Kingsport, Tennessee: A Planned American City* (Lexington, Ky., 1987), 38.

23. Nolen, *St. Petersburg Today, St. Petersburg Tomorrow,* 11.

24. Ibid., 11–13.

25. Ibid., 31, 25, 12.

26. John Nolen, *New Ideals in the Planning of Cities, Towns, and Villages* (New York, 1919), 43.

27. Nolen, *St. Petersburg Today, St. Petersburg Tomorrow,* 12.

28. Ibid., 28.

29. John O. Simonds, *Earthscape: A Manual of Environmental Planning and Design* (New York, 1978), 13–17, 263–66; Ian McHarg, *Design with Nature* (Garden City, N.Y., 1969), 105–10.

30. Nolen, *St. Petersburg Today, St. Petersburg Tomorrow,* 28.

31. Ibid., 15, 27; PCPD, *Pinellas County Historical Background* (Clearwater, Fla., 1986), 79; Walter P. Fuller, *This Was Florida's Boom* (St. Petersburg, 1954), 45.

32. Nolen, *St. Petersburg Today, St. Petersburg Tomorrow,* 28.

33. Ibid., 17.

34. Ibid., 18.

35. Ibid., 25.

36. Ibid., 29.

37. Ibid., 14.

38. Ibid., 13–14.

39. Ibid.

40. Ibid.

41. Frank Williams to Nolen, Oct 4, 1922, Box 75, NP.

42. Raymond Arsenault, "City Charters and Forms of Municipal Government in St. Petersburg, 1892–1992" (St. Petersburg, 1992), 2; Luther J. Carter, *The Florida Experience: Land and Water Policy in a Growth State* (Baltimore, 1974), 43.

43. Nolen, *St. Petersburg Today, St. Petersburg Tomorrow*, 20.

44. Straub to Nolen, January 16, 1923, Box 75, NP.

45. Nolen to Straub, January 24, 1923, Box 75, NP. Southern cities found city planning an especially effective and "progressive" governmental device for separating the races. St. Petersburg's plan, however, reflected the people of St. Petersburg's views more than Nolen's. For instance, when planning the new town of Kingsport, Tennessee, Nolen vigorously protested his clients' demands for the construction of a "Negro Village." Although he eventually relented, Nolen tried to soften some of the system's harsher strictures. While the plan's sponsors wanted a rental community for blacks located next to an industrial area, Nolen had a different idea. He designed a pleasant, landscaped neighborhood located on high ground away from the factories and protected from industrial encroachment by stands of oak trees and a winding creek. The plan's sponsors quickly dismissed this proposal. They felt it was "bad to give the colored people such a fine piece of land." Within a few years the black living area was a blighted slum located next to a dye plant (Brownell, *The Urban Ethos in the South*, 182–84; Hancock, "John Nolen and the American City Planning Movement," 466; Wolf, *Kingsport, Tennessee: A Planned American City*, 51–53). In 1926, Nolen followed a similar strategy in a plan for the new town of Venice, Florida. Once again, Nolen's desire to build a segregated yet high-quality community for blacks was deemed impractical and a waste of money (Glass, "John Nolen and the Planning of New Towns," 404).

46. Nolen, *St. Petersburg Today, St. Petersburg Tomorrow*, 29.

47. Ibid., 30.

48. Ibid., 7.

49. Straub to Nolen, August 23, 1922, Box 54, NP.

50. In 1915, voters passed a new charter that replaced the city council with an eight-member commission and a salaried mayor. Although the mayor lacked veto powers, this "strong mayor" format allowed Pulver to set the budget, direct the city's affairs, and appoint or suspend the chief of police, the city attorney, and the fire chief (Arsenault, "City Charters and Forms of Municipal Government," 2).

51. William Leuchtenberg, *The Perils of Prosperity* (Chicago, 1959), 198–99.

52. *St. Petersburg Independent*, August 25, 1923.

53. *St. Petersburg Times*, November 14, 1922.

54. Nolen to Straub, March 7, 1923; Straub to Nolen, March 14, 1923, Box 75, NP.

55. Earle Draper, quoted in Hancock, "John Nolen and the American City Planning Movement," 296.

56. Hancock, "John Nolen and the American City Planning Movement," 234–37.

57. *St. Petersburg Times*, March 30 and April 1, 1923.

58. Ibid.

59. Ibid.

60. After the 1921 hurricane destroyed the existing pier, Brown led a group of businessmen that lent the city $18,000 to rebuild. After construction was completed in 1922, the city's engineers reported that the new pier's pilings had only a few years left. The *St. Petersburg Independent* immediately launched a campaign to build a massive pier that would rival the nation's largest, Atlantic City's famous Steel Pier. Brown pushed his agenda with the same fervor that Straub used to promote planning. When Nolen presented his plan, Brown was receiving pledges for his million-dollar dream (Arsenault, *St. Petersburg and the Florida Dream*, 138; Walter P. Fuller, *St. Petersburg and Its People* [St. Petersburg, 1972], 162).

61. Fuller, *St. Petersburg and Its People*, 156. At this time St. Petersburg Beach occupied only the northern third of the present-day city.

62. *St. Petersburg Times*, March 30, 1923.

63. Ibid., April 1–3, 1923.

64. McRae to Nolen, April 5, 1923, Box 75, NP.

65. *St. Petersburg Times*, April 3, 1923.

66. Nolen to Straub, April 16, 1923, Box 75, NP.

67. Nolen to McRae, May 11, 1923, Box 75, NP.

68. Arsenault, *St. Petersburg and the Florida Dream*, 195; *St. Petersburg Times*, April 17, August 23, 1923.

69. Brian W. Blaesser and Alan C. Weinstein, eds., *Land Use and the Constitution: Principles for Planning Practice* (Chicago, 1989), 16, 8.

70. Chapter 9915, *1923 Florida Statutes*.

71. St. Petersburg City Commission Minutes, June 1923, City Clerk's Office.

72. Nolen to Williams, June 26, 1923, Box 75, NP.

73. *St. Petersburg Times*, June 10, 1923.

74. Ibid., June 21, August 23, September 5, 1923; McRae to Nolen, August 4, 1923, Box 75, NP.

Chapter 4

1. Raymond Arsenault, *St. Petersburg and the Florida Dream* (Norfolk, Va., 1987), 138.

2. *St. Petersburg Times*, June 22 and July 1–4, 1923.

3. Ibid., July 7–10, 1923.

4. Ibid., June 17, 1923.

5. Ibid., June 19, 1923.

6. Ibid., June 20, July 1–7, 1923.

7. Arsenault, *St. Petersburg and the Florida Dream*, 194; *St. Petersburg Times*, August 12, 1923.

8. Karl Grismer, *The Story of St. Petersburg* (St. Petersburg, 1948), 238–39; Walter P. Fuller, *St. Petersburg and Its People*, (St. Petersburg, 1972), 178–83.

9. *St. Petersburg Times*, July 25, 1923, November 11, 1925.

10. Fuller, *St. Petersburg and Its People*, 180–83; *St. Petersburg Times*, May 12, 1927.

11. Grismer, *The Story of St. Petersburg*, 308–10; *St. Petersburg Times*, March 1, 1916.

12. *St. Petersburg Times*, June 22 and July 25, 1923; Walter P. Fuller, *This Was Florida's Boom* (St. Petersburg, 1954), 63; Grismer, *The Story of St. Petersburg*, 156–58.

13. C. M. Hunter, "The Florida Boom," Florida Writers Project (USFSC).

14. *St. Petersburg Times*, August 12, 1923; Fuller, *St. Petersburg and Its People*, 262–63; Farris Bryant, *The Government and Politics of Florida* (Gainesville, Fla., 1957), 128–29.

15. Arsenault, *St. Petersburg and the Florida Dream*, 194; Fuller, *St. Petersburg and Its People*, 262; Grismer, *The Story of St. Petersburg*, 238.

16. *St. Petersburg Times*, July 25, 1923, August 9, 1925.

17. Ibid., August 12, 1923; Fuller, *St. Petersburg and Its People*, 181.

18. *St. Petersburg Independent*, August 21 and 27, 1923.

19. *St. Petersburg Times*, August 23, 1923.

20. Ibid., August 21–29, 1923.

21. Ibid., August 5 and September 5, 1923.

22. Ibid., June 10 and July 24, 1923.

23. Ibid., August 5, 1923.

24. McRae to Nolen, August 4, 1923, Box 75, NP.

25. Justin Hartzog to McRae, August 7, 1923, Box 75, NP.

26. *St. Petersburg Times*, August 23, 1923.

27. Ibid., August 21 and 25, 1923.

28. Ibid., August 22, 1923.

29. Ibid., August 25–26, 1923.

30. Ibid.

31. Ibid., August 29, 1923; *St. Petersburg Independent*, August 29, 1923.

32. *St. Petersburg Independent*, August 28, 1923.

33. Ibid., August 29, 1923.

34. *St. Petersburg Times*, August 29, 1923.

35. Ibid., September 5, 1923.

36. For a history of city planning in Los Angeles, see R. M. Fogelson, *The Fragmented Metropolis: Los Angeles, 1850–1930* (Cambridge, Mass., 1967), 247–72.

37. *St. Petersburg Times*, February 21, 1924.

38. Frank Pulver to Nolen, January 7, 1924, Box 94, NP.

39. *St. Petersburg Times*, May 26, 1927, August 26, 1923; Nolen to J. P. Lynch, April 13 and 17, 1923, Box 75, NP.

40. *St. Petersburg Times*, March 19, 1925, February 28, 1924.

41. *St. Petersburg Times*, February 28, 1924.

42. Ibid., March 5, 1924.

43. John K. Galbraith, *The Culture of Contentment* (Boston, 1992), 20.

44. Jonsberg to Nolen, January 24, 1928, Box 34, NP.

45. Ibid.

46. Charles D. Fox, *Florida in the Making* (New York, 1925), 12.

47. *St. Petersburg Times*, March 21, 1926.

48. Arsenault, *St. Petersburg and the Florida Dream*, 202.

49. *St. Petersburg Times*, May 3, 1925.

50. John Rothchild, *Up for Grabs: A Trip through Time and Space in the Sunshine State* (New York, 1985), 80.

51. Ibid., 78–79; Fuller, *This Was Florida's Boom*, 24–25.

52. Nolan, *Fifty Feet in Paradise*, 200–201; Hancock, "John Nolen and the American City Planning Movement," 152.

53. Grismer, *The Story of St. Petersburg*, 152; *St. Petersburg Times*, March 18 and May 5, 1923.

54. Fuller, *This Was Florida's Boom*, 22; Nolan, *Fifty Feet in Paradise*, 213.

55. David Nolan, *Fifty Feet in Paradise: The Booming of Florida* (Orlando, 1984), 211–14.

56. *St. Petersburg Independent*, June 10, 1925.

57. *St. Petersburg Times*, March 21, 1926.

58. Perriton Maxwell, writing in an editorial in *Suniland* (July 1925).

59. Irving Howe, *A Margin of Hope: An Intellectual Biography* (New York, 1982), 36–38.

60. Blaine Brownell, *The Urban Ethos in the South, 1920–1930* (Baton Rouge, 1975), xix, 39–40, 219.

61. Arsenault, *St. Petersburg and the Florida Dream*, 138.

62. *St. Petersburg Independent*, October 9, 1925.

63. Ibid., February 7, 1924, and October 14, 1923; Grismer, *The Story of St. Petersburg*, 154.

64. Grismer, *The Story of St. Petersburg*, 372–73.

65. *St. Petersburg Times*, March 22, 1925.

66. Richard H. Pells, *Radical Visions, American Dreams: Cultural and Social Thought in the Depression Years* (New York, 1973), 26; Ellis W. Hawley, *The Great War and the Search for Modern Order* (New York, 1979), 136–46; Roderick Nash, *The Nervous Generation* (Chicago, 1970), 126–50.

67. Robert S. Lynd and Helen M. Lynd, *Middletown* (New York, 1929), 496–502.

68. Pells, *Radical Visions, American Dreams*, 27.

69. St. Petersburg Chamber of Commerce, "The Sunshine City, 1926."

70. *St. Petersburg Times*, March 18, 1923.

Chapter 5

1. *St. Petersburg Times*, February 3, March 2, and March 5, 1924.

2. Ibid., March 2, 1924; Walter P. Fuller, *This Was Florida's Boom* (St. Petersburg, 1954), 62–63.

3. *St. Petersburg Times*, April 2, 1926.

4. Straub to Nolen, July 14, 1925, Box 94, NP; City Planning File, December 20, 1924, City Clerk's Office, St. Petersburg.

5. John Hancock, "John Nolen and the American City Planning Movement, 1900–1940" (Ph.D. diss., University of Pennsylvania, 1964), 390–400.

6. *Special Acts of Florida 1925*, Chapter 11046.

7. St. Petersburg City Commission Minutes, June 8, 1925; *St. Petersburg Times*, June 7, 1925; City Planning File, July 13, 1925.

8. Straub to Nolen, August 4, 1925, Box 94, NP.

9. Straub to Nolen, July 14, 1925, Box 94, NP.

10. James A. Glass, "John Nolen and the Planning of New Towns" (master's thesis, Cornell University, 1984), 396–400.

11. Hartzog to Nolen, August 21, 1925, Box 94, NP; *St. Petersburg Times*, November 10, 1925.

12. Straub to Nolen, November 25, 1925, Box 94, NP.

13. *St. Petersburg Times*, November 22, 1925.

14. Planning Board Minutes, November 9, 1925, City Clerk's Office, St. Petersburg; *St. Petersburg Times*, January 9, 1939.

15. Nolen to Straub, September 19, 1925.

16. Flavel Shurtleff to Nolen, Box 6, NP.

17. Mel Scott, *American City Planning since 1890* (Berkeley, 1969), 235.

18. Hancock, "John Nolen and the American City Planning Movement," 400.

19. Fuller, *Florida's Boom*, 13–15, 36–39.

20. Raymond Arsenault, *St. Petersburg and the Florida Dream* (Norfolk, Va., 1987), 199.

21. Frank Jonsberg, "Address of Welcome," in *Planning Problems of Town and Region: Papers and Discussions of the Eighteenth National Conference on City Planning* (St. Petersburg, 1926), 1–4.

22. Frederick L. Olmsted Jr., "The Planning of Pleasure Resort Communities," in *Planning Problems of Town and Region*, 92–104.

23. Nolen was designing a new town at Venice. See Glass, "John Nolen and the Planning of New Towns," 396–404.

24. John Nolen, "New Communities Planned to Meet New Conditions," in *Planning Problems of Town and Region*, 5–16.

25. Mrs. Robert M. Seymour, "A State Plan for Florida," in *Planning Problems of Town and Region*, 197–201.

26. G. Gordon Whitnall, "The Place of the East Coast in a State Plan for Florida," in *Planning Problems of Town and Region*, 204.

27. Ibid., 209.

28. *St. Petersburg Times*, April 2, 1926.

29. "Remarks," *Planning Problems of Town and Region*, 211.

30. *St. Petersburg Times*, April 2, 1926.

31. *St. Petersburg Times*, April 2 and February 3, 1926; Karl Grismer, *The Story of St. Petersburg* (St. Petersburg, 1948), 309.

32. George Tindall, "The Bubble in the Sun," *American Heritage* (August 1965): 110; "Editorial," *Suniland* (October 1925): 80; *St. Petersburg Times*, September 1, 1925;

David Nolan, *Fifty Feet in Paradise: The Booming of Florida* (Orlando, 1984), 211–12; Charlton W. Tebeau, *A History of Florida* (Coral Gables, 1972), 386.

33. R. M. Fogelson, *The Fragmented Metropolis: Los Angeles, 1850–1930* (Cambridge, Mass., 1967), 65, 74.

34. *St. Petersburg Times*, February 3, 1926.

35. Nolan, *Fifty Feet in Paradise*, 211–12.

36. Ibid., 213–14.

37. *St. Petersburg Times*, November 21, 1925.

38. Tebeau, *A History of Florida*, 386–87; Nolan, *Fifty Feet in Paradise*, 212–22.

39. Tindall, "The Bubble in the Sun," 110; Tebeau, *A History of Florida*, 385; *St. Petersburg Times*, November 1–8, 1925, February 1, 1926.

40. Crosley, quoted in Tindall, "The Bubble in the Sun," 111.

41. *St. Petersburg Times*, March 21, 1926.

42. Ibid., March 21 and 24, 1926.

43. Ibid., March 21, 1926.

44. Fuller, *Florida's Boom*, 60.

45. Ibid., 62.

46. *St. Petersburg Independent*, August 2, 1928, November 4, 1924.

47. *St. Petersburg Times*, March 21, 1926.

48. Ibid., August 31, 1926, May 29, 1932; Fuller, *Florida's Boom*, 62–63; Walter P. Fuller, *St. Petersburg and Its People* (St. Petersburg, 1972), 178–79.

49. Fuller, *St. Petersburg and Its People*, 181.

50. Ibid., 179; Fuller, *Florida's Boom*, 63.

51. *St. Petersburg Times*, June 9, 1927.

52. Ibid., May 10–11, 1927.

53. Fuller, *Florida's Boom*, 62.

54. Ibid.

55. *St. Petersburg Times*, December 14, 1927.

56. Ibid., April 10–17, 1927.

57. Ibid., May 10, 1927.

58. Jonsberg to Nolen, January 13, 1927, NP.

59. Jonsberg to Nolen, January 28, 1927; Nolen to Jonsberg, January 31, 1927, Box 34, NP.

60. Nolen to Jonsberg, March 14, 1927, Box 34, NP.

61. Justin Hartzog, *A Report on City Planning Proposals for St. Petersburg, Florida* (Cambridge, Mass., 1927). Henceforward in this chapter, all quoted material is from this report unless otherwise noted.

62. *St. Petersburg Times*, September 21, 1927.

63. Nolen to Jonsberg, April 26, 1927, Box 34, NP.

64. Jonsberg to Nolen, April 23, 1927, Box 34, NP.

65. While a map was drafted for the Tampa Bay Regional Plan, the project never moved any further. Jonsberg to Nolen, June 18, 1927, Box 34, NP.

66. Nolen to Jonsberg, June 22, 1927, NP; Hartzog to Jonsberg, July 29, 1927, Box 34, NP.

67. Hancock, "John Nolen and the American City Planning Movement," 433; Nolen to Jonsberg, August 15, 1927, Box 34, NP.

68. Jonsberg to Nolen, August 18, 1927, Box 34, NP.

69. Ibid., January 24, 1928.

70. Ibid.

71. St. Petersburg Times, December 12 and January 23, 1927.

72. Ibid.

73. St. Petersburg Times, November 21, 1975; Fuller, St. Petersburg and Its People, 179.

74. Nolen to Jonsberg, November 13, 1928, Box 34, NP.

75. Ibid., April 1, 1929.

76. St. Petersburg Times, May 12 and 21, 1929.

77. St. Petersburg Independent, March 29, 1929.

78. Ibid., May 20, 1929.

79. Ibid., August 12, 1929.

80. St. Petersburg Times, August 12 and December 30–31, 1929.

81. Ibid., August 19, 1929, January 1, 1930, December 30, 1929.

82. St. Petersburg Independent, January 1, 1930; Fuller, Florida's Boom, 55; Fuller, St. Petersburg and Its People, 254.

83. Fuller, Florida's Boom, 54.

84. St. Petersburg Times, May 29, 1932, November 21, 1975. St. Petersburg's indiscriminate outlays on public improvements, particularly roads, made it an oddity among American cities. In 1940, 336 miles of paved streets ran through St. Petersburg, and nearly 60 percent—three times the national average—of the city's 11,000 developed acres were occupied by streets. By contrast, Richmond, a city of 190,000, contained only 114 miles of paved streets; Des Moines, a city with 100,000 more residents and a larger area than St. Petersburg, had paved 327 miles of roads. Harland Bartholomew and Associates, St. Petersburg Comprehensive Plan (St. Louis, 1941). Government Publications, Washington University, St. Louis, Missouri.

85. Nolen to Jonsberg, February 2, 1929, and May 21, 1930, Box 34, NP.

86. Jonsberg to Nolen, May 31, 1930, Box 34, NP.

87. St. Petersburg Times, January 9, 1939.

88. Nolen, quoted in Hancock, "John Nolen and the American City Planning Movement," 560; also see page 439.

89. Ordinance Number 773-A, City Commission Minutes, July 1933, City Clerk's Office, St. Petersburg.

90. John Hancock, "The New Deal and American Planning," in Two Centuries of American Planning, edited by Daniel Schaffer (Baltimore, 1988), 221.

91. St. Petersburg Times, December 3, 1976; Arsenault, St. Petersburg and the Florida Dream, 258–60.

92. John Harvey, "Introductory Remarks to Workshop on Proposed 1990 Land Use Plan" (St. Petersburg, 1971), 4.

93. *Laws of Florida 1935*, Chapter 17275, Senate Bill Number 783; *St. Petersburg Times*, July 7, 1936.

94. Arsenault, *St. Petersburg and the Florida Dream*, 258–72.

95. Fuller, *St. Petersburg and Its People*, 185–96.

96. *St. Petersburg Times*, March 20, 1936.

97. Ibid., April 20, 1936.

98. Ibid., September 20, 1936, and January 27, 1929.

99. Hancock, "John Nolen and the American City Planning Movement," 606–7.

Chapter 6

1. Harland Bartholomew and Associates, *St. Petersburg Comprehensive Plan* (St. Louis, 1941). Government Publications, Washington University, St. Louis, Missouri.

2. St. Petersburg City Clerk's Office, City Commission File, Drawer 2.

3. *St. Petersburg Times*, October 6, 1938.

4. Ibid., January 9, 1939.

5. Christopher Silver, *Twentieth Century Richmond: Planning, Politics and Race* (Knoxville, 1984), 160.

6. Bartholomew, *St. Petersburg Comprehensive Plan*. Unless otherwise noted, all quoted material in this section comes from this document.

7. Walter P. Fuller, *St. Petersburg and Its People* (St. Petersburg, 1972), 195.

8. Norman J. Johnston, "Harland Bartholomew: Precedent for the Profession," in *The American Planner*, edited by Donald Krueckeberg (New York, 1983), 280–99; Eldridge Lovelace, *Harland Bartholomew: His Contributions to American Urban Planning* (Urbana, Ill., 1993), 81.

9. Lovelace, *Harland Bartholomew*, 17.

10. Bartholomew did not travel to Europe until after World War II, when he was well along in his career (Lovelace, *Harland Bartholomew*, 92).

11. Harland Bartholomew, *Land Uses in American Cities* (Cambridge, Mass., 1955), 3.

12. Norman J. Johnston, "Harland Bartholomew: His Comprehensive Plans and Science of Planning" (Ph.D. diss., University of Pennsylvania, 1964), 97.

13. Christine Boyer, *Dreaming the Rational City* (Cambridge, Mass., 1983), 154.

14. Lovelace, *Harland Bartholomew*, 19, 35–58, 81–83; Johnston, "Harland Bartholomew: His Comprehensive Plans," 99, 103, 106–8.

15. Harland Bartholomew, *Urban Land Uses* (Cambridge, Mass., 1932), v, 3–5; Lovelace, *Harland Bartholomew*, 35–37, 81.

16. Bartholomew, *Urban Land Uses*, 3–5.

17. Ibid.

18. Johnston, "Harland Bartholomew: His Comprehensive Plans," 103, 106–8.

19. Lewis Mumford, "The Next Twenty Years in City Planning," *Proceedings of the Nineteenth Conference on City Planning* (Washington, 1927), 47; Carl Abbott, *Portland:*

Planning, Politics, and Growth in a Twentieth Century City (Lincoln, Nebr., 1983), 104; Blaine Brownell, *The Urban Ethos in the South, 1920–1930* (Baton Rouge, 1975), 179.

20. Forests covered 95,000 acres of the peninsula, and there were 732 farms covering 28,607 additional acres (Pinellas County Planning Department [PCPD], *Pinellas County Historical Background* [Clearwater, Fla., 1986], 45–47).

21. William Straub, *The History of Pinellas County* (St. Augustine, 1930), 13.

22. Walter Fuller to Nelson Poynter, November 9, 1943, FP.

23. Robert N. Pierce, *A Sacred Trust: Nelson Poynter and the* St. Petersburg Times (Gainesville, Fla. 1993), 261.

24. Nelson Poynter to Walter Fuller, October 21, 1943, FP.

25. Walter Fuller to Nelson Poynter, November 9, 1943, FP.

26. Ibid.

27. Nelson Poynter to Walter Fuller, November 11, 1943, FP.

28. Pierce, *A Sacred Trust: Nelson Poynter and the* St. Petersburg Times, 134.

29. Fred Bair, "Batting Average for Prophets," *Newsletter of Florida Planning and Zoning* 7 (March 1956): 2.

30. Fred Bair, "Planning News," *Newsletter of Florida Planning and Zoning* 5 (July 1954): 6; Raymond Arsenault, *St. Petersburg and the Florida Dream* (Norfolk, Va., 1987), 310–11.

31. Arsenault, *St. Petersburg and the Florida Dream*, 308; Fuller, *St. Petersburg and Its People*, 198–224.

32. PCPD, *Pinellas County Historical Background*, 43.

33. James Cobb, *The Selling of the South: The Southern Crusade for Industrial Development, 1936–1980* (Baton Rouge, 1985), 92–93; Bureau of the Census, *Census of the United States, 1940* (Washington, 1940); Fuller, *St. Petersburg and Its People*, 216–17.

34. U.S. Department of Commerce, *1960 City and County Data Book* (Washington, 1960), 484–86.

35. Louise Weaver, "Florida Vernacular Architecture," St. Petersburg Historical Museum Exhibit (January 21, 1993); Arsenault, *St. Petersburg and the Florida Dream*, 309; David Rochlin, "The Front Porch," in *Home Sweet Home: American Domestic Architecture*, edited by Charles W. Moore, Kathryn Smith, and Peter Becker (New York, 1983), 24–29.

36. Cynthia L. Girling and Kenneth I. Helphand, *Yard, Street, Park: The Design of Suburban Open Space* (New York, 1994), 83; Pierce, *A Sacred Trust: Nelson Poynter and the* St. Petersburg Times, 134; PCPD, *Pinellas County Historical Background*, 45–47; Straub, *The History of Pinellas County*, 14–15.

37. Alex Kreiger and William Lennertz, eds., *Andres Duany and Elizabeth Plater-Zyberk: Towns and Town-Making Principles* (New York, 1991), 7.

38. Michael Southworth and Eran Ben-Joseph, "Street Standards and the Shaping of Suburbia," *Journal of the American Planning Association* 61 (Winter 1995): 77–78.

39. Pierce, *A Sacred Trust: Nelson Poynter and the* St. Petersburg Times, 135.

40. *St. Petersburg Times*, August 18, 1985.

41. Walter P. Fuller, *This Was Florida's Boom* (St. Petersburg, 1954), 14–15.

42. Jan P. Lofton, "Rediscovering the Value of Wetlands," *Florida Water* 1 (Fall 1992): 19.

43. The rate of runoff increased by 74 to 86 percent. PCPD, *Conservation Element of the Pinellas County Comprehensive Plan* (Clearwater, Fla., 1989), 139; Jonathan M. Harbor, "A Practical Method for Estimating the Impact of Land Use Change on Surface Runoff, Groundwater Recharge and Wetland Hydrology," *Journal of the American Planning Association* 60 (Winter 1994): 103–4. The sixteen-county Tampa Bay Region has lost 35,000 acres of wetlands because of groundwater depletion. *Orlando Sentinel,* April 10, 1995; "Water Woes," Florida Public Radio, April 11, 1995.

44. PCPD, *Pinellas County Historical Background,* 63b.

45. Fred Bair, "The Future," *Newsletter of Florida Planning and Zoning* 7 (November 1956): 4.

46. Telephone interview with John Harvey, August 4, 1990. Harvey was hired after St. Petersburg received federal matching grants for "general urban planning."

47. Pierce, *A Sacred Trust: Nelson Poynter and the* St. Petersburg Times, 239–40.

48. Bair, "Rezone the City and Broaden the Tax Base," *Newsletter of Florida Planning and Zoning* 7 (February 1956): 4.

49. Ibid. (March 1956), 3–6.

50. Interview with John Harvey; St. Petersburg Planning Department (SPPD), *1974 Conceptual Plan* (St. Petersburg, 1974), 14.

51. *St. Petersburg Times,* April 13, 1958; LeRoy Collins Papers, USFSC.

52. *St. Petersburg Times,* April 3, 1957.

53. John Harvey, "Introductory Remarks, Proposed 1990 Land Use Plan" (St. Petersburg, January 1974), 4.

Chapter 7

1. Samuel P. Hays, *Beauty, Health and Permanence: Environmental Politics in the United States, 1955–85* (New York, 1987), 35.

2. Ibid., 1–39.

3. Donald Worster, *Nature's Economy: A History of Ecological Ideas* (New York, 1985), 205–20. For an analysis of the evolution of ecological theory, see William Cronon, *Changes in the Land: Indians, Colonists and the Ecology of New England* (New York, 1983), 8–13; Donald Worster "Ecology of Order and Chaos," *Environmental Review* 14 (Spring 1990): 1–18.

4. Robert F. Hutton, *The Ecology of Boca Ciega Bay, with Special Reference to Dredging and Filling Operations* (St. Petersburg, 1956), 7.

5. Nelson Blake, *Land into Water, Water into Land: A History of Water Management in Florida* (Tallahassee, 1980), 38–59.

6. The problem of filling is first documented in *Florida Water Resources Study Commission Report on Water Problems* (Tallahassee, 1956).

7. Tom Wagy, *Governor LeRoy Collins of Florida: Spokesman for the New South* (University, Ala. 1985), 74–83, 120–43.

8. Sheldon Plager and Frank Maloney, *Controlling Waterfront Development* (Gainesville, Fla., 1968), 30–31.

9. Telephone interview with Ney Landrum, August 7, 1990.

10. John Rothchild, *Up for Grabs: A Trip through Time and Space in the Sunshine State* (New York, 1985), 33.

11. *St. Petersburg Times*, March 13, 1957.

12. Ibid., February 13, 1957. The Pinellas County Commission also served as the Pinellas Water and Navigation Control Authority by a special act of the state legislature, passed in 1955.

13. Robert N. Pierce, *A Sacred Trust: Nelson Poynter and the* St. Petersburg Times (Gainesville, Fla., 1993), 261.

14. *St. Petersburg Times*, February 22, 1956.

15. Ibid.; Pierce, *A Sacred Trust: Nelson Poynter and the* St. Petersburg Times, 260–61.

16. *St. Petersburg Times*, February 22, 1956.

17. Hutton, *The Ecology of Boca Ciega Bay*, 7–9.

18. According to E. O. Wilson, "The loss of a keystone species is like a drill accidentally striking a power line. It causes lights to go out all over" (Wilson, in G. Tyler Miller, *Living in the Environment* [Belmont, Calif., 1994], 101).

19. Interview with Kenneth Woodburn, August 6, 1990; Hutton, *The Ecology of Boca Ciega Bay*, 81.

20. Rothchild, *Up for Grabs*, 32.

21. Plager and Maloney, *Controlling Waterfront Development*, 13.

22. *St. Petersburg Times*, April 3, 1957.

23. Ibid., March 6, 1957.

24. Ibid.; Rothchild, *Up for Grabs*, 83–103.

25. Rothchild, *Up for Grabs*, 84–86; Jonathan Raban, "The Gaudy Green Eden," in Florida Leadership Forum, *Progress or Decline: Issues of Growth Management* (Tallahassee, 1986), 181–86.

26. Rothchild, *Up for Grabs*, 96.

27. *St. Petersburg Times*, April 12, 1957.

28. Ibid., October 13, 1958.

29. Ibid., April 14, 1957.

30. Ibid., May 17 and June 5, 1957.

31. Plager and Maloney, *Controlling Waterfront Development*, 26–39.

32. All quoted material is from Pinellas County Commission, *Excerpts from Furen–Ratner Fill Hearings* (Clearwater, Fla., 1957), unless otherwise noted.

33. Woodburn interview, August 6, 1990.

34. *St. Petersburg Times*, January 7, 1958.

35. Ibid., September, 28, 1958.

36. Ibid., January 17, 1958.

37. Ibid., January 9, 1959.

38. Ibid., February 27, July 10, and August 19, 1959.

39. Roy R. Lewis, "Impacts of Dredging in the Tampa Bay Estuary, 1876–1976," in *Conference of the Coastal Society: Time Stressed Environments*, edited by E. L. Pruitt (Arlington, Va., 1977), 47–51; J. L. Taylor and C. H. Saloman, "Some Effects of Hydraulic Dredging and Coastal Development in Boca Ciega Bay," *U.S. Fish and Wildlife Service Bulletin* 67 (February 1968): 213–41.

40. Blake, *Land into Water*, 197; Luther J. Carter, *The Florida Experience: Land and Water Policy in a Growth State* (Baltimore, 1974), 53–54.

41. Pinellas County Planning Department (PCPD), *The History of Pinellas County* (Clearwater, Fla., 1986), 44; *St. Petersburg Independent*, May 23, 1969.

42. Joseph Siry, *Marshes on the Ocean Shore* (College Station, Tex., 1984), 178–82.

43. Taylor and Saloman, "Hydraulic Dredging and Coastal Development"; *St. Petersburg Times*, May 5 and November 30, 1966.

44. Rutherford H. Platt, *Land Use Control: Geography, Law, and Public Policy* (Englewood Cliffs, N.J., 1991), 330.

45. *Zabel v Tabb*, 430 F2d 199 (1970).

46. *St. Petersburg Times*, March 28, 1970.

47. Tampa Bay Regional Planning Council, *The Future of Tampa Bay* (St. Petersburg, 1985), 151–56.

48. *St. Petersburg Times*, February 12, 1985; *St. Petersburg Independent*, April 15, 1986; R. R. Lewis and E. Estevez, *The Ecology of Tampa Bay, Florida: An Estuarine Profile* (Washington, 1988), 89–127.

49. Telephone interview with former Florida governor LeRoy Collins, July 11, 1990.

Chapter 8

1. John Egerton, *The Americanization of Dixie* (New York, 1974), 3–13.

2. James Cobb, *The Selling of the South: The Southern Crusade for Industrial Development, 1936–1980* (Baton Rouge, 1985), 229–53; James Cobb, *Industrialization and Southern Society, 1877–1984* (Lexington, Ky., 1984), 121–35; Charles P. Roland, *The Improbable Era: The South since World War II* (Lexington, Ky., 1975), 434–53.

3. Egerton, *The Americanization of Dixie*, 13.

4. Pinellas County Planning Department (PCPD), *Water Supply Element of the Pinellas County Comprehensive Plan* (Clearwater, Fla., 1978), 7, 23.

5. Ibid., 9; John DeGrove, *The New Frontier for Land Policy: Planning and Growth Management in the States* (Cambridge, Mass., 1992), 8.

6. St. Petersburg Citizens' Goals Committee, *Citizens' Goals Report* (St. Petersburg, 1973), 1–5.

7. *St. Petersburg Times*, July 23, 1973.

8. Nelson Blake, *Land into Water, Water into Land: A History of Water Management in Florida* (Tallahassee, 1980), 287; T. R. Alexander and A. G. Crook, "Recent Vegetational Changes in South Florida," in *Environments of South Florida: Present and Past II*, edited by J. P. Gleason (Coral Gables, 1984), 199–210; J. J. Ewel, "Invasibility:

Lessons from South Florida," in *Ecology of Biological Invasions of North America and Hawaii*, edited by H. Mooney and J. Drake (New York, 1986).

9. See articles by James A. Kushlan, Robert J. Livingston, William E. Odom and Carole C. McIvor, and Clay L. Montague and Richard G. Wiegert in *Ecosystems of Florida*, edited by Ronald L. Myers and John J. Ewel (Orlando, 1990), 357–63, 568–72, 545, 512–16.

10. Jacob B. Stowers, "Water Wars: Will They Ever End?" in Florida Chamber of Commerce, *Growth Management Short Course* (Tallahassee, 1995), 562–64; Blake, *Land into Water*, 289–90.

11. Luther J. Carter, *The Florida Experience: Land and Water Policy in a Growth State* (Baltimore, 1974), 118–24; Fred Ward, "The Imperiled Everglades," *National Geographic* (January 1972): 1–27.

12. Arthur Marshall, "South Florida—A Case Study in Carrying Capacity." Paper delivered to the American Association for the Advancement of Science, Washington, December 29, 1972, 1.

13. Askew, quoted in John DeGrove, *Land, Growth and Politics* (Washington, 1984), 111.

14. The Florida Audubon Society had the largest membership, followed by the Sierra Club, the Florida Defenders of the Environment, and the Florida Conservation Foundation.

15. Tom Ankersen, "Coping with Growth: The Emergence of Environmental Policy in Florida" (master's thesis, University of South Florida, 1983), 62; DeGrove, *The New Frontier for Land Policy*, 10; Carter, *The Florida Experience*, 41–55.

16. Carter, *The Florida Experience*, 125–32; DeGrove, *Land, Growth and Politics*, 99–176; Ankersen, "Coping with Growth," 40–82.

17. Bob Graham, "A Quiet Revolution: Florida's Future on Trial," *Florida Naturalist* 45 (October 1972): 147; DeGrove, *Land, Growth and Politics*, 106–126. For an overview of the "Quiet Revolution," see F. Bossleman and D. Callies, *The Quiet Revolution in Land Use Controls* (Washington, 1971).

18. Planning Advisory Service, *Urban Growth Management Systems* (Chicago, 1975), 19; Stowers, "Water Wars: Will They Ever End?" 562; *St. Petersburg Times*, November 3, 1973; PCPD, *Water Supply Element*; Carter, *The Florida Experience*, 133.

19. Ankersen, "Coping with Growth," 71.

20. John Harvey to Daniel W. O'Connell, May 23, 1973; Donella H. Meadows et al., *The Limits to Growth: A Report for the Club of Rome's Project on the Predicament of Mankind* (New York, 1972).

21. Carter, *The Florida Experience*, 40.

22. *St. Petersburg Times*, September 21, 1972.

23. Ibid., November 11–15, 1973; Blake, *Land into Water*, 239–41.

24. *St. Petersburg Times*, November 11 and 22, 1973.

25. Ibid., November 22, 1973.

26. Ibid., July 23, 1973.

27. Ibid.

28. Ibid., October 13, 1976.

29. Ibid., October 16, 1973; Planning Advisory Service, *Urban Growth Management Systems*, 20.

30. *St. Petersburg Times*, October 31, 1973; Pinellas County Administrator, *Position Statement No. 2: Resource Needs and Managed Growth for Pinellas County* (Clearwater, Fla., October 30, 1973).

31. The plan for Ramapo, New York, was the primary focus of study. In November 1973, Robert Freilich, one of the authors of the Ramapo plan, spent several days working with Pinellas officials on "a policy of controlled growth" (*St. Petersburg Times*, November 2, 1973).

32. St. Petersburg Planning Department (SPPD), *1974 Conceptual Plan*; SPPD, *1982 Land Use Plan*, 1.

33. John B. Harvey, "Interim Growth Policy for St. Petersburg" (November 2, 1973).

34. Ibid.

35. Welford Sanders, *The Cluster Subdivision: A Cost-Effective Approach* (Chicago, 1980).

36. U.S. Constitution, amend. 5; Rutherford H. Platt, *Land Use Control: Geography, Law, and Public Policy* (Englewood Cliffs, N.J., 1991), 227–34; Richard J. Roddewig and Christopher J. Duerksen, *Responding to the Takings Challenge* (Chicago, 1989); Brian W. Blaesser and Alan C. Weinstein, eds., *Land Use and the Constitution: Principles for Planning Practice* (Chicago, 1989).

37. John Harvey, "Introductory Remarks to Workshop on Proposed 1990 Land Use Plan," (St. Petersburg, 1971), 1.

38. John Harvey to Hendrix Hearn, January 11, 1973.

39. *St. Petersburg Times*, June 16, 1973; Environmental Task Force, *Land Resources Assessment* (St. Petersburg, 1974), 1.

40. The precedent-setting case in growth management at this time was New York Court of Appeals (State Supreme Court) *Golden v Township of Ramapo*, 285 NE2d 291. For a ruling against population caps, see *Boca Raton v Boca Villas Corp.*, 371 So2d 254.

41. Ian McHarg, *Design with Nature* (New York, 1969); William Thompson, "A Natural Legacy: Ian McHarg and His Followers," *Planning* 57 (November 1991): 14–20; Ian McHarg, "Mr. McHarg's Opus," *Planning* 62 (May 1996): 12–13.

42. McHarg, *Design with Nature*, 55–56.

43. SPPD, *1974 Conceptual Plan*. All quoted material is from this document unless otherwise specified.

44. John Nolen, *St. Petersburg Today, St. Petersburg Tomorrow* (St. Petersburg, 1923), 18.

45. *St. Petersburg Independent*, February 28, 1974; *St. Petersburg Times*, September 2, 1975.

46. *St. Petersburg Times*, March 21, 1974.

47. "St. Petersburg Votes to Exile," *Florida Trend* 17 (May 1974): 95.

48. *St. Petersburg Times*, March 22–31, 1974.

49. Ankersen, "Coping with Growth," 94.

50. SPPD, *Vision for a Decade* (St. Petersburg, 1984), 2–3; *St. Petersburg Times*, September 28, 1975.

51. DeGrove, *Land, Growth and Politics*, 120.

52. SPPD, *Citizen Participation* (March 1989), 2.

53. SPPD, *Vision for a Decade*, 1–5; on the costs of growth management, see David E. Dowall, *The Suburban Squeeze* (Berkeley, Calif., 1984), 1–13.

54. *St. Petersburg Times*, October 13, 1974.

55. Ibid.

56. SPPD, *Land Use Plan Update* (St. Petersburg, 1982), 14.

57. SPPD, *1974 Conceptual Plan*, 25–26.

58. *St. Petersburg Times*, October 13, 1976, and September 28, 1975.

59. *St. Petersburg Times*, September 28, 1975.

60. Ibid.

61. Ibid., October 13, 1976.

62. Ibid., November 11, 1975.

63. Wisconsin Supreme Court, 210 NW2d, at 770–71.

64. Blaesser and Weinstein, *Land Use and the Constitution*, 81–83.

65. *St. Petersburg Times*, October 10, 1976.

66. Ibid., October 13, 1976, October 3, 1975.

67. Ibid., October 12, 1976.

68. The planning staff used the standards set forth in Urban Land Institute, *Community Builders Handbook* (Washington, 1968), 264–67.

69. John Harvey, "The Need to Establish a Growth Policy for Pinellas County," County Planning Workshop, September 29, 1971; PCPD, "Conceptual Plan Analysis" (Fall 1978). The staff estimated that approximately 25 percent of urban areas in Pinellas are utilized for rights-of-way. Given parking demands, a figure of 25 percent of paved land may be conservative.

70. PCPD, *Pinellas Planning Council Annual Report, 1978–79* (Clearwater, Fla., 1979).

71. *St. Petersburg Times*, March 21–22, 1978, June 13, 1975.

72. Ibid., June 24, 1975.

73. Ibid., April 9, 1975.

74. PCPD, *The Conservation of Natural Resources Element of the Pinellas County Comprehensive Plan* (Clearwater, Fla., 1980), 5.

75. *St. Petersburg Times*, January 20, 1988.

76. Orange County Conservation and Recreation Lands Committee, *Land Acquisition and Implementation Strategies* (Orlando, 1991), appendix D.

77. Planning Advisory Service, *Urban Growth Management Systems*; Lawrence B. Burrows, *Growth Management: A Planner's Perspective* (New York, 1981).

78. *St. Petersburg Times*, March 21–22, 1978.

79. PCPD, *Water Supply Element*, 23.

80. *St. Petersburg Times*, March 21–22, 1978.

81. PCPD, *Conservation Element*, 265.

82. DeGrove, *The New Frontier for Land Policy*, 10; Douglas Strong, *Tahoe: An Environmental History* (Lincoln, Nebr., 1984), 195–200; Michael Hough, *Out of Place: Restoring Identity to the Regional Landscape* (New Haven, Conn., 1990), 84.

Chapter 9

1. St. Petersburg Planning Department (SPPD), *1983 St. Petersburg Land Use Plan* (St. Petersburg, 1983), 10.

2. SPPD, *Land Use Plan Update* (St. Petersburg, 1982), 101–2; David Salvesen, *Wetlands: Mitigating and Regulating Development Impacts* (Washington, 1990), 50–52.

3. Pinellas County Commissioners, "Work Session Agenda," October 6, 1987; telephone interview with Ellyn Kadel, manager, Pinellas County Real Estate Management Division.

4. Will Abberger, "Growth Management through Land Acquisition," in *Balanced Growth: A Planning Guide for Local Government*, edited by John DeGrove (Washington, 1991), 66–68; Gladding and Lopez, "Good Management Planning," *Florida Public Lands* 1 (Orlando, Fla., 1994): 1–3; Pinellas County Planning Department (PCPD), *Pinellas Gazette* (Summer 1993): 1–3; Institute for Environmental Studies at the University of South Florida (IESUSF), *Brooker Creek Management Plan* (Tampa, 1995).

5. Florida Department of Environmental Protection, *Preservation 2000: A Ten-Year Land Acquisition Plan* (Tallahassee, 1994), 3–8; "Preservation 2000 May Lose a Chunk of Budget," *Orlando Sentinel*, February 17, 1995.

6. *Florida Statutes*, § 373.59.

7. PCPD, *Pinellas Gazette*, 1.

8. IESUSF, *Brooker Creek Management Plan*, 13; see also William Cronon, *Changes in the Land: Indians, Colonists and the Ecology of New England* (New York, 1983), 131–32.

9. IESUSF, *Brooker Creek Management Plan*, 22–41.

10. Pinellas Trail, "The History of the Pinellas Trail," *On the Trail* (Summer 1993); Pinellas County Parks Department, "The Pinellas Trail," brochure (1993).

11. Charles Little, *Greenways for America* (Baltimore, 1990), 4–5.

12. Taped interview with Keith Bergstrom, April 11, 1993.

13. Charles A. Flink and Robert M. Searns, *Greenways: A Guide to Planning, Design, and Development* (Washington, 1993), 56, 88; Pinellas Trail, *On the Trail* (Summer 1993); "The Pinellas Trail," *Planning* 58 (December 1992): 48.

14. *St. Petersburg Times*, March 21, 22, 1978.

15. Lisa Wormser, "Enhancements: Getting Up to Speed," *Planning* 61 (September 1995): 10–14; interview with Linda Chapin, March 17, 1994; interview with Forrest Michael, Florida RTC, March 18, 1994.

16. Pinellas Trail, *On the Trail*.

17. Pinellas County Parks Department, "The Pinellas Trail."

18. Environmental Protection Agency, "A Water Success Story" (Washington, 1977).

19. *Orlando Sentinel*, March 30, 1994.

20. Jacob B. Stowers, "Water Wars: Will They Ever End?" in Florida Chamber of Commerce, *Growth Management Short Course* (Tallahassee, 1995), 562; Karen E. Jones, "Local Residents Getting a Sinking Feeling over Water Scarcity." University of South Florida, Geography Department (March 1996).

21. *Orlando Sentinel*, April 10, 1995; "Water Woes," Florida Public Radio, April 11, 1995.

22. *St. Petersburg Times*, January 10, 1985.

23. PCPD, *Pinellas County Historical Background* (Clearwater, Fla., 1986), 66.

24. *Orlando Sentinel*, November 5 and 11, 1990; John N. Simons, "Mercury in the Everglades," *Florida Naturalist* 64 (Spring 1991): 7–9; Florida Department of Environmental Regulation, "Mercury, Largemouth Bass, and Water Quality: A Preliminary Report" (Tallahassee, 1990); Carl J. Waters and John W. Huckabee, eds., *Mercury Pollution: Integration and Synthesis* (Boca Raton, Fla., 1994).

25. F. Probst, *The Governor's Task Force on Urban Growth Patterns* (Tallahassee, 1989).

26. Stowers, "Water Wars: Will They Ever End?" 562–63.

27. R. R. Lewis and E. Estevez, *The Ecology of Tampa Bay, Florida: An Estuarine Profile* (Washington, 1988), 114.

28. SPPD, *Conservation Element: Technical Support Document* (St. Petersburg, 1989), 16–18; Deborah Gordon, *Steering a New Course: Transportation, Energy, and the Environment* (Washington, 1991), 25.

29. Carl Hiaasen, *Tourist Season* (New York, 1986), 24.

30. *Tampa Tribune*, March 6, 1985.

31. *St. Petersburg Times*, January 20, 1988.

32. John DeGrove, *The New Frontier for Land Policy: Planning and Growth Management in the States* (Cambridge, Mass., 1992), 9–10.

33. Ibid., 7; John DeGrove, "Introduction," in *Balanced Growth: A Planning Guide for Local Government*, xiii.

34. Donald Connors, "State and Regional Planning: Summary of Selected Recent Acts and Initiatives," in *State and Regional Initiatives for Managing Development*, edited by D. Porter (Washington, 1992), 228.

35. C. Simeon, "Growth Management in Florida: An Overview and Brief Critique," in *State and Regional Initiatives for Managing Development*, edited by D. Porter (Washington, 1992), 43.

36. John DeGrove and Julian Juergensmeyer, eds., *Perspectives on Florida's Growth Management Act of 1985* (Cambridge, Mass., 1986); Ivonne Audirac, A. Shermyen, and M. Smith, "Ideal Urban Form and Visions of the Good Life: Florida's Growth Management Dilemma," *Journal of the American Planning Association* 56 (Autumn 1990): 470–82; Woody Price, "Florida's Growth Management Act," and John

DeGrove, "Growth Management: What It Portends for the Future," in *Liveable Cities for Florida's Future* (Tallahassee, 1988), 15–19, 37. John Koenig, "Down to the Wire in Florida," *Planning* 56 (October 1990): 4–9.

38. SPPD, *Recreation and Open Space Technical Support Document* (St. Petersburg, 1989), 61.

39. R. D. R. Hoffmann, "St. Petersburg: The Comeback Continues," *Florida Business* (January 1990): 24–29; SPPD, *Intown Redevelopment Plan* (St. Petersburg, 1982).

40. *St. Petersburg Times*, August 21, 1988.

41. Hoffmann, "St. Petersburg: The Comeback Continues," 25–27, "Tampa Bay," *Florida Trend* 34 (April 1992): 71–72.

42. Martin J. Normile, "The Bay Plaza Program," *Urban Land* 48 (January 1989): 14–17.

43. The Bay Plaza Company, *Final Plan* (St. Petersburg, 1988).

44. Ibid.

45. The Bay Plaza development was styled after the Country Club Plaza, built by J. C. Nichols in Kansas City during the 1920s. Nichols worked with John Nolen before building the plaza. William S. Worley, *J. C. Nichols and the Shaping of Kansas City* (Columbia, Mo., 1990), 303, 237.

46. *St. Petersburg Times*, August 21, 1988.

47. Save Our St. Petersburg (SOS), "Issues" 1 (July 1988): 1.

48. Ibid., 4–5.

49. Ibid., 9–10.

50. *St. Petersburg Times*, August 21, 1988; Ronald Thomas, *Taking Charge: How Communities Are Planning Their Futures* (Washington, 1988).

51. *St. Petersburg Times*, August 21, 1988.

52. "Tampa Bay," *Florida Trend* (April 1992), 72.

53. "Tampa Bay," *Florida Trend* (April 1993), 70.

54. "Tampa Bay," *Florida Trend* (April 1992), 72.

55. "Tampa Bay," *Florida Trend* (April 1993), 70.

56. Richard O'Brien, "Scorecard," *Sports Illustrated* (November 29, 1992).

57. SPPD, *Land Use Plan Update* (St. Petersburg, 1982), 198.

58. This figure is derived from the city's 1982 estimates for boulevard landscaping and acquisition of rights-of-way. The original boulevard plan called for transit lanes as well. Since bicycle lanes require only ten-foot rights-of-way, the costs would fluctuate in relation to right-of-way acquisition. According to the city's estimates, it would have cost between $750,000 and $1,000,000 per mile to construct boulevards (SPPD, *Land Use Plan Update*, 198–99). Federal ISTEA funding and matching state funds, which helped construct the Pinellas Trail, would have been available for this project as well.

59. Figures are from the Pinellas County Real Estate Management Division.

60. World Commission on Environment and Development, *Our Common Future* (New York, 1987), 1–42.

61. Daniel Boorstin, *The Image; Or, What Happened to the American Dream?* (New York, 1962), 6.

62. PCPD, *Pinellas County Historical Background*, 45–47; PCPD, *Future Land Use Element* (Clearwater, Fla., 1989), 12, 163.

63. Orange County CARL Committee, *Land Acquisition and Implementation Strategies*, (Orlando, 1991), appendix D.

64. J. H. Balsillie, "Post-Storm Report: Hurricane Elena," Florida Department of Natural Resources (Tallahassee, Fla., 1985). Information on potential hurricane damage can be found in *St. Petersburg Times*, May 27, 1979; Robert H. Simpson and Herbert Riehl, *The Hurricane and Its Impact* (Baton Rouge, 1981), 317–36; Tampa Bay Regional Planning Council, *Tampa Bay Region Loss and Contingency Planning Study* (St. Petersburg, 1980); Don G. Friedman, *Computer Simulation in Natural Hazard Assessment* (Hartford, 1974).

65. *Orlando Sentinel*, May 10, 13, and 23, 1995.

66. *St. Petersburg Times*, May 27, 1979.

67. John MacDonald, *Condominium* (New York, 1977), 247.

68. Jonathan Raban, "The Gaudy Green Eden," in Florida Leadership Forum, *Progress or Decline: Issues of Growth Management* (Tallahassee, 1986), 187.

69. *Orlando Sentinel*, March 30, 1994.

70. Robert Putnam, "Bowling Alone: America's Declining Social Capital," *Journal of Democracy* 6 (January 1995): 65–78.

71. Lewis Mumford, *The Story of Utopias* (New York, 1922), 268, 300.

Epilogue

1. Ruth E. Knack, "Repent, Ye Sinners, Repent," *Planning* 55 (August 1989): 6; Andres Duany, quoted in Andres Duany and Elizabeth Plater-Zyberk, "The Second Coming of the Small Town," *Wilson Quarterly* 16 (Winter 1992): 19–48.

2. Alex Kreiger and William Lennertz, eds., *Andres Duany and Elizabeth Plater-Zyberk: Towns and Town-Making Principles* (New York, 1992); David Mohney and Keeler Easterling, eds., *Seaside: Making a Town in America* (New York, 1991); Todd Bressi, "The Neo-Traditional Revolution," *Metropolis* 9 (March 1990); "Post-Tonica," *Zelo* 2 (Summer 1987): 20–21; Philip Langdon, "A Good Place to Live," *Atlantic Monthly* (March 1988): 39–60; Lloyd W. Bookout, "Neotraditional Town Planning: A New Vision for the Suburbs," *Urban Land* 51 (January 1992): 20–26; Beth Dunlop, "Our Towns," *Architectural Record* 179 (October 1991): 110–12; James R. Hagy, "Back to Basics: Small Town U.S.A.," *Florida Trend* 32 (October 1990): 46–50; William Fulton, "The Newest Idea: Old-Style Neighborhoods," *Governing* 3 (October 1990): 72–73.

3. "After Opal, Seaside Diamond Bright," *Seaside Times* (Winter 1995), 1–3.

4. John Nolen, *St. Petersburg Today, St. Petersburg Tomorrow* (St. Petersburg, 1923), 31.

5. *Florida Planning* 2 (December 1990): 1.

6. Phil Patton, "In Seaside, Florida, the Forward Thing Is to Look Backward," *Smithsonian* 21 (January 1991): 85; Witold Rybczynski, *Looking Around* (New York, 1992), 110.

7. Sam H. Kaplan, "The Holy Grid: A Skeptic's View," *Planning* 56 (November 1990): 10–11.

8. Ivonne Audirac and Anne H. Shermyen, "Neotraditionalism and Return to Town Life: Postmodern Placebo or Remedy for Metropolitan Malaise?" Paper delivered at AESOP Conference, Oxford, England, July 1991.

9. David Salvesen, *Wetlands: Mitigating and Regulating Development Impacts* (Washington, 1990), 1–20; David E. Dowall, *The Suburban Squeeze* (Berkeley, Calif. 1984), 12. In "Ideal Urban Form and Visions of the Good Life: Florida's Growth Management Dilemma," *Journal of the American Planning Association* 56 (Autumn 1990): 477, Ivonne Audirac, Anne Shermyen, and M. Smith argue, "Unless state and local governments buy large tracts of land to remove them from future agricultural and urban uses and fund effective stormwater management systems, accommodating growth more compactly will not improve Florida's water quality."

10. William Fulton, "Addicted to Growth," *Governing* 3 (October 1990): 68–73.

11. American Planning Association, *1996 APA National Planning Conference* (Chicago, 1996), 1.

12. Bruce Stephenson, "Bellair, Florida: Florida's Old, New Town." Paper presented at the 1996 National Planning Conference, Orlando, Florida, April 16, 1996.

13. Nolen, *St. Petersburg Today, St. Petersburg Tomorrow*, 31.

Index

Index

Tourism (*continued*)
    communities, 119; and *St. Petersburg Today, St. Petersburg Tomorrow*, 55–58, 65
Trustees Internal Improvement Fund (TIIF), 128, 130–31, 134–36, 138–39
Tyrone Boulevard, 122

University of Miami, 132, 146, 192
University of Pennsylvania, 40
University of South Florida, Institute for Environmental Studies, 168
Unwin, Raymond, 43–44, 89, 192
Updike, John, 1
Urban Land Institute, 162
U.S. Army Corps of Engineers, 128, 140–41
U.S. Department of Commerce, 64, 142
U.S. Fish and Wildlife Service, 132

Van Bibber, W. C., 16
Venice, Fla., 105, 207n, 211n
Vinoy Hotel, 81, 89, 182

Wallace, Henry, 107
Wallace, John, 107
Weedon Island, 168
West Orange Trail, 173–74
Whitnall, Robert, 88, 91, 97
Williams, Frank B., 46–47, 55, 63–64, 69, 76–78
Williams, Lloyd B., 162
Windom, William, 135
Winter Park, Fla., 5
Woodburn, Ken, 132, 134, 138
Woodward, C. Vann, 144

Zabel, Alfred, 140–41
Zabel v. Tabb, 140–41

Urban Life and Urban Landscape Series
Zane L. Miller and Henry D. Shapiro, General Editors

The series examines the history of urban life and the development of the urban landscape through works that place social, economic, and political issues in the intellectual and cultural context of their times.

Polish Immigrants and Industrial Chicago: Workers on the South Side, 1880–1922
Dominic A. Pacyga

The New York Approach: Robert Moses, Urban Liberals, and Redevelopment of the Inner City
Joel Schwartz

Designing Modern America: The Regional Planning Association and Its Members
Edward K. Spann

Hopedale: From Commune to Company Town, 1840–1920
Edward K. Spann

Welcome to Heights High: The Crippling Politics of Restructing America's Public Schools
Diana Tittle

Washing "The Great Unwashed": Public Baths in Urban America, 1840–1920
Marilyn Thornton Williams